SECOND THAT
EMOTION

Jeremy D.
Holden

SECOND THAT
EMOTION

How
DECISIONS,
TRENDS, *&*
MOVEMENTS
Are Shaped

Prometheus Books

59 John Glenn Drive
Amherst, New York 14228–2119

Cover image © 2012 HuHu/Shutterstock.com
Cover design by Jacqueline Nasso Cooke

Inquiries should be addressed to
Prometheus Books
59 John Glenn Drive
Amherst, New York 14228–2119
VOICE: 716–691–0133
FAX: 716–691–0137
WWW.PROMETHEUSBOOKS.COM

16 15 14 13 12   5 4 3 2 1

Library of Congress Cataloging-in-Publication Data

Holden, Jeremy D., 1964–
    Second that emotion : how decisions, trends, and movements are shaped /
Jeremy D. Holden.
        p.   cm.
    Includes bibliographical references and index.
    ISBN 978–1–61614–664–1 (hardcover : alk. paper)
    ISBN 978–1–61614–665–8 (ebook)
    1. Emotions. 2. Decision making—Psychological aspects. 3. Social
contract. 4. Social movements. I. Title.

BF531.H645 2012
155.9'2—dc23
                                                            2012018455

Printed in the United States of America on acid-free paper

To my wife, Natalie, and my children, Lily and Sam.
Thank you for your love, your patience, and your inspiration.

"Life is a state of mind."

Closing line from the 1979 movie *Being There*

CONTENTS

An Invitation to *Second That Emotion* 9

Chapter 1   The Role of Social Contracts   13

Chapter 2   Players in a Movement: 37
Zealots, Disciples, and the Congregation

Chapter 3   I Follow the Leader. He Follows Me.   61

Chapter 4   The Psychology of Illogical Leaps   85

Chapter 5   Social Media's Emotion Beacon   113

Chapter 6   The Sanctuary of Certainty   135

Chapter 7   Signs, Symbols, and Icons   157

Chapter 8   Breaking a Social Contract Can Be Terminal   185

Chapter 9   Creating a Culture Shift in the Age of Illogic   209

Acknowledgments   231

Notes   235

Index   257

AN INVITATION TO
SECOND THAT EMOTION

Like most authors, with the help of my editor I went back and forth on the name of the book, and finally we settled on something quite literal but nonetheless evocative in choosing *Second That Emotion*. In everything I've done and experienced in my life there has been a common thread—namely a deep-rooted curiosity in the emotional basis for why people choose to make fundamental changes in their actions and affiliations, and how they establish the beliefs that determine their choices.

I've been involved in marketing and advertising for some of the biggest and most influential brands in the world, I've run for political office, I've written and taught college-level courses, I've studied graphic design and law, I'm an avid history and movie buff, I've performed improvisational comedy, and I've sold paintings door to door in Italy (it would have helped if I'd spoken Italian). In each of these experiences and pursuits I've been fascinated by the strange psychology of how people become persuaded and the role that group dynamics play in the adoption of an idea, a personality, or a product. This book represents the sum of my learning from these experiences so far, and by shining a spotlight on the phenomenon of movements, my intent is to reveal how these movements are created and perpetuated, the roles that different groups and individuals play in them, and the illogical beliefs that often underpin them.

Second That Emotion is a book for businesspeople that isn't primarily about business, as the stories and cases are drawn equally from history, politics, sports, and popular culture, as well as from the business and branding world. With the exception of brand marketing and advertising, from which I've made a living for almost a quarter of a century, I don't consider myself an expert on many things, and indeed in many ways I'm the ultimate generalist. But they say you should write about your passions, and so I've brought the sum of my broad interests and experiences to bear in this book. I once had a spirited discussion with a client who argued that when people go to work they leave behind those things that aren't purely work related. Well, I don't subscribe to that, and it's been my experience that most of us are full of diverse ideas and passions, which we can't simply switch off when we arrive at the workplace. And whether or not you agree with me on that point will likely determine whether you enjoy reading *Second That Emotion.*

In some respects, *Second That Emotion* is for the "ADHD generation," as it's not in every book that you can read about a single theme through stories and examples as diverse as Julius Caesar, Winston Churchill, Barack Obama, Steve Jobs, Angelina Jolie, Jeffrey Dahmer—as well as the iPhone®—and often in a single chapter! It certainly doesn't follow a tried-and-true formula, and it took a leap (I hope not an illogical one) for Prometheus Books to let me take you on this often-winding but I hope ultimately rewarding journey.

Emotion drives our decisions, drives trends as well as movements, and influences every facet of our personal and professional lives. Some shifts we recognize, while others are still in the process of forming and are as yet unseen. Emotion is the engine that drives our history, our politics, and is present in the world of celebrities and sports, as well as in the commercial realm. As a businessman or businesswoman, if you want to see your company or brand break through, I hope my insights into how emotion-driven illogical leaps underpin movements and how to perpetuate your own cultural shift will make this book both essential and entertaining reading.

And if you simply find this topic as fascinating as I do, I've tried to provide a window into our own decision-making processes and how we support personalities and join movements based on emotion. So I invite you to read *Second That Emotion,* and I hope you enjoy reading it as much as I've enjoyed researching and writing it. If you do enjoy it, or even if you don't, please let me know by posting a comment at http://jeremydholden.com.

—Jeremy D. Holden

CHAPTER 1

THE ROLE OF SOCIAL CONTRACTS

"Half the promises people say were never kept, were never made."

—Edgar Watson Howe,
E. W. Howe's Monthly, 1911–1937

Social contracts represent the essential ingredient in creating movements, whether those movements are historical, political, populist, or commercial.

There was a moment in the 2008 election campaign when a rather shambolic woman approached the platform at one of Senator John McCain's rallies to express her concerns about Senator Barack Obama as a future president. After some inaudible words of support for the candidate, she stumbled toward the real emotional basis of her opposition to Senator Obama: "I have read about him and he's an Arab!"

In that moment, the truth behind the cause she felt she was part of—and the basis of her illogical beliefs—was revealed. The fact that it shocked Senator McCain was evident. In an unguarded moment, he spontaneously countered her words: "No ma'am, no ma'am. He's a decent family man and a citizen that I just happen to have disagreements with."

The disappointment among the assembled crowd was audible and palpable. Senator McCain's gracious and reasonable statement literally sucked the life out of the room. In that moment, the senator had broken the terms of a social contract that a group of his supporters had entered into with him, but which he wasn't fully aware of. In a heightened emotional state, these supporters had taken a set of facts and morphed them into a reality that was meaningful to them. The terms of their social contract with the Republican nominee stated: *I will support you if you recognize that Senator Obama is a Muslim who seeks to destroy America from the inside out.*

At the core of the contract was an illogical leap: *Senator Obama's ethnicity is unclear from his appearance and he spent time in a Muslim country in his early years. Arabs attacked us on September 11, 2001. Therefore Senator Obama is an Arab who seeks to destroy America.*

Senator Obama's ethnicity *isn't* obvious from his appearance. He had spent part of his early life in the primarily Muslim country of Indonesia, although this was mostly unknown when he started his campaign. Arabs did attack the United States on September 11. The (illogical) conclusion was that he was an Arab, and because he was an Arab he was an enemy of America bent on destroying the United States and her citizens, from the inside out.

In February 2011, the Pew Research Center found that 31 percent of Republicans polled believed that Barack Obama was a Muslim[1] while 39 percent responded that they didn't know. Only 27 percent believed Obama when he said—and demonstrated on numerous occasions—that he was a Christian. The fact that the campaign had highlighted his attendance at the incendiary Reverend Wright's church in Chicago was known consciously, but it only added fuel to the fire. Almost a third of Republicans demanded that their candidate recognize the threat to national security that Senator Obama posed—more than enough to deflate the Far Right, limit their turnout, and shape the election.

Only in that moment did Senator McCain truly comprehend the basis of support that he had from that group. His surprise and concern was evident in his reaction, and from then on his campaign, to his credit—or at least the elements of his campaign that he fully controlled—never sought to perpetuate that type of myth and misinformation.

Senator McCain had seen hateful propaganda peddled against

him in the 2004 Republican primary, where leaflets and e-mails had been routed suggesting that his daughter, whom he had adopted from Bangladesh, was actually the product of an illicit affair.[2] He had also seen his friend and fellow Vietnam veteran, Senator Max Cleland, branded as soft on national security and therefore lacking in patriotism.[3] Mr. Cleland is a triple amputee as a result of injuries sustained during his tour of duty in Vietnam and clearly was, and is, a patriot.

The natural reaction for many of us is to shake our heads and condemn both the ignorance of our fellow citizens and the immoral and exploitative nature of the propaganda peddlers. But what if these kinds of mass illogical leaps are not exclusively the result of manipulative propaganda, and what if they aren't just limited to those who are malleable or uninformed? What if each of us—every day—build belief systems based on illogic that impact our affiliations, as well as our brand and lifestyle choices?

As the example of the woman at Senator McCain's rally illustrates, social contracts are formed when a large swathe of society is in a heightened emotional state, and its passion for an idea, politician, celebrity, or brand gives rise to a set of illogical beliefs as the basis for a movement. Social contracts are pivotal to the creation of culture shifts, and my purpose in this book is to explain the strange psychology behind how they are formed, how they spawn passionate Zealots and committed Disciples—how they are universally celebrated and perpetuated through social media—as well as how they can be broken.

Conventional wisdom has it that spin doctors and Madison Avenue are responsible for manipulating our thoughts, causing us to endorse ideas or buy products that we'd otherwise reject outright. But while advertising and propaganda can provide a spark, and social media provides the kindling, it's we who create the terms for a social contract, more often than not based on thinking that we know logically to be flawed. We choose to enter into the contract, we perpetuate it, and we determine when its terms have been broken.

Recognizing and nurturing an emerging social contract is essential for any businessman or businesswoman if he or she wants to see his or her company or brand break through and create a culture shift. And for the rest of us, social contracts can provide a window into our own decision-making process and how emotion-based illogical leaps drive the personalities we support and the movements we choose to become part of—whether they be political, populist, or commercial. Let's look at some more examples from the world of politics.

When President Clinton left office, his approval rating was 66 percent, as high a poll number as any president had received upon departing the White House in living memory. And yet the last two years of his presidency had been overshadowed by the scandal surrounding his relationship with White House intern Monica Lewinsky, his subsequent denial, and the resulting impeachment proceedings.

By all rights, his supporters should have felt deeply resentful of the national disgrace and distraction that his actions had caused, and wished to punish him accordingly. After repeated denials that he had had a sexual relationship with Lewinsky, under pressure from the special prosecutor, Clinton was forced to publicly acknowledge having had an "inappropriate relationship" with her—and through the intensely embarrassing reporting about stains on Lewinsky's dress, it became clear that he'd engaged in a sexual act with her in a small corridor just off of the Oval Office itself.[4] His own administration members and political partners clearly felt angry about the lost opportunity of his last year in office and the embarrassment that his actions had caused. It created a cooling in his relationship with Prime Minister Tony Blair, who had put his own credibility on the line in vouching for Clinton. It also created a rift between the president and Vice President Al Gore, as Gore felt the scandal would undermine his chances in the forthcoming election. As a result, Gore damaged his own chances by hardly involving the still-popular president Clinton in the 2000 election campaign against then governor George W. Bush.

Yet the response of Clinton's supporters, who overwhelmingly maintained their support for the president, was anything but logical. President Clinton has stated that people were able to see beyond the scandal and focus on the bigger picture of his presidency, specifically the relative period of peace and prosperity under his leadership. Yet people have always struggled to take a broader view and see beyond near-term events when judging their political leaders, so by all rights there should have been an outpouring of righteous indignation reflected in Clinton's approval rating.

Perhaps the true nature of the social contract that American voters had originally entered into with Bill Clinton helps to explain their puzzling reaction. The social contract stated: *You are a smart, hardworking, charismatic leader who will represent our country well at home and abroad, and so I will overlook your obvious character flaws, most notably your rampant infidelity, which was quite apparent even before you were first elected as president.* After all, even Hillary Clinton (former senator and then secretary of state) once acknowledged that her husband was "a hard dog to keep on the porch."[5]

Against this criterion, President Clinton had not broken his social contract and thus continued to receive widespread approval. Perhaps the illogical leap in this case was to assume that someone with his evident character flaws—which had been apparent before his election during his time as governor of Arkansas—wouldn't inevitably compromise himself in such a way as to undermine his ability to function as president. But the nature of social contracts do not allow for that type of reasoned or predictive thinking.

To further emphasize this point, contrast the public's reaction to President Clinton's infidelity with that of another politician and former presidential candidate, Senator John Edwards of North Carolina. Senator Edwards cheated on his wife with an employee (Rielle Hunter), and President Clinton also had cheated on his wife with an employee. Both attempted to lie about it and were eventually discovered and forced to admit it.[6] Conventional wisdom has it that Senator Edwards was treated more harshly in the court of public opinion because he cheated on his late wife, Elizabeth—at a time when she was battling breast cancer—and certainly his behavior didn't exactly endear him to the average woman voter, in particular.

The real answer can be found in the nature of the social contract that had been established with Senator Edwards in his first presidential campaign in 2004, based in large measure on his own personal biography. The social contract stated: *You are a clean-cut, morally upstanding family man with small-town values, who used your legal talents to fight for the little guy and got rich in the process. I'll support you because of your moral character and because I think you can bring the country prosperity.*

In Senator Edwards's case the illogical leap was evident from the outset. Ask any person whether they think the average class-action attorney follows a strict moral code, and they'll probably laugh in your face. I know a number of lawyers who are both wholly ethical and morally upstanding, but that is not the general public perception, as lawyers fall just below politicians and just above advertising executives in the table of least trusted professionals. Nevertheless, the contract Senator Edwards's supporters entered into with him demanded that he adhere to the moral terms that his supporters had laid down. His actions broke those terms in spectacular fashion, and he paid the price with his political career.

With reference to the figure whose shadow loomed across the American political landscape for almost fifty years, I had the pleasure of watching the Clint Eastwood–directed movie *J. Edgar* (2011) about the life and times of the founder of the FBI. And if anyone is still laboring under the misperception that Leonardo DiCaprio is getting by on his good looks alone, they should watch his moving portrayal of a deeply private, complex, and contradictory man. I went to see the film primarily to learn more about the origins of the G-men, but the lasting takeaway was of a sensitively observed and portrayed love story between Hoover and his longtime colleague and companion, Clyde Tolson.

My perceptions of Hoover walking in were probably similar to many in terms of the social contract he'd established during his life with the average American, and which has now been passed down to this generation. Hoover's social contract stated:

You were secretive and scary, and many believed you were the most powerful man in the country because of the sensitive information you kept on the presidents you served. I heard some weird stuff about you being a cross-dresser and they said you kept all the credit for the bureau's success for yourself. But you rooted out militant extremists, tackled organized crime, battled the communists, and kept us safe for almost five decades, so I'm glad they named a building after you.

Whether it's a public figure, a media celebrity, or a consumer brand, it really doesn't matter what was intended when one first came to prominence. The only thing that matters is the illogical and jumbled concoction that becomes fixed in the mind of the consumer. My perception of J. Edgar Hoover didn't change fundamentally after seeing the film, but rather it expanded. I came away with a richer picture of this secretive and at times misguided American patriot who was able to function because of the emotional stability offered by Clyde Tolson, the love of his life. Public images are illogical and contradictory, and marketers and image makers, who still advocate a linear approach, would do well to broaden their perspective.

When we establish a social contract with a political figure, we bundle our hopes and beliefs onto them, and we expect them to live up to the standards we've set. The nature of politics is such that a candidate tends to be relatively ambiguous in stating his or her positions in order to appeal to the widest electorate—and that opens the door for us to project views and values onto them that ultimately they'll be unable to live up to. Of course, most politicians just want to get elected and generally are happy to receive our votes on pretty much any terms. But as with the examples I've cited, when politicians fail to understand the nature of the social contract that voters have established with them, the results are often terminal, and the movement they've created is fatally undermined.

SOCIAL CONTRACTS IN HISTORY

When Margaret Thatcher became the first female leader of a major political party in the United Kingdom—after unseating former Conservative Party prime minister Ted Heath—and then won a national election to become Britain's first woman prime minister in 1979,[7] she didn't so much break the glass ceiling as demolish the entire building.

Thatcher was the daughter of a middle-class grocer from the largely forgotten town of Grantham, in the middle-eastern region of England. Bright and ambitious, she went to Oxford University and became a barrister (lawyer) before entering politics and being elected to the UK Parliament in 1959, where she represented the North London district of Finchley. She rose up through the party ranks to become education secretary before ultimately challenging and defeating the then leader and former prime minister Ted Heath, and becoming leader of the Conservative Party in 1974.[8] The notion of a woman prime minister at that time was unusual enough, but for a middle-class woman from Grantham to ascend to the leadership of the oldest and most elitist political party in Britain—whose former leaders had included William Pitts, Benjamin Disraeli, Sir Winston Churchill, and Sir Anthony Eden—was an extraordinary achievement in itself.

People tend to embrace dramatic change only in times of crisis, and Britain's economy and the resulting unrest at the time certainly warranted that label. The so-called winter of discontent,[9] in the United Kingdom in 1978–1979, with the resulting labor strikes, sky-high taxation, and record unemployment under the Labour government of Prime Minister Jim Callaghan, opened the door for dramatic change and reform, paving the way for Thatcher's Conservative Party to win the 1979 election and make her Britain's first woman prime minister.

A series of historic events and memorable statements, and a nickname that stuck, helped to define the nature of the social contract that the British people established with Margaret Thatcher—as the basis for the culture shift that came to be known as Thatcherism. She was Maggie, the "Iron Lady" who stared down the powerful miner's union, stood up to the mighty Soviets alongside President Reagan, liberated the Falkland Islands from Argentina, survived a brutal assassination attempt by the Irish Republican Army (IRA) in a Brighton hotel, and "handbagged" the mostly male members of Parliament and her cabinet into submission. One of her famous handbags recently sold for almost $40,000 in June 2011 at a London charity auction. She once famously commented that, "If you want something said, ask a man, but of you want something done, ask a woman."[10] Whatever your political persuasion, you cannot but acknowledge that Margaret Thatcher was a formidable political operator.

She was an ordinary yet extraordinary woman, who rose to the apex of national and world politics by being true to her conservative principles and following her version of the economics of common sense—which she spoke to in a way that the average family sitting around the kitchen table could understand. She was utterly intractable and her famous comment at the 1980 Conservative Party conference helped define her for a decade in power: "You turn if you want to. The lady's not for turning!"[11]

Thatcher's social contract stated: *Maggie is one of us made good. She took on the elitists and the militants at home and beat them. She stared down the communists and the IRA. She rescued the Falkland Islands and put the economy back on track. She isn't everyone's cup of tea, but she's our Iron Lady, so don't mess with her.*

By 1983 the UK economy had begun to turn around, with stronger growth, lower inflation, and reduced mortgage rates. But Thatcherism wasn't working for everyone in the United Kingdom: manufacturing output dropped by 30 percent from five years earlier and unemployment reached record levels. Indeed, Thatcherism represented a British version of trickle-down economics, and for the poor and those on the lowest rung of the societal ladder, it was less of a trickle and more of a slow drip.

The illogical leap for the lower and lower-middle classes in the United Kingdom was that someone with a staunchly conservative viewpoint who was committed to the privatization of industry and the resultant reduction in manufacturing, who had been educated in one of England's most elite universities, and who had demonstrated that she didn't view tackling growing unemployment as a priority, should be a friend of the workingman and workingwoman. But the nature of social contracts has always been illogical, and Thatcher's entrenched image as someone who "took on the establishment" convinced ordinary people that she was indeed a kindred spirit, despite much evidence to the contrary.

Within Thatcher's own party and her own cabinet there had always been muted voices of resentment against some of her policies and particularly her brusque style of leadership. She was highly skeptical of European integration in all its forms—and particularly economic integration, which she believed had the potential to undermine British sovereignty—and she had become somewhat of a caricature for many with her power suits, her carefully cultivated low speaking voice, and her use of the "royal" *we* in referring to herself. There were even whispers that Queen Elizabeth II had taken exception to her perceived image as a sort of alternate monarch. However, because of the power of Thatcher's social contract with the British people, Margaret Thatcher never lost a national election, although at times her polling numbers during the midterm periods dipped below that of her party.

In 1990, Thatcher's long-serving cabinet minister, Sir Geoffrey Howe, resigned over a disagreement about entry into the European monetary system, and in his resignation speech Howe made a damning statement about Thatcher's style of leadership—using a cricket analogy to suggest she had "broken her players' bats before sending them out to play." Michael Heseltine, a self-made millionaire and former cabinet minister who had held the position of secretary of state for both the Environment and Defense, had subsequently resigned from Thatcher's government over frequent disagreements with her.[12] Heseltine was a charismatic figure who was seen by many within the conservative movement as a more "suitable" leader in waiting, and after Howe's resignation, Heseltine took the opportunity to challenge Thatcher—boosted by polling numbers that suggested he would be a more popular leader going into the 1992 election.

The nature of a social contract is such that it's the people that both establish the contract and set the terms, not the other way around. Thatcher's supporters may have been tiring of her style of leadership and sought a new direction and a fresh face, but she was still their Iron Lady and it was they who would vote to decide when it was time for her to go—just as they had done with Churchill after World War II—and not a small clique of Conservative Party members of Parliament.

Heseltine was popular and a talented leader, but for him to be seen to have unseated Thatcher, rather than the people who put her there, left them feeling disenfranchised and angry, and they let the Conservative members of Parliament know it in no uncertain terms. The result was that Thatcher was forced to step down after failing to defeat Heseltine in the leadership contest. Ultimately, however, Heseltine was defeated in the next ballot by the compromise candidate John Major—who with Thatcher's endorsement went on to succeed her and ultimately win the 1992 election.[13]

Perhaps the ultimate loser of the coup against Margaret Thatcher was the Conservative Party itself. The party's failure to understand the true nature of the social contract that the British people had established with Margaret Thatcher resulted in the Conservative Party losing not one but two strong leaders. And while John Major was able to scrape a narrow victory at the national election in 1992, at the following election in 1997, Tony Blair's Labour Party tossed the Conservatives out of power in a landslide victory.[14] Successive Labour governments then governed until 2010, when a repackaged Conservative Party under David Cameron, in coalition with Nick Clegg and the Liberal Democrats, regained power.[15]

Ordinary voters are the creators and owners of the social contract, deciding not just the terms but also when it is time to end the contract—and in failing to understand that, the Conservatives paid a heavy price in the political wilderness for thirteen long years.

As will become evident, I am a hopeless movie buff with a particular interest in political biographies. In writing about political and historical figures that I may not have largely agreed with, I have attempted to present their achievements and influence objectively. It was from this perspective that I had looked forward to seeing the 2011 film *The Iron Lady* about the life of Margaret Thatcher, having grown up in the United Kingdom through the turbulent years of her leadership.

While I, like many, had mixed feeling about Thatcher's influence on Britain, no one could argue that she wasn't a formidable figure on the world stage for more than a decade. I was looking forward to seeing the lion's share of the film deal with her role in the formative events surrounding her premiership: the miner's strike, the Falklands War, the revival of London as one of the world's key financial centers, the fall of the Berlin Wall, the escalation of IRA violence, and the eventual defeat of communism and the winding down of the Cold War.[16] These were matters of enormous consequence, the impact of which still reverberates today.

Yet director Phyllida Lloyd chose to center her film around a depiction of Thatcher as a vulnerable and elderly old woman reflecting on mostly private snippets of her extraordinary life while engaged in a dialogue with her deceased husband, Denis! Lloyd seemed to miss the irony within her own screenplay when Thatcher, gracefully portrayed by the peerless Meryl Streep, berated her physician for asking how she was feeling, instead of what she was thinking. Whether or not you agreed with Thatcher's ideas, it was her ideas, which became known as Thatcherism, that defined both her and her legacy. She wanted to make a difference and live a purposeful life, and she certainly did that, becoming one of the most beloved (and hated) political figures of the twentieth century. And making a film of Thatcher's life that, in most cases, barely referenced the pivotal events themselves, or her political partnerships with towering figures such as Ronald Reagan and Mikhail Gorbachev, seemed both petty and a wasted opportunity. Streep, however, did win an Academy Award for Best Actress for her portrayal of Thatcher.

Thatcher had little time for those she termed "vacillators" who either didn't know their own minds or who wouldn't defend their views and enter the fray. The only certainty around this disappointing film was that Thatcher herself would have found it vacuous and trivial, and would have quickly moved on to more important matters. At the same time, however, you can bet she'd have enjoyed coaching Meryl Streep on her accent.

In a strikingly similar, although far more bloody, scenario than the Thatcher coup many centuries earlier, Brutus, Cassius, and the other senators who stabbed Julius Caesar to death in 44 BCE on the fateful Ides of March (March 15 in the Roman calendar) paid the ultimate price for breaking a social contract that also wasn't theirs to sever.

While I cannot hope to do justice to the extraordinary and complex man who shaped our world as much as any other, suffice it to say that Julius Caesar was a unique and complex individual. After his successes in conquering Gaul, and following his defeat of Pompey the Great in the civil war at Pharsalus in 48 BCE, Caesar returned to Rome and was appointed dictator by the Senate.[17]

In returning to Rome from his various successful campaigns, Caesar saw how central government had become powerless, the provinces had turned into independent principalities under strong governors, and the army had become the main weapon in accomplishing political aims. So he established a new constitution to achieve three goals: he wanted to quash resistance in the provinces, create a strong central government, and knit the empire back into a cohesive whole.

In order to achieve his vision, Caesar enacted a series of reforms—much to the chagrin of the Senate—which included the restructuring of debt laws that effectively eliminated a quarter of all debts, redistributed land to his military veterans and other supporters, and even changed the calendar to match the Egyptian calendar, inserting three extra months (which is almost identical to the calendar we use today). He became the Prefect of Morals, the Father of the Fatherland, and the Imperator whose likeness appeared on Roman coins.

For members of the Senate, which had governed the Roman Republic for almost five hundred years, this was a dictatorship that undermined everything they had stood for. But for many of the people of Rome, who saw a reduction in crime and corruption, the opportunity for land and advancement, and the strengthening of the empire, Caesar was a liberating figure.

Their social contract with Caesar stated: *Caesar has conquered Gaul, brought wealth and unity to the empire, tackled the crime and corruption that the Senate had failed to, staged games, and made it easier for us to buy food and land. The Senate may have been elected by the people, but it isn't working for the people—so what if we have a dictator? I'm better off under Caesar, who seems to have my best interests at heart.* Of course, the illogical leap that the Roman mob was taking was to assume that any action Caesar took wasn't entirely self-serving, but still their day-to-day existence was made easier under his dictatorship.

So as Brutus and Cassius emerged from the Senate after the murder of Caesar and loudly proclaimed "We are free," it's little surprise that they were met with absolute silence as Romans stayed in their homes, in no mood to celebrate the death of the man who had improved their lot, and afraid of the wrath that would follow from Caesar's loyal military generals, Marc Antony and Octavian—Caesar's nephew and named successor.[18] Brutus's and Cassius's homes were attacked, and they were forced to flee Rome. Antony and Octavian (later to become Augustus, Rome's first emperor) brought back the practice of proscription, which sanctioned the murder of Caesar's assassins as well as their political opponents. The seizing of their wealth also enabled the generals to fund forty-five legions employed in the civil war against Brutus and Cassius, who were ultimately defeated and killed at the battle of Philippi.

So a parallel can be drawn with the assassination of Caesar and the hounding of Brutus and Cassius. Like Heseltine and Howe centuries later, Brutus and Cassius believed they were doing the right thing for the country and for the people. But the people had established the terms of the social contracts with their leaders, and if anyone was going to oust those leaders from power—or in Caesar's case, to assassinate him—that fell to the people and not to their leader's political opponents.

History is littered with examples of would-be leaders claiming to act in the name of the people but really acting toward their own agendas. These examples remind us that the power of a social contract is such that if you forcibly sever something that the people don't believe is broken, it's you who will ultimately pay the price.

SOCIAL CONTRACTS WITH CELEBRITIES

The phenomena of social contracts aren't just limited to the world of politics. Social contracts are equally present in the powerful connections that we form with our favorite celebrities and athletes.

In 2009, when his contract with the Cleveland Cavaliers expired, LeBron James, like many NBA free agents, decided to explore other options of where to play basketball.[19] James's approximate understanding of his commitment to the Cavaliers and to the city of Cleveland stated: *I will play hard, be a model ambassador for the NBA and the city of Cleveland, and try to win a championship.*

However, LeBron James's social contract with the people of Cleveland was somewhat different. It stated: *You are a symbol that Cleveland is a city at the forefront, rather than a city in decline, and in that sense you represent far more than success on the basketball court—you represent hope for Cleveland's renewal in the future.* Setting aside the indelicate handling of James's decision to move to the Miami Heat, there was something unnatural and visceral about the outpouring of anger directed at someone who, until then, had been a model player in the NBA and a model ambassador for Cleveland. If he had understood the true nature of the social contract he had entered into with the people of the city—and the depth of emotion his decision would generate—he would surely have handled his departure differently.

When James chose to leave Cleveland, he took hope for the future of that city with him in a way that transcended basketball and left fans feeling abandoned and betrayed. The illogical leap stated: *LeBron must understand what he represented to the city, therefore his failure to inform the Cavaliers before he announced his decision to join Miami in a one-hour television special must have been staged to intentionally embarrass the club, the city, and the people of Cleveland.*

In a logical world, James's actions would have been seen as clumsy but not malicious. But the nature of social contracts is anything but logical. As consumers, customers, and fans, we decide the terms of our social contracts, no matter how illogical those terms may be. Yet in the context of a social contract, just because people have a heightened level of emotional engagement doesn't mean that they cannot still be forgiving. Contrast LeBron James's social contract with that of the actor Robert Downey Jr.

Robert Downey Jr. made his screen debut at age five in his father's film *Pound,* and he first achieved a greater level of recognition in the Brat Pack film *Less Than Zero* (1987)—in which, as a prelude to his future struggles, he played a teenage drug addict. In the early 1990s, Downey's film-acting career began to blossom with roles in *Air America* and later *Natural Born Killers.* But Robert Downey Jr. came into the full public and critical spotlight for his portrayal of Charlie Chaplin in *Chaplin,* chosen for the lead role by the esteemed British director Sir Richard Attenborough, of *Gandhi* fame. Downey received an Academy Award nomination for Best Actor for his performance in *Chaplin.*[20]

Downey's father first gave marijuana to Robert Jr. at the age of six.[21] Thus drugs became a central plank of the younger Downey's life from a very early age and became the means through which he felt able to communicate with, and relate to, his father.

In the late 1990s, Robert Downey Jr.'s critical drug problem began to take over his life, and he suffered frequent arrests and was subsequently admitted into various drug rehabilitation clinics. In 2000, after being released from the California Substance Abuse Treatment Facility and State Prison, he landed a part in the popular TV series *Ally McBeal* as the title character's new love interest. Again he received popular and critical acclaim, but he had to be written out when his drug problem inevitably resurfaced.[22]

For many actors or sporting celebrities, to fall so hard and so often would have meant the end of their careers, but the nature of the social contract that people established with Robert Downey Jr. helps to explain why they have been so patient and so forgiving in his case.

His social contract states: *You were a child protégé and are an acting genius who brings immense pleasure to moviegoers. That level of creative talent often goes hand in hand with emotional instability, particularly as you were brought up surrounded by drugs and in the public spotlight. We know you are a drug addict, but as long as you continue to battle it and entertain us, we'll forgive your relapses.*

So people have continued to accept Downey, indeed his popularity has soared, and he now has the title role in two successful movie franchises, *Iron Man* and *Sherlock Holmes,* the latter for which he won the Golden Globe Award for Best Actor in 2009.

One of the things that separate us from every other animal is our capacity to project our feelings and values onto others, and in many ways it's a positive attribute because it's been the basis of our morality as human beings. This instinct was developed at a time before mass communications and the digital age, and it allowed us to both empathize and establish community-based moral practices and codes. But as we view celebrities through social media and other digital portals, and come to feel like we know them, this instinct to project our feelings and values kicks in, and as a result we unknowingly take illogical leaps.

In a logical world, Robert Downey Jr.'s ongoing drug battle and frequent arrests would have earned the scorn of the public, which is quick to label celebrities as spoiled, weak, and selfish, and unworthy of the talents they've been given. Instead, his popularity is now such that when his friend Mel Gibson's public image nose-dived after a spate of negative publicity, it was Downey who asked the public to give Gibson another chance. But the nature of social contracts are such that while one individual can be lauded for the way he has battled his demons, another can be condemned for the far lesser public infraction of being insensitive and appearing arrogant. Indeed, when LeBron James's Miami Heat team lost to the Dallas Mavericks in the 2011 NBA Championship, the universal reaction seems to have been one of delight and a sense of validation in LeBron's failure.

SOCIAL CONTRACTS WITH OUR FAVORITE BRANDS

The relationship that we have with our favorite brands carries a degree of emotional fervor similar to the way we feel about an actual person, whether they be a friend, a politician, or a celebrity. We choose brands to help define our own personal image, and as such the connection can be charged and deeply personal to us. As a result, brand relationships have the potential to rise to the level of a social contract as the basis for creating a culture shift, with all the emotion and illogic that it entails.

In 2004 the Dove® brand Campaign for Real Beauty®[23] was launched worldwide by Unilever in tandem with its advertising agency Ogilvy & Mather. The campaign included traditional and digital advertising, an extensive social-media initiative, as well as workshops, the publication of a book, and even the production of a play.[24]

The campaign featured normal women of different shapes and sizes, and it showcased photography from Rankin, the firm featuring John Rankin Waddell, who had made a career out of subverting fashion photography. Rankin's gift was to bring out the essential humanity in his subjects, and he preferred to work with ordinary-looking woman rather than with fashion models. For as long as there has been a women's rights movement, the advertising industry has been justifiably condemned for blatantly stereotyping women, creating a false and unattainable portrayal of feminine beauty. Female

stereotyping and the advertising industry have been blamed for creating low self-esteem among women, causing depression and even
teen suicides. In a bold and ambitious move, the Dove Campaign for
Real Beauty sought to reverse not just the industry's perspective on
female beauty but also society's viewpoint of it.

The campaign quickly sparked interest from passionate Zealots
(profiled in the next chapter) who became engaged through
various social-media platforms including Twitter®, Facebook®, and
YouTube™—and used digital advertising and PR as a means of
driving support and interest. Viral videos were created to demonstrate how the media as a whole had contributed to society's distor-
tion of beauty—some of which were seeded by Unilever, and others
generated organically by the Zealots themselves. As the campaign's
appeal broadened, hundreds of thousands engaged, with the Dove's
YouTube hub alone receiving over eleven million hits.

In every respect, Dove's campaign met the criteria of a culture
shift, as a large swathe of society was worked up into an emotional
fervor, driven by an underlying desire to change societal norms.
Dove's passionate consumers created the "Dove Beauties" and established a social contract with the brand that stated: *For as long as I can
remember, advertisers have been portraying an unrealistic image of female
beauty, creating insecurity and feelings of inferiority among women. Finally,
Dove has given us an honest picture of female beauty, and I will buy their
products and support their brand in gratitude and recognition.*

The illogical leap in this case was to assume that Unilever—
Dove's parent company and the Anglo-Dutch behemoth that rivals
Procter & Gamble worldwide for dominance in the personal beauty
category—would primarily have the greater good of society in mind,
rather than purely commercial motives. Like any successful global
organization, Unilever is first and foremost beholden to its shareholders, and while taking this stand was ethically desirable, it was primarily about differentiation and making a smart business decision.[25]

Indeed, dig a little deeper into Unilever's stable of personal
beauty products and brands and you'll find Axe® (or Lynx® as it's

known in the United Kingdom), which is targeted at a young male audience and has long featured advertising that blatantly stereotypes women and female sexuality. Unilever is also the parent of Fair & Lovely®, which is a skin-lightening product marketed around the world to dark-skinned women. Against charges of corporate hypocrisy, in Unilever's defense, Unilever is simply marketing each of its brands to their respective audiences in the way that makes them most likely to resonate—and Unilever has made no particular effort to mask the fact that it is the parent of each of these brands.

As I discuss in the next chapter, Zealots like to dig deep and be the knowledge owners and opinion leaders of whatever subject or topic they are engaged in. To that end, it's highly likely that the Zealots were fully aware of Dove's connection to Unilever—and therefore to Axe. The Zealots' level of passion would have ensured that they revealed all of the Dove brand's corporate connections, and shared that information via social media. But because Dove was doing something that these Zealots supported with such passion, and because in part these consumers were defining themselves through that support, the Zealots appear to have collectively turned a blind eye to the apparent contradictions of Dove's corporate parent, Unilever.

Such is the nature of a social contract—since it's individuals and not companies who create the terms, it's individuals who determine when a brand has broken the social contract—and in this instance, perhaps illogically, they chose to continue their support and perpetuate the Dove Beauties movement. As I'll discuss later in the chapter on broken social contracts, the Dove example of consumers turning a blind eye when it comes to social contracts tends to be the exception rather than the rule.

In Dove's case, the creation of a social contract was underpinned by a pent-up emotional desire for change, in the way women were portrayed in society. In the climate created by the great recession of 2009–2010, the effects of which are ever present today, the underlying societal need was for the government and companies alike to find innovative ways to help ordinary people.

Sometimes it's the most unlikely of candidates that emerges as a champion. With the amount of TARP money pumped into the American automotive industry in order to shore up ailing companies like Chrysler and GM (notably Ford chose to weather the storm without taking public funds), you'd think it would be an American company that would have found an innovative way to restore consumer confidence and kick-start the stalled car market. Instead, it was a hard-to-pronounce Korean company that had the insight to realize that the true barrier to car buying wasn't price, it was the fear of losing your job.

Hyundai, pronounced *Hunday* in the United States and *Hi-und-i* in the United Kingdom (I've no idea how it's actually pronounced in Korea), had struggled since it entered the American market in 1986 to convince American consumers of the quality of its products. Partly that was self-induced, with early models like the Excel® in the United States and the Stellar in the United Kingdom that, while undoubtedly cheap, hardly lived up to their prestigious-sounding names in terms of performance and features. They also struggled in part because of consumer's lack of knowledge about the nature of the company, let alone the overall quality of Korean manufacturing. David Letterman in his Top 10 pranks to play in space (in referring to the space shuttle) memorably included at No. 8, "Pasting a Hyundai logo on the main control panel"! For the average American consumer, being wary of products from overseas markets that they knew little about, was not a new phenomenon—after all it was only twenty years ago that US consumers viewed Japanese cars with disdain, believing them to be inferior to American-made brands. And as Indian and Chinese car manufacturers begin to enter the US market over the next decade, no doubt history will continue to repeat itself as American consumers initially question their overall quality.

Nevertheless, from their earliest days in the US market, Hyundai had shown an insightful ability to understand and act upon the perceptions of American car buyers. In 1998, in a bold move designed to prove the quality of its cars, it initiated a ten-year and 100,000-mile comprehensive warranty, at a time when the best competitive warranty was five years and 50,000 miles. In 2008, to the skepticism of many within the automotive industry, Hyundai announced it would be launching the Genesis® sedan[26]—a true luxury vehicle with all the requisite performance and technology bells and whistles—but at a lower price than competitive Japanese luxury vehicles like Lexus®, Acura®, and Infiniti®, and far below the traditional German luxury brands like Mercedes-Benz®, BMW®, and Audi®.[27]

So given this entrepreneurial spirit, perhaps it shouldn't have been a surprise that as consumer confidence reached an all-time low in December 2008, and the car market slowed down to walking pace—while competitors showered the category with employee pricing and "red tag" sales—Hyundai dug deeper into people's psyches in order to find a solution. The number-one fear in any recession is that you will lose your job and therefore be unable to make your payments and meet your commitments. Whether it's having your house foreclosed or your car repossessed, it's that visceral fear of being vulnerable and shamed that underpins a consumer spending freeze—and Hyundai conceived of a way to begin to create a thaw.

The Hyundai Assurance program was launched a day after Hyundai's own year-on-year sales were down by almost 50 percent and created new momentum for the brand and for the US automotive industry. Hyundai Assurance guaranteed that if you bought or leased a car and then lost your job and couldn't make the payments, you could bring the car back without having to meet any special conditions. You simply had to prove that you'd recently lost your job or your source of income, and you were completely at liberty to hand back the car with no questions asked. The program immediately garnered massive mainstream media attention as people applauded Hyundai for trying to kick-start the car market. The program also generated enormous word-of-mouth discussion via social media, as people sought reassurance from their friends and peers that there wasn't some loophole they should be wary of—as for many, Hyundai Assurance sounded almost too good to be true![28]

The program went straight to the heart of consumers' anxiety and created the basis for a social contract with Hyundai that stated: *When other car companies were taking our tax dollars and trying to get us into more debt with crazy deals, Hyundai took a stand for ordinary people by allowing us to get new cars without worrying about losing our jobs. Whether they are from Korea or wherever, they seem more on the side of ordinary Americans than the US car companies.*

Hyundai Assurance certainly enabled the company to weather the worst of the recession far better than most of its competitors, seeing a healthy sales increase in 2009 compared to 2008. But the true benefit of the program lived in the creation of a social contract with a section of the American people, who have now come to view Hyundai as a borderless company that was both innovative and on the people's side when consumers most needed a company to be. Of course, positive brand image and goodwill can carry you only so far, and Hyundai's line of new car models (including the 2011 Elantra®, Sonata®, as well as the Genesis) have all won international awards for both their design and overall quality—and there is no doubt that its cars now have heightened appeal on the road, when they drive up to a stoplight. Nevertheless, the fact that Hyundai's US recorded sales in 2010 were 538,228 (up from 435,064 in 2009), and their highest recorded year by far to date,[29] likely relates in large measure to the social contract they'd been able to establish through Hyundai Assurance.

Perception is reality, and while it may seem illogical to think Hyundai Assurance was nothing more than a brilliant promotion, American consumers took it as something more—and the long-term benefit to the company of having established a social contract will be realized over the coming years, assuming Hyundai can continue to innovate. But what made the success of the program particularly gratifying is the fact that it actually cost Hyundai almost nothing in real financial terms, as only a handful of customers nationwide ever handed their cars back!

SOCIAL CONTRACT TERMS ARE NON-NEGOTIABLE

As I've hoped to illustrate and will continue to expand upon in the rest of the book, there are certain criteria and conditions that are usually required in order for a social contract to form, which are as follows:

- Social contracts are often underpinned by an emotional desire for change or to challenge societal norms.
- Illogical leaps are often the central currency of social contracts.
- Social contracts spawn passionate Zealots (the first group in establishing the contract; profiled in detail in chapter 2).
- Social contracts today are universally celebrated and perpetuated through social media.
- Social contracts represent the essential ingredient in the creation of movements, whether they are historical, political, populist, or commercial in nature.

As the Edgar Watson Howe quote states, "Half the promises people say were never kept, were never made."[30] So it really doesn't matter what was intended when your brand, celebrity persona, or political candidacy was launched—the only thing that matters is how it was received and processed, and the nature of the social contract that was established in order to create a movement.

As consumers, customers, and fans, *we* decide the terms of our social contracts, no matter how illogical those terms may be.

CHAPTER 2

PLAYERS IN A MOVEMENT

Zealots, Disciples, and the Congregation

"The whole world loves a maverick and the whole world wants the maverick to achieve something nobler than simple rebellion."

— Kevin Patterson,
Mother Jones magazine, 2007

Movements are driven and perpetuated by three groups that are defined by distinct attitudes and behaviors.

Almost everyone who took a marketing course in college is familiar with the adoption curve wherein a brand progresses through different audiences beginning with the early minority, through the early majority, to the late majority, and ultimately reaching the late minority audience. In each category you would use demographics and socioeconomic factors to profile each group.

From my experience having spent many years working both as a researcher and as a professional culture and societal watcher, it's clear that today this model has changed. Three distinct groups have emerged, each defined by common attitudes or psychographics that play a central role in the creation of a movement—whether it happens to be political, populist, or commercial in nature. In broad terms, I would describe each of these groups as having the following attitude-based profiles:

Zealots. Zealots are likely to be hostile toward institutions on principle, whether public or private, political or commercial; they tend to take more extreme positions expressed through digital and social media; they are motivated to stand for something, whatever the consequences; they like to be viewed as influential outsiders; they hate to compromise and can be highly vocal and militant about their beliefs; they tend to reject majority views and populism; they like to be the knowledge owners and to make discoveries; they enjoy decoding mysteries and exposing conspiracies; they believe in the purity of ideas and always seek a better way. Therefore, in evaluating new product technology, a Zealot will want to have done his or her homework ahead of the pack in order to become the knowledge owner whom others look to for advice and guidance, often via social media. A Zealot will enjoy the sense that he or she has picked through the hype to find the truth of a product's true performance, and will share that opinion without any filtering. If they buy into the product, they'll be staunch advocates until they see any evidence of compromise or dilution, at which point they're likely to become the product's fiercest critic.

Disciples. Disciples prefer to be right rather than first. They are vocal advocates for political or commercial causes or brands that allow them to participate through digital and social media; they will stand for something only once they've fully evaluated what they'll be standing against; they are motivated to assess the downside of every decision before offering their support; they prefer consensus but aren't afraid to break ranks when they believe strongly in the rightness of a cause or an idea; they think change comes from the inside out; they accept the necessity of being pragmatic and strive to make considered, well-informed decisions; they reject innovation for its own sake and believe an idea is as good as one's ability to implement it. Disciples believe in activism but with a moderate tone. In contrast to a Zealot, in evaluating new technology a Disciple will only buy in once the benefits of the new product have been weighed against the negatives and he or she has all the requisite facts and data. Therefore, the Disciples won't be concerned if they aren't the first to be seen with a new product, but once they have made their choice they will be its staunchest and most loyal advocate.

The Congregation. The Congregation is rarely vocal or active in support of their preferred brands. They absorb a large amount of information and are actively engaged in social media; they hold firm beliefs but take a moderate stance; they welcome pragmatic compromise and tend to feel more comfortable in the majority position; they like to consult widely before making decisions and they don't like to be guinea pigs; they embrace proven and purposeful innovation. The Congregation will fall into alignment only when the case has been convincingly made. So in evaluating the same new technology, first and foremost the Congregation won't want to be the ones to be leading the evaluation. They also will be extremely cautious about the first reports, believing that time and organic adoption will be the best indicators of the product's usefulness and effectiveness. When the Congregation seeks information and advice it looks to those who take a calm and considered approach to evaluating a product's strengths and weaknesses. They instinctively gravitate away from extremist positions, both positive and negative, as well as hyperbole. As a result, they find the Disciple persona far more appealing and convincing as a messenger, and tend to be wary of Zealots. Indeed, the very fact that a Zealot community has endorsed a particular product is more likely to make the Congregation skeptical rather than to engage, and they'll wait for the more reasoned voice of the Disciples to wade in with an opinion.

Zealots, Disciples, and the Congregation are interrelated and interdependent in the creation of a movement. Without the Zealots to light the spark and create initial interest and engagement, the Disciples wouldn't be moved to do their own evaluation—and without the measured endorsement of the Disciples, the Congregation would be loathe to consider becoming involved. Although their styles and processes of adoption are different, each group nevertheless plays an active role in the creation of movements, distinct from the remainder of society which simply reacts passively—without consciously embracing those movements, or even recognizing the real nature of what they are part of.

The events of January and February 2011 surrounding the

Egyptian uprising that led to the ouster of President Mubarak are illustrative of the distinct roles played by each of these subgroups, as well as providing a window into each group's unique characteristics. When Wael Ghonim, a marketing manager at Google, used Facebook to administer his now-infamous "We Are All Khaled Said" page, in reference to the young businessman who died at the hands of undercover police,[1] he planted the initial anti-Mubarak propaganda that motivated the Zealots to rise up.

In the uprising the Zealots were a group of twenty-something, heavy social-media-using, relatively well-educated Egyptians who took their pent-up frustration at the daily restrictions and often brutal nature of the Mubarak regime and coalesced around the death of Khaled Said. They used social media as their primary tool, to both incite others and to organize the protests.

The defining characteristics and persona of the Zealots were on display in those early hours of the uprising. The Egyptian populace as a whole was shocked by the extreme nature of the antigovernment propaganda being expressed. The call was for the ouster of Mubarak, rather than for something or someone else. The early protestors were viewed as extremists and therefore as outsiders, and there was no sense given of the possibility for compromise. Indeed, in those early hours the populace as a whole might easily have turned against the Zealots, as most were absent from social media, and the people sensed a militancy that had the potential to wash away not only the Mubarak regime but also any benefits they valued under the regime. There was a puritanical quality to the uprising while the Zealots drove it, which was at once invigorating while at the same time frightening for the Congregation.

On the third day, the Disciples found their voice. Men like Mohammed ElBaradei, the 2005 Nobel Peace Prize winner and former director general of the International Atomic Energy Agency, became fully engaged.[2] And as the Disciples joined, the tone of the rhetoric around the uprising changed from simply calling for the ouster of Mubarak to becoming pro democracy. Information went from being shared exclusively through social media to being shared via more traditional media such as the use of leaflets. ElBaradei and other voices that emerged on the third day showed all the characteristics of the Disciple persona. They hadn't been the instigators, but they were able to better express the emotion of the Congregation.

They appeared strong and impassioned, and indeed ElBaradei continued the call for Mubarak's immediate departure. There was a forceful yet pragmatic aspect to their protest, which appeared to be well informed about how the regime would likely respond. The Disciples were activists but with a moderate tone, and interestingly it wasn't until they became vocal that the Mubarak regime truly sensed the threat and organized the counter protests that ultimately caused its demise.

Assuming the military keeps its promise to hold truly democratic elections in 2012, in the end it will be the Congregation that will determine the future of Egypt, but they will be led by Disciples rather than Zealots—and no doubt many of the early Zealots will consider the outcome to be a poor compromise against the purity of their ideals and the passion that led to the initial uprising. As new violent protests erupted in January 2011 in Cairo against the slow pace of reform, one could already see that frustration bubbling under the surface.[3] And when in the same month ElBaradei confirmed he wouldn't be seeking the presidency because he didn't believe the forthcoming elections would be free and open, it sent a further ominous signal. Certainly the movement cannot realize its goals until a true leader has emerged as a rallying point, and the formation of a new social contract with the Egyptian people is established.

Contrast the success achieved by the Egyptian protestors with what appeared momentarily to be the seismic events that began in late 2011 in New York City in the form of the Occupy Wall Street (OWS) protests. OWS proved to be a fascinating illustration of the group dynamics that shape and ultimately define a movement. The protests that initially coalesced around a July 13, 2011, blog and a poster in the July/August 2011 edition of *Adbusters* magazine calling for people to occupy Wall Street on September 17, 2011, then spread to numerous towns and cities around the United States as well as around the world. Yet the movement almost seemed to be happening in an alternate reality to the daily lives of most Americans.

If you lived your life on Twitter and listened to Keith Olbermann's every utterance on Current TV®, then OWS and the apparent culture shift it represents seemed like the center of the universe. Indeed opinion leaders like renowned author and *New York Times* columnist Thomas L. Friedman were asking you to weigh-in on whether you believed OWS was evidence of Paul Gilding's somber predictions of societal breakdown from his book *The Great Disruption,* or illustrative of the more optimistic view of John Hagel III in alluding to "The Big Shift" in his book *The Power of Pull.*

The honest answer to Friedman's question at that time was to wait and see, but we now know there were some key factors in determining the ultimate outcome, as events played out over days and weeks. The predominantly youthful group driving OWS—using social media as an organizing tool and comparing the protest to the uprising in Egypt—was viewed by most in the population at large as "Zealots." The Congregation felt the same sense of disillusion with the frozen political system that the Zealots felt. They had the same frustration over unemployment and the same resentment toward the corporations that took TARP money and then continued to pay exorbitant executive salaries and bonuses, while failing to lend to small businesses. However, they didn't engage because they saw no reasoned agenda put forward, nor did they hear the OWS message delivered through the informed and constructive voice of Disciples.

There was also an uneasy concern that some of the OWS protestors were playing at civil disorder, just as had seemed to be the case during the London riots of late 2011. In that instance, beyond the opportunistic criminality, perhaps the most cynical cultural aspect was the fact that some of those involved simply seemed to be having fun as they stole and terrorized. Following the Tweets it was possible to see how thrilling some of the rioters found this experience, as they sought to mirror Egyptian protestors, ignoring the fact that they lived in a democracy rather than under a dictatorship.

For the OWS movement to broaden its appeal, it was crucial that there be an acknowledgment that this was an entirely different type of uprising. America was and is not a totalitarian regime but rather a progressive democracy, flawed and economically moribund of late, but a democracy nonetheless. The Zealots leading the movement failed to understand this distinction and the nuances of the argument they needed to make to broaden the OWS movement.

Lawrence Lessig, the brilliant author of *Republic, Lost,* wrote about the principle of "non-contraction" in his article published in the *Huffington Post* on December 29, 2011. In pointing out the contradictions on both sides of the political divide, Lessig argued for the youth of America to unite in challenging corruption. He was speaking to the root cause of the OWS movement—namely the flow of money that had been seen to take Congress out of the hands of the people and given it to a handful of well-funded special-interest groups. This was something that an overwhelming majority of Americans recognized and distained. If OWS could have spawned more vocal Disciples like Lessig and focused the collective voices (and actions) on removing this most destructive of congressional practices, then the Congregation would likely have marched beside them. Only in that way could the now-deflated OWS protest have created a culture shift and effected the kind of political and societal change it was ultimately seeking.

THE ROLE OF EACH GROUP IN VIRAL MOVEMENTS

In the digital realm, the distinct role of Zealots, Disciples, and the Congregation are apparent in relation to campaigns that have spread virally and created culture shifts. The first example of a digitally driven viral program to go mass wasn't an advertising campaign for a brand—it related to the launch of the movie *The Blair Witch Project* in 1999.

The Blair Witch Project was essentially a horror film faux documentary produced by Haxan Films[4] that was developed on a relatively shoe-string budget by piecing together supposedly-real amateur footage. The plot centered around three student filmmakers who hiked into the Black Hills near Burkittsville, Maryland, to investigate a local legend known as the Blair Witch. According to the legend, the Blair Witch was the ghost of Elly Kedward, who had been banished for witchcraft in 1785. The audience was told that the three young filmmakers were never heard from again and that the film had been constructed from harrowing footage they had shot at the time—which subsequently had been discovered a year later and then pieced together.[5]

The Blair Witch Project was not the first movie of its kind by any means, and it bore a striking similarity to the 1998 film *The Last Broadcast*.[6] Both films were faux documentaries that featured characters that entered the wilderness to unravel a legend and subsequently vanished in mysterious circumstances. *Cannibal Holocaust*, a widely banned Italian film from 1980, also had distinct similarities, in this case centered around a group of filmmakers who ventured into the jungles of South America to make a documentary about a tribe of cannibals—with predictably gruesome consequences.[7] Again, the premise was that their actual footage had been found and used to make a significant portion of the film.

So given that there was nothing particularly new about either the script or the premise behind *The Blair Witch Project*, how is it that this little film with minimal studio backing, that cost around $500,000 to make, became a global phenomenon grossing almost $250 million worldwide? The answer lies in the brilliant viral campaign that preceded its launch, which first activated Zealots, and then Disciples, who eventually engaged the wider Congregation to create the most unlikely of movie blockbusters.

Co-directors Daniel Myrick and Eduardo Sánchez, in tandem with Artisan Entertainment, were largely responsible for creating the interest and rumor around the film that spread virally through each group—and *The Blair Witch Project* became the first movie to be primarily marketed via the Web. In truth, they had very little choice other than to rely on the Web, in order to compete with movies carrying $200 million price tags and $50 million advertising budgets—like the woeful *Wild Wild West,* starring Will Smith, which launched at the same time.

Recognizing the enduring appetite for urban legend both in the United States and internationally, Artisan Entertainment began by creating a website for Haxan Films in the summer of 1998, in order to perpetuate the myth of the Blair Witch. Demonstrating many of the characteristics of Zealots in seeking to make discoveries, and being first to unravel mysteries—those who initially engaged explored the site and related links, and began to craft their own content and blog about their discoveries. By the time Artisan Entertainment picked up the movie at the Sundance Film Festival and relaunched the website as Blairwitch.com in April 1998, the Zealots were already driving three million hits a day.

Artisan Entertainment continued to feed the myth with fake newspaper clippings about the filmmaking trio's disappearance, folklore about the Black Hills, and police photos from the trio's car. Footage from the woods was released in increments, the movie's trailer was leaked to select websites and *MTV*—and was presented as an entertainment scoop. The line between reality and fiction began to blur as flyers appeared all over college campuses seeking information about the missing trio while discreetly touting the movie. When the Sci-Fi Channel aired *Curse of the Blair Witch* four days prior to the movie's launch—and garnered the channel's highest ratings ever—it was evident that the movie had moved beyond the initial Zealots and created its own crop of Disciples, and had successfully established a social contract.

Although the film's actual release was supported with suitably cryptic advertising and trailers that featured little more than darkness and screams, the paid promotional effort was almost unnecessary as the movie banked $29 million in its first weekend of release—evidence that the Disciples' influence had persuaded the Congregation of the power of the film. Endorsements from influential critics including Roger Ebert in the *Chicago Sun-Times,* and Filmcritic.com listing *The Blair Witch Project* as the fiftieth best movie ending of all time, assured the Congregation that this was a must-see movie. And the phenomenon continued with a successful book, games, soundtrack, and DVD releases, and it continues today with a potential remake to be based in Scotland, under review.

The Blair Witch Project created a new Web-based template for rolling engagement designed to attract first the Zealots and then the Disciples, who would ultimately provide the assurance and credibility to draw in the wider Congregation. The rollout happened in the form of a slow and calculated reveal, more than a year before the movie launched. Cumulatively, if you engaged in full, there were few secrets about the myth of the film that you couldn't discover—in fact, there was so much content made available that it caused concern about giving the plot away prior to launch.

The first brand marketer to take the template that *The Blair Witch Project* had established and refine it was Audi, the German luxury automaker that is owned by Volkswagen. Rather like an indie film-maker, Audi in the United States typically was being outspent by its luxury competitors by as much as five to one when it came to launching new car models. Audi also had some other tough challenges in relation to launching its new A3 compact luxury vehicle. For one thing, the A3 was a hatchback design rather than a sedan, and many car manufacturers had gambled and lost betting that they could get US car buyers to choose a luxury hatchback.

So in close partnership with its advertising agency McKinney, Audi set out to challenge the traditional brand-advertising world by creating an experiential marketing campaign (or alternate-reality game) for the A3, in the vein of *The Blair Witch Project*—and in the process cement its brand position in the United States. The campaign began with the theft of the first Audi A3 to arrive in the United States from Audi's dealership on Park Avenue in New York. The story revolved around two invented characters, Nisha Roberts and Ian Yarborough, who ran an art-retrieval business and who were brought in to try to retrieve the stolen A3. In the process, working with Nisha's friend Virgil Tatum (who appeared to be the prime suspect for some time), they revealed a highly sophisticated art heist orchestrated by a shadowy figure known only as Archlight. It transpired that the stolen A3 had been one of six cars where the criminals had secretly hidden key pieces of information related to the heist. By piecing together all the information found in the cars, Nisha and Ian were able to reveal the full scope of the world's biggest art heist.

"The Art of the Heist campaign," as it was known,[8] was live for several months in the lead-up to the launch of the A3 in May 2005 and offered multiple points of entry, from credible-seeming websites such as Lastresortretrieval.com to physical events where you could meet the characters being played by actors, to traditional advertising. However deeply you wanted to dig into the Heist, a mechanism was available—or you could simply create your own content.

The interplay between the three target groups was in full evidence throughout the campaign and beyond. The Zealots proved to be a group of relatively affluent young people in their late twenties who loved complex entertainment and games, and who wanted to discover the latest phenomenon to share with their circle of friends and contacts. Typically this group had rejected brands on principle and disdained the idea of being marketed to, but in this instance, while they recognized that the Art of the Heist was a brilliantly veiled marketing program, they continued to share and blogged about their experiences because they found the whole process of decoding the mystery so compelling.

As the message spread virally and the Disciples became involved, they began to vocalize not only their enjoyment of the Heist campaign but also their support for Audi as a progressive marketer—and there were various exchanges in which Disciples were active via social media in defending both the campaign and Audi against detractors. The intense digital dialogue, availability of campaign entry points and opportunities to engage—coupled with the air cover of traditional advertising—worked in tandem to draw in the Congregation. The organic effect meant that the Audi A3 wasn't viewed as just another car launch—it was seen as a progressive movement that helped to cement a social contract with Audi for a new generation of car buyers.

There was ample evidence that this digitally centered approach, designed to create a groundswell of interest that moved organically through the three target groups, had worked beyond all expectations. Through the period of the campaign and beyond, Audi saw positive brand measures increase dramatically, PR impressions and hits to its website explode, and—most important—Audi far exceeded its ambitious sales goals in the first three months. The Art of the Heist became the most awarded marketing and advertising campaign of 2006 and one of the most formative and celebrated of the decade.

COMMERCIAL LESSONS TRANSLATE TO POLITICS

Both *The Blair Witch Project* and the Art of the Heist were characterized by the organic transitions they were able to achieve from initial engagement among the Zealots to capturing and enlisting the Disciples to using them as advocates to bring in the Congregation. In the 2008 Republican and Democratic primaries, two campaigns in particular went viral and caught the imagination of younger voters— but only one of them was able to achieve a similar transition and move beyond the Zealots in capturing Disciples and the Congregation.

In 2008 Representative Ron Paul made a second attempt at running for the presidency, after an unsuccessful bid in 1988. A medical doctor and congressman for the Texas Fourteenth District, Paul still serves on the House Foreign Affairs Committee and Joint Economic Committee, as well as being chairman of the House Financial Services Committee's Domestic Monetary Policy Subcommittee.[9] Known for his libertarian positions, and founder of the advocacy group Campaign for Liberty, he's often clashed both with the Democrats as well as his own Republican leadership in Congress. Paul's been called the intellectual grandfather of the Tea Party movement, and he's the first representative in history to serve in Congress alongside his son, Rand Paul, who was elected as a senator for Kentucky in 2010.

In February 2007, a month after Ron Paul formed his presidential exploratory committee and a month before he officially entered the race, a CNN landline poll found that he had the least name recognition of any Republican candidate in the race, other than the little-known John H. Cox. From that position in the course of Ron Paul's ultimately unsuccessful bid for the Republican nomination, he shocked the field in Iowa by finishing fifth and receiving 9 percent of the vote[10]—having visited the state only three times, he still beat out Tommy Thompson, who'd visited over one hundred times.

Ron Paul garnered huge publicity not only in Boston but also in other cities across the nation with his reenactment of the Boston Tea Party, when he and his supporters dumped boxes containing banners that read "Tyranny" and "No Taxation without Representation" into Boston Harbor. He exceeded expectations in almost every state he competed in, taking 4 percent of the popular vote in all of the "Super Tuesday" states, 5 percent in Texas and Ohio, and 7 percent in Vermont and Rhode Island.[11] By most objective measures he won the Republican primary debate at the Reagan Presidential Library, and by February 2008 he'd won sixteen delegates to the Republican National Convention. By the time he suspended his campaign in June 2008,[12] Ron Paul was able to invest $4.7 million in Campaign for Liberty, the new advocacy group he had formed.

After Representative Paul suspended his campaign, traffic to his website continued to exceed that of either Senators Clinton or Obama. That wasn't a great surprise, as traffic to Paul's website in the course of the campaign had consistently outstripped that of all of his major Republican challengers, as well as the Democratic front-runners. In much the same way as Governor Howard Dean had in 2004 (which I discuss in a later chapter), Ron Paul's campaign marshaled support from Zealots through his inventive use of social media. Paul came in third among all candidates, ahead of all Republicans in the January 2008 Facebook elections—he had more than one hundred and thirty thousand Myspace® friends—and he had the most YouTube views of any Republican candidate, with his

YouTube channel becoming among the top forty most subscribed to of all time. Paul's Zealots created their own viral content including the popular "Ron Paul Girl" video, and somewhat bizarrely, numerous *World of Warcraft* players who had named themselves after him, going so far as to stage an in-game support match.

But undoubtedly Paul's greatest advocates were the one hundred and five thousand grassroots members who supported him on Meetup .com®, who collectively planned more than thirty-one thousand terrestrial (offline) events. By comparison, Senator Obama, the leading Democratic candidate on Meetup.com, had less than 5 percent the number of Ron Paul's members. Through these members, who became known as the Paulites, Ron Paul raised almost $20 million, set the largest single-day donation of any Republican in the race, and twice received the most money via the Web of any presidential candidate in history.

In noting the disparity between Paul's Web support and his performance in the primaries, David Thorburn, director of the Massachusetts Institute of Technology Communications Forum, suggested that "support from an intellectually elite minority that lives in cyberspace does not translate into support among the general population."[13] Whatever the validity of Thorburn's point, it still doesn't explain how Senator Obama—the only candidate with a comparable Web and social-media following—was able to convert his grassroots Web popularity into a fundamental culture shift, while Representative Paul remained a relative fringe candidate in 2008.

Perhaps the answer is less about the weight of traditional media dollars that Senator Obama was able to throw at his campaign than it is about the way Representative Paul's candidacy and his supporters were characterized in the mainstream media. The noted blogger Tommy Christopher spoke of the success that Paul's critics had in painting his supporters as being "cult-like." And there was ample ammunition to paint the Paulites with that brush, from their incendiary "American Revolution" campaign slogan to stunts like the reenactment of the Boston Tea Party to their success in overwhelming

Republican post-debate online polls. CNN's Jack Cafferty even suggested that Ron Paul's supporters "at any given moment can almost overpower the Internet."[14]

For African Americans in particular, there was also the specter of racism hovering around the campaign from selected newsletters published under Paul's name and brought to light by the *New Republic.* This, coupled with the comparatively extreme nature of some of Paul's policy positions—for example, as part of his nonintervention foreign policy he had called for the United States to withdraw from the United Nations and NATO. And he'd voted against almost every new government spending initiative or tax. Indeed, Paul was responsible for two-thirds of the lone negative votes in the House between 1995 and 1997, proving that as a true Zealot he wasn't just prepared to stand on principle but to stand alone!

Representative Paul appears to embrace the label of outsider, and his Zealots follow suit in supporting him, and his social contract with them states: *You are unlike other politicians in that you take stands on principle and seem to have a fundamentally different idea for the direction of America than most Democrats or Republicans. Your policies, while rooted in the Constitution, are refreshingly contrarian, especially when delivered by someone who appears to be so unassuming. You are both a traditionalist and a progressive, as your empowering use of social media demonstrates. In supporting you I feel as though I'm part of a revolutionary movement rather than a political campaign.*

Although Ron Paul has been staunch in reaffirming that he is a Republican, it's perhaps not surprising that some of his positions and actions led the Libertarian Party to reach out to him as a potential third-party presidential candidate after it became clear he wasn't going to become the Republican candidate in 2008. Nevertheless, Paul became a candidate for the Republican Party nomination again in 2012, having announced the formation of his exploratory committee in Iowa in April 2011—and he won the Tea Party Patriots summit straw poll in March 2011, suggesting that he'd have their backing as he moved forward. But Paul's ultimate success in securing the Republican nomination rested on whether this time around he could move his support beyond the Zealots and appeal to Disciples—as President Obama did successfully in 2008 in establishing his broader social contract—or whether he'd remain on the populist fringe again.

There were aspects to Representative Paul's campaign in 2008 that appealed to the psyche of Disciples. For example, these Disciples were vocal advocates for causes or brands that allowed them to participate through digital and social media, which Paul's campaign did. But at the same time they accepted the necessity of being pragmatic, even conciliatory, and believed in activism but with a moderate tone. They preferred consensus although they weren't afraid to break ranks, but if these Disciples sensed that a candidate seemed to relish extremism or consistently took polarizing positions, they would likely be turned off. Most of all they believed an idea was only as good your ability to implement it—and if they felt that a position like withdrawal from NATO would never appeal to the wider Congregation, they took it as a sign that Representative Paul preferred to remain on the fringes rather than influence the center!

The Kevin Patterson quote, "The whole world loves a maverick and the whole world wants the maverick to achieve something nobler than simple rebellion,"[15] could have been written for Disciples and provides the lens through which they have viewed Ron Paul's candidacy in 2012. If he had been able to follow in the footsteps of other great rebellion leaders and shed the polarizing skin of a revolutionary Zealot, he conceivably may have be able to ride the coattails of his grassroots movement to the Republican nomination against an unusually weak field, and challenge President Obama for the White House.

Another striking example of the degree to which garnering support from Zealots alone is ultimately self-defeating can be seen in the ongoing saga of WikiLeaks and its release of almost seventy-seven thousand documents about the war in Afghanistan that had not previously been available to the public. The July 2010 leaks detailed individual incidents of friendly fire and civilian casualties related to the conflict. Julian Assange is the editor in chief of WikiLeaks and the public face of the company, and he has described himself as being "the heart and soul of the organization."[16] Founded in October 2006 by a group it describes as Chinese dissidents, journalists, mathematicians, and entrepreneurial technologists, WikiLeaks' stated purpose is to expose oppressive regimes around the world and assist people who wish to reveal unethical behavior in governments and corporations. Others have variously described WikiLeaks as a crusading global whistle-blower and a radical organization bent on undermining NATO, capitalism, and Western democracy—depending on your politics and perspective. Secretary of State Hillary Clinton commented that the leaks "put people's lives in danger" and "threaten national security."[17]

One thing that's certain is that in releasing numerous documents that the US government considered to be both classified as well as highly embarrassing in some instances, WikiLeaks cemented its outlaw credentials in the eyes of the Obama White House, and the administration has not been reticent in going after both the organization and Julian Assange specifically. Soon after the leak of diplomatic cables began, Attorney General Eric Holder opened a criminal probe of both WikiLeaks and Julian Assange, and the US Justice Department is reportedly considering charges under the Espionage Act—while Federal prosecutors are also allegedly considering prosecuting Assange for trafficking in stolen government property. One complication in prosecuting Assange in the United States is related to rape charges he is facing in Sweden—one of his lawyers stated that they had resisted extradition to Sweden from Great Britain, where Assange resided for several years, in part because they feared it would ultimately lead to his extradition to the United States. With Assange appealing the extradition order to Sweden, it will be fascinating to see whether his lawyer's prediction comes true.

Not everyone considers Julian Assange to be a pariah, however. Legal expert Dr. Ben Saul has suggested that he believes Assange is the target of a global smear campaign to demonize him as a criminal or a terrorist, while the Center for Constitutional Rights issued a statement pinpointing the "multiple examples of legal overreach and irregularities" related to Assange's arrest in Britain. But whatever your personal stand on the rights and wrongs of WikiLeaks—whether you believe it helps facilitate open government by revealing truths that ordinary people have a right to know or whether you believe it is guilty of reckless endangerment of people's lives—support for the organization will never spread beyond a minority of Zealots world-wide who support WikiLeaks' stand because of the radical manner in which it goes about pursuing its stated agenda.

The Disciple persona prefers to be right rather than first, and would seriously question whether the upside of releasing such an overwhelming number of highly sensitive documents is warranted. Disciples also believe that change comes from the inside, and they would consider WikiLeaks' actions to be that of an outsider at best—and more likely they'd simply consider those actions to be reckless. Most important, Disciples believe in activism but with a moderate tone, and nothing about Julian Assange, the public face of WikiLeaks, would strike them as moderate. The degree to which citizens should have open access to classified government information is a serious and important debate, but as long as WikiLeaks and Julian Assange continue to be seen to behave as an outlaw group they will limit their support to a minority of Zealots—and alienate the Disciples who could theoretically enable support from the wider Congregation.

One of the areas where a leader needs to tread a fine line between being seen as a Zealot versus a Disciple relates to the business and practice of political consulting. For companies and organizations paying political consultants to wield insider influence over Washington's legislators, they hope and expect to see a Zealot-like commitment to the cause they are paying them to be advocates for. While lobbying is a fundamental right guaranteed under the US constitution—as the first amendment states, "Congress shall make no law abridging the freedom to petition the government for a redress of grievances"—that doesn't mean that lobbyists' clients, who in some cases are paying hundreds of millions of dollars to influence the five thousand bills that are introduced into Congress every session, want their efforts to be made public and be written about.

Until his conviction for mail fraud and conspiracy in 2006,[18] along with US Representative Bob Ney and nine other lobbyists and congressional aids, Jack Abramoff was the darling of K Street and the poster child for the power of Washington lobbyists. His rise and crashing fall were chronicled in the 2010 movie *Casino Jack*, which starred Kevin Spacey as Abramoff.[19] Nicknamed Casino Jack in part because of his lobbying efforts on behalf of the gaming rights of various Native American tribes, including the Choctaws and the Coushattas, Abramoff ultimately pled guilty to two criminal felony counts of defrauding the tribes of tens of millions of dollars.

While rightly incarcerated for his criminal acts, perhaps Abramoff's style of doing business and Zealot-like persona eventually ruffled enough feathers to ensure that an unwelcome spotlight would be shone on both his elicit activities and the practice of lobbying—much to the chagrin of the K Street community, and members of Congress, who were fully aware that the practice was deeply unpopular with the American public. In many ways Jack Abramoff did for lobbying what John Gotti did for organized crime—by making it seem glamorous and bringing the practice out into the open, he raised public consciousness and ultimately paid the price when the spotlight he'd created revealed his illegal activities. In truth, a successful lobbyist may need to have the heart of a Zealot to be successful, but he or she needs to adopt the style and manner of a Disciple to be effective in the longer term.

PERSONIFYING LEADERS AND GROUPS

So if you are evaluating a public figure like Julian Assange or Jack Abramoff, or a political candidate like Ron Paul, or even your own company's CEO, how can you decode how they are wired as a leader? Or conversely, in reviewing your political supporters, brand advocates, or celebrity fans, how can you determine whether they are Zealots, Disciples, or members of the Congregation?

Neuro-Linguisitic Programming™ (NLP™) is widely used by management trainers, life coaches, and the self-help industry to enable people to improve their ability to communicate by helping them to better understand their own wiring and that of others.[20] NLP is also used by covert government services like the CIA and the FBI as a tool to draw out people's unconscious feelings and profile them. You'll see NLP techniques on display in recent hit television shows such as *Lie to Me, The Mentalist,* and *Hawaii Five-0.*

Richard Bandler developed NLP in the early 1960s while he was a student at the University of Santa Cruz in tandem with his professor John Grindler. "Neuro" relates to how we process information through our senses. "Linguistic" relates to how we use language to communicate. "Programming" connotes how we organize information to achieve desired results. In combining these components, they came up with a process that has helped people both decode as well as communicate with others by observing their styles of speech and actions.

Following the principles of NLP, each of us has a preferred communication modality that can be visual, auditory, or kinesthetic. Once you become proficient in reading someone's primary modality, you're able to communicate more effectively. For example, as a father, knowing that my daughter is auditory, I will make a particular effort to choose language that matches her wiring in order to get my point across: "I hear you. It sounds like . . . Listen to this." My son, on the other hand, is visual, so conversely I'll make a particular effort to use seeing words with him: "I see what you mean. Let me paint a picture for you. It looks like . . ." It doesn't solve all our communication issues, but at least we can start from the same page.

Often the most revealing aspect of NLP in trying to decode a person's wiring, however, is called *cue framing.* Cue framing is based on the principle that people are motivated by certain cues that influence their decision making, whether choosing a brand, supporting a candidate, or becoming a fan of a particular celebrity. One particularly instructive cue when evaluating a leader relates to whether he or she is wired to *move away* from something or to *move toward* something, as

I'll explain. In society we're roughly an even split between the two. Some of us instinctively move away from negative consequences in seeking to resolve a problem, while others simply move toward a positive outcome without first considering the potential downside. People who are "move away" are sometimes mistakenly labeled as being negative, when in reality you can be wired to move away from negative consequences and still be an inspiring leader, or vice versa.

This simple cue can be enormously instructive in trying to profile the type of leader a person is, or may become in the future. For example, in Jon Meacham's excellent portrait of the friendship between Roosevelt and Churchill, *Franklin and Winston*, it is striking how their partnership worked so well[21]—in part because Roosevelt was "move away" while Churchill was "move toward." As we reflect on Churchill's extraordinary leadership through World War II, it's easy to forget that his early political life was marked by relative failure caused in large measure by consistent overreaching.

Many historians attribute Churchill's poor decision making and overreaching to the Allies' tragic setback at Gallipoli, during World War I, while he was First Lord of the Admiralty. Churchill's greatest strength was his ability to inspire others with a sense that anything was possible. But it wasn't until he found a partner in Roosevelt, who could temper Churchill's tendency to rush in, that Churchill appears to have become truly successful in his decision making. In essence, Churchill's early leadership was clouded by his unchecked "move toward" tendencies, which marked him as more Zealot than Disciple. Although his style and temperament clearly evolved over time, in part because of his partnership with Roosevelt, perhaps it isn't surprising that prior to World War II the British people had become wary of Churchill's extremist positions and rhetoric, and his apparent tendency to act like a proverbial "bull in a china shop."

The other tempering influence in Churchill's life, and certainly the most constant, was Clementine, his beloved wife and the source of much of his strength, stability, and compassion. *The Gathering Storm* was a charming and insightful 2002 BBC and HBO film that dramatized the period leading up to the outbreak of World War II while Churchill was in the political wilderness—fighting what at times appeared to be a lone battle to get Parliament and the rest of Britain to recognize the threat that Hitler and a re-armed Germany posed. Exquisitely portrayed by Albert Finney and Vanessa Redgrave, Churchill's bluster and instinct to charge in and confront an issue head on and the valiant attempts by his wife, Clementine, to put a check on his bravado is beautifully captured in the interplay between the couple.[22]

In the 2009 sequel to the original film, *Into the Storm,* with Brendan Gleeson and Janet McTeer now playing Winston and Clemmie,[23] void of the influence of the now-deceased Roosevelt and ignoring the pleadings of his wife, Churchill made a fatal error in his first national election radio broadcast in suggesting that a Labour (socialist) government wouldn't allow free expression of public discontent, stating that "they would have to fall back on some form of Gestapo." The phrase was taken to mean that Churchill was comparing the British Labour Party to the detested Nazi secret police, and is widely considered to have been central to the defeat of Churchill's Conservatives, and to his own removal as prime minister in the 1945 election. Churchill's Zealot-like inability to compromise, even in his choice of language in this case, was more illustrative of his early years as a leader than of his Disciple-like stewardship through World War II.[24]

Some historians maintain that at the Yalta Conference in February 1945, the perception was that President Roosevelt (FDR) gave in to Stalin over the post-war borders of Poland, while Churchill was willing to launch a war against Stalin, as Churchill stated, ". . . to prevent Europe from being saved from one tyrant only to be handed over to another." FDR took a more pragmatic approach, not because he didn't appreciate the threat that Stalin posed or because he misjudged Stalin's character, but because he recognized that both the United States and Europe needed the USSR to enter the Pacific war with the Allies.[25] In compromising, Roosevelt was demonstrating the characteristics of a Disciple, by moving away from a greater threat while solving an immediate problem.

Churchill wasn't the only successful leader to morph his style and approach over time to match the persona of a Disciple. Freedom fighters and revolutionaries like Nelson Mandela in South Africa and Lech Walesa in Poland gave up the mantle of a Zealot in order to lead the wider Congregations in their countries. There are also examples of leaders in history who have shown all the characteristics of a Disciple in ascending to power, only to govern as a Zealot—as Robert Mugabe in Zimbabwe exemplifies today. Churchill and Roosevelt are also not the only examples of a successful partnership in which one leader is "move toward" and the other "move away," although often it isn't apparent until sometime after they've left office. President Clinton's decision-making process, revealed in his memoir *My Life,* is suggestive of a Disciple with "move away" traits, while Vice President Gore is revealed both from the memoir as well as from his career since leaving office as having more Zealot-like tendencies.[26] While they were in office, however, it appeared from a distance as though the reverse was true.

Understanding these distinctions isn't valuable only in trying to understand how a leader or an individual is wired—they can also apply to entire groups of people in both the commercial and political realms. When trying to establish a social contract, it's important to recognize that the early Zealots will be predominantly the ones who move toward, with passion and energy and the desire to be first to make their case and state their terms—as was the case in Egypt when the early Zealots took to the streets without having framed their demands or agenda, simply calling for the overthrow of President Mubarak. The Disciples in the Egyptian uprising were slower to take to the street, considering the downside as well as the upside of the uprising—demonstrating the classic tendency to "move away" from any unintended consequences before reaching for a positive outcome. In the case of the Egyptian uprising, the Zealots were the voices *for* the removal of Mubarak, but the Disciples were the voices *against* the dismantling of the state that ultimately paved the way for the broader Congregation to embrace the pro-democracy movement.

BE PREPARED TO ABANDON THE ZEALOTS

Kevin Patterson's quote, "The whole world loves a maverick and the whole world wants the maverick to achieve something nobler than simple rebellion," speaks to the desire we all have to see a popular movement gather momentum and realize its ultimate purpose. After an initial uprising, such as we've seen in the Middle East, what's required is a more pragmatic and less puritanical approach. Unless Zealots are able to evolve and adopt the persona of Disciples, it can be necessary to abandon them—as it's the Disciples who will ultimately persuade and engage the wider Congregation and perpetuate a culture shift.

This may seem callous, as the Zealots typically are your original and most vocal supporters and the ones who helped you become established in the first place. But the nature of Zealots is such that they have a polarizing influence, and in the end can serve to limit broader participation.

The Disciples who took more time to finally support you did so because they were studying you before making a commitment. When they did come on board they made a positive choice, believing in your ability to fulfill your purpose, and as a result will be longer-term advocates—assuming you don't break the terms of the social contract. Disciples are your greatest asset in convincing the wider Congregation to become part of the movement, and the more your efforts and decisions are geared toward arming the Disciples to make the case for you, the more efficient you can be and the more success you'll ultimately achieve.

CHAPTER 3

I FOLLOW THE LEADER.
HE FOLLOWS ME.

"As we look into the next century, leaders will be those who empower others. "

—Bill Gates, opening
the Gates Foundation Library, Oregon, 1997

There can be only one leader.

Rome was a republic for almost five hundred years before the emperors. Two consuls would be elected from the Senate to serve together for a period of one year, at which point two new consuls were then elected. While in theory there was no single leader or figurehead, upon returning from successful campaigns in Gaul, Germania, and Britannia, successful generals were able to dictate terms to the Senate because of their standing among the Roman people.

Even the greatest senators and consuls like Cicero—who had the wisdom, wit, and political savvy to preserve the republic—fought an uphill battle trying to impose restraints on Rome's most popular generals. No general could enter the gates of Rome with anyone other than his personal guard unless the Senate had invited him to do so. In addition, as a general led his troops back into a city in triumph, a slave always accompanied him who was charged with constantly whispering reminders to him that the victorious general was just a man and not a god. The same practice continued under the emperors of Rome, and similarly failed to keep their egos in check as the deranged Caligula famously proved, eventually declaring himself a god.[1] This was not a huge leap for an emperor who had previously appointed his favorite horse to be a senator.

Perhaps it was inevitable that eventually one general, with limitless ambition and the adoration of the general population—due to his extraordinary military accomplishments and genius for propaganda—would seek to elevate himself to the position of emperor. Although Julius Caesar was never pronounced emperor, he functioned in that capacity and paved the way for his nephew Octavian, who became known as Augustus, to become Rome's true patriarch and its first emperor, after he defeated Marc Antony and Queen Cleopatra at the Battle of Actium[2] and reunified the empire.

You would think that after enduring the obscene excesses and barbarism of the lunatic Caligula's rule, the people of Rome would have preferred anything to another emperor, particularly when the only available candidate at the time, Claudius, was thought by most to be mentally unsound. Robert Graves's *I, Claudius*, a leading candidate for the greatest historical novel ever written, illuminates the character of the emperor who was considered an imbecile when he was elevated almost by chance after Caligula was assassinated—and yet returned sanity and prosperity to Rome during his reign.[3]

While it is understandable that the largely Germanic Praetorian Guard which benefited most from the patronage of the emperor would have sought to elevate Claudius, it is revealing that the Senate, legions, and people of Rome quickly accepted Claudius, rather than forcing a return to the republic. After all, even Claudius had been an advocate for the republic for most of his life. But if history teaches us anything, it's that the nature of societies is such that we seek to elevate one individual above all others, even when a political culture shift has occurred, driven by need to oust one individual from power, as evidenced in 2011 in Tunisia, Egypt, and Libya.

The Russian Revolution of 1917 ousted Tsar Nicholas II and soon voted in Vladimir Lenin as chairman of the Council of the People's Commissars of Russia and the undisputed first among equals. France dispensed with its monarchs, only to replace them with presidents who came to wield regal powers. Many have questioned why Britain and the commonwealth of former colonial countries continue to have a monarchy. It can't be simply because it's good for tourism and the movie industry, as the Oscar-winning success of *The King's Speech* might suggest. It certainly isn't cheap maintaining a monarchy with the accompanied pomp, royal weddings, and required maintenance of properties, and the Queen is still the richest woman in the world. As for why Australia retains Queen Elizabeth II as its head of state, a great Aussie friend of mine suggested that "it would be extremely mean-spirited to fire an elderly lady, when she'll be retiring soon enough"—the implication being that Australia may well reconsider becoming a republic when Prince Charles ascends to the throne, having last rejected the idea of breaking ties with the British monarchy in 1999 by a vote of 55 percent to 45 percent.[4]

Somewhat counterintuitively, however, having a monarchy can actually be quite good for a modern democracy. Because our instinct is to elevate one individual above all others, when the monarch fulfills that ceremonial function it is less likely that the highest-elected leader—whether he or she be a prime minister or a president—will be treated with reverence and placed on a pedestal. In truth, they seem far more likely to be held accountable by the people who put them there. That's one potential benefit, of course, another being we get to enjoy the pomp and ceremony of a royal wedding every so often, as we did on April 29, 2011, with the marriage of Prince William and Kate Middleton, now the Duke and Duchess of Cambridge.[5]

Many of my friends in the United States look with envy at prime minister's question time in the British House of Commons, wishing that their presidents could be similarly tested and grilled by congressional colleagues on a weekly basis. While it's undoubtedly good political theater, it's also a study in democracy and accountability. If it was the political equivalent of a staged wrestling match, it's doubtful that prime ministers, past and present, would have dreaded it as much as they did and sought to limit the number of such encounters—something Tony Blair finally managed to do. Those who witnessed it won't soon forget the spectacle of Margaret Thatcher's final prime minister's question time after a decade in power, and after her resignation to avoid being ousted by Conservative Party members of Parliament, in 1989. What many thought might be a somber affair turned into an amusing romp as the departing prime minister demonstrated her mastery of the forum while spraying caustic charm and wit around the House of Commons chamber, at one point leaning back on her lectern and remarking, "I'm enjoying this."[6]

While Mr. Blair was still a humble backbench member of the UK Parliament, in the early 1980s a new political party was formed called the Social Democratic Party (SDP), in reaction to the increasing shift to the far left that the Labour Party was making at that time.[7] Led by the respected veteran Labour minister Roy Jenkins and the charismatic former foreign secretary, Dr. David Owen, the SDP lacked the political infrastructure to fight an election, and so they chose to partner with the Liberal Party to fight the national elections in 1983 and 1987.

While the SDP initially saw polling numbers as high as 30 percent soon after their inception—reflecting the desire in the United Kingdom for a strong third-party alternative—they failed to take significant parliamentary seats from either of the major parties in the national election, in large measure because they ran their campaign with two equal party leaders, David Owen and David Steel.

British voters struggled to understand the direction and core values of the Liberal–SDP alliance, as is the case with all political groups when there isn't a single leader that personifies them. Soon after the 1987 election, the alliance bowed to the inevitable and merged, appointing David Steel as its single undisputed party leader.[8]

ONLY A DISCIPLE CREATES MASS PARTICIPATION

When a political culture shift develops, the first question tends to be who is leading it—and that inevitably frames our perspective of the nature of the uprising, and goes a long way in determining our willingness to support it. Would the Russian or Cuban Revolution have succeeded without Lenin or Castro? Would the Velvet Revolution in the former Czechoslovakia or Solidarity in Poland have succeeded without Havel or Walesa? Would South Africa's relatively peaceful transition to majority rule have been possible without Mandela?

Although each of these leaders began as a Zealot for their cause, each consciously or unconsciously adopted the persona of a Disciple in order to bring their Congregations along with them. Conversely, who can name the leader of the Tiananmen Square protests that were ruthlessly crushed by the Chinese authorities? We remember the young man who stood bravely in front of the tanks, in part because our instinct is to personify any culture shift through a single individual; but there was no leading Disciple around whom people could coalesce.

And while the Egyptian people were successful in ousting Mubarak, history suggests their political movement will fail to achieve its ultimate democratic goals unless an acceptable leader with the persona of a Disciple emerges to nudge the military leadership to give up the powers they've inherited.

The story of Nelson Mandela's imprisonment for twenty-six years during the apartheid period in South Africa, and his eventual release by then president F. W. de Klerk, is well documented.[9] But the actions of the secret police through that period in systematically eliminating every moderate leader that emerged—through murder or imprisonment—are less well known. While other African National Congress (ANC) activists stayed underground and fought a violent insurgency against the apartheid regime, Steve Biko was the classic voice of a Disciple for the freedom movement in South Africa. His story and tragic murder is movingly told in the book and film *Cry Freedom,*[10] written by his friend, the noted journalist Donald Woods.

By imprisoning the more moderate voices like Mandela and Walter Sisulu, successive apartheid governments ensured that the only resistance leaders left were militant Zealots. This helped to ensure that the armed conflict continued and intensified. It wasn't until February 11, 1990, when Mandela appeared at the gates of Victor Verster Prison in Paarl to be cheered by thousands of supporters overjoyed at his release,[11] that the ANC was fully able to come together behind a now-moderate Disciple, and the opportunity for a peaceful transition of power versus a civil war emerged.

In the United States, the grassroots Tea Party movement that emerged and gained traction after the 2008 election—in large measure as a protest against what was viewed as too much government[12]—has struggled to find a leader with the profile of a Disciple, one around whom all members of the party can unite. Of the various candidates, former governor Sarah Palin of Alaska has the highest profile after being Senator John McCain's vice presidential nominee in 2008 and continuing to receive media exposure. But she is viewed as a polarizing figure and for many, lacking in gravitas—traits she is seen to share with another potential leader, Representative Michele Bachmann of Minnesota. Senator Jim DeMint of South Carolina and Senator Rand Paul of Kentucky both have the credence that comes with elected office, but they are known more for what they stand against than for what they stand for. Representative Ron Paul, Rand Paul's father and the man considered the spiritual leader of the Tea Party movement, would also need to evolve from his perceived Zealot-like persona (as discussed in the previous chapter), based in part on some of his more radical policy positions. Rush Limbaugh and Glen Beck both have powerful broadcast platforms but little credibility as political leaders outside of the journalism industry, and plenty of baggage within it.

All have important voices but none is seen as the undisputed leader. For the Tea Party to sustain its momentum, it needs to anoint a unifying Chief Disciple, requiring that a new leader emerge or that one of these prospective leaders shed the polarizing skin of a Zealot. The 2012 Republican primary campaign provided a platform for someone to emerge as the new undisputed leader of the Tea Party. However, with the rise and seemingly immediate fall of Representative Bachmann, former Texas governor Rick Perry, and least likely of all, former Godfather's Pizza CEO Hermann Cain, no one was able to dislodge Ron Paul as the Chief Disciple. But given Paul's polarizing persona, the party's influence is in danger of waning in the longer term, as a political movement can emerge without a unifying leader, but it cannot perpetuate and achieve its potential without one.

THE ACCIDENTAL DISCIPLE

The need for someone with the persona of a Disciple to emerge as a leader isn't limited just to politics, but is equally important in the context of culture shifts that are humanitarian in nature, and sometimes the Disciple who does emerge is seemingly the least likely candidate.

On October 23, 1984, BBC News in Britain aired a story by a young reporter named Michael Buerk from Korem in Ethiopia (Buerk went on to become the prime-time news anchor for the BBC).[13] Largely hidden from the Western world until then, a famine of biblical proportions had developed in Ethiopia, and the pictures carried in the television news report first stirred a nation and then the world. Tragically, then as now, there are people starving throughout the world—more than one billion according to United Nations estimates.[14] People in the West can become immune to images of starvation and suffering from developing countries. But what made the global response to this catastrophe so different from similar events was, in large part, because one highly motivated, highly persuasive, and extremely well-connected rock star had been watching and was moved to do something about it.

In many ways, Bob Geldof was an unlikely global leader of the Live Aid movement that he launched. He wasn't a global superstar like Sting or Bono, and he wasn't well known as a humanitarian activist. His band, the Boomtown Rats, had emerged during the punk era of the late 1970s, and its star was already fading.[15] Geldof was initially a Zealot who raged against the injustice of starvation being tolerated in the late twentieth century, but he quickly found his Disciple voice and inspired people to believe that this time something could be done. He partnered with Midge Ure from the band Ultravox in writing "Do They Know It's Christmas," and he convinced many of Britain's biggest rock and pop stars at that time to record it, including Sting, Bono, Paul Young, Paul Weller, Simon Le Bon, George Michael, and Boy George. The success of the single inspired a comparable US release of the song "We Are the World," written by Michael Jackson, with a catalog of American stars recording it, including Stevie Wonder, Dionne Warwick, Willie Nelson, and Bruce Springsteen.

In 1985, Geldof partnered with Harvey Goldsmith, the successful promoter and producer, to stage groundbreaking back-to-back concerts at Wembley Stadium in London and John F. Kennedy Stadium (aka JFK Stadium) in Philadelphia. The concerts inspired similar events in Australia and Germany. More than seventy thousand people (including myself) attended the Wembley concert, while almost one hundred thousand attended in Philadelphia. Phil Collins, lead singer and drummer of the band Genesis, performed in London, jumped on the Concorde immediately afterward, and performed in New York. The title of "world's biggest band" informally passed from the Police to U2, and the late Freddie Mercury—the consummate showman—proved that he was peerless as he and his band Queen proceeded to steal the show. It was initially hoped that the London concert would raise $1.5 million, but in the end the combined concerts raised about $230 million. Donations flooded in from all over the world, including a $1.5 million donation from the ruling family of Dubai. Live Aid became one of the world's largest charitable organizations overnight, and Bob Geldof was knighted as a result.[16]

Could Live Aid have happened if another rock star or celebrity had stepped forward to lead it? Another leader would have had to match Geldof's energy and passion, as well as his ability to inspire participation. In the age before the Web, the only way to participate—other than financially—was through physical action, and Geldof's tirelessness and ability to get any organization or person to participate inspired people to become active themselves in donating not just money but also their time.

Another essential and often-overlooked enabler of a successful Chief Disciple is the individual who often remains in the shadows, allowing the Chief Disciple to lead and shine. In Geldof's case it was Midge Ure, the little-discussed former leader of the band Ultravox, whose presence appeared to be a calming and guiding influence for Geldof as the Live Aid movement rose to undreamed-of heights in the national psyche. These "shadow men and women" play a pivotal role both functionally and psychologically in guiding their political, business, sporting, and business leaders to glory.

The comments of Steve Williams, Tiger Woods's former caddy and Aussie Adam Scott's current man on the bag, after his new boss's dominant win at the WGC Bridgestone Invitational on August 8, 2011, were striking. Having caddied for Tiger for most of Woods's major wins and having walked in the shadows as Tiger won seven Bridgestone titles, Williams described Scott's 2011 Bridgestone win as the "best win of my [thirty-three-year professional] career as a caddy," thereby delivering his former boss a subtly aimed left hook! It will be fascinating over the next few years to compare Adam Scott's fortunes with those of Tiger Woods, as a way to judge the crucial nature of Williams's role in their partnership, and Tiger's unprecedented success during that period.

Many English soccer (football) fans will have enjoyed the 2009 film *The Damned United,* which dramatized the career of legendary manager (coach) Brian Clough and his hate-love-hate relationship with Leeds United Football Club. The film brilliantly revealed Clough's emotional and practical reliance on his coaching "sidekick" Peter Taylor. Having partnered with Clough to great effect at Derby County Football Club, Taylor refused to join him at Leeds, and without the foil and emotional balance he provided, Clough's reign at the then league champions lasted just forty-four days. Clough may have been a Chief Disciple in his various managerial roles, but he clearly couldn't function and succeed without Taylor.

And shadow men and women aren't just limited to the sporting world. Would Vincent Van Gogh be celebrated today if his brother Theo hadn't made it his life's mission to provide the emotional and financial support necessary for Vincent to work and function? Even after his brother succumbed to mental illness and took his own life, Theo maintained his commitment to ensuring that his brother's work was seen and revered, in much the same way as the great American abstract expressionist Jackson Pollock's wife, Lee Krasner, did. Van Gogh's famous self-portrait is now believed to actually have been the only portrait of Theo ever completed, offering some legacy for Theo's valiant efforts in the shadows.

Golf caddies, artists' reps, comedic straight men, sports agents, political spouses, right-hand men, and the list goes on of shadow men and women who enable the Chief Disciple to flourish. So why do we leave them in the shadows and fail to celebrate their pivotal contributions? Why must only the stars be allowed to shine and not their enablers, with the fictional exception of Tom Cruise's *Jerry Maguire*? Perhaps we are afraid that if we acknowledge that the extraordinary requires the merely exceptional in order to flourish then their star will be diminished. Of course this is illogical, as the reverse tends to be true. When a Chief Disciple acknowledges his or her limitations and raises someone up from the shadows, it only makes his or her star shine more brightly. Certainly a key component of Geldof's appeal as the Chief Disciple of the Live Aid movement was his authentic humility in the midst of a host of typically egotistical rock stars.

It's fun to imagine how much money could be raised today by a comparable star-studded global effort, with the power of social media. Watching the story of yet another biblical famine unfolding in Somalia in September 2011, it's natural to feel ashamed that this generation hasn't been able to move us forward enough in the last quarter century to make famine on this scale a thing of the past. It's also natural to wonder if the current generation of celebrity musicians and entertainers will step up and inspire today's children as Bono, Sting, Springsteen, and Geldof did in the past.

Among today's artists and producers, who has the influence and charisma to rally the world's greatest entertainers together to perpetuate this movement? Jay-Z, Sean Combs, Chris Martin of Coldplay, Lady Gaga, or perhaps Katy Perry could become the new Chief Disciple. In Katy Perry's case that's probably much easier now that she has separated from her actor husband Russell Brand, ensuring that there wouldn't be any unfortunate associations with his spoof "African Child" music video from the raucous 2010 movie, *Get Him to the Greek.*

With the myriad of traditional, digital, and social distractions today it would be a herculean task to focus the attention of the world's youth on Somalia; but then we could have said that back in 1984 about Ethiopia, yet Geldof made it happen.

It's little wonder that charitable organizations like the UN Refugee Agency (UNHCR) appoint celebrity goodwill ambassadors to promote their efforts in specific parts of the world, helping to generate support and raise funds. As with any popular cause, the more a charity remains faceless and leaderless, the less inclined the Congregation will be to participate and donate. As with all seismic culture shifts, Live Aid would not have succeeded on the scale it did without a leader with the persona of a Disciple who became the driving force behind it and caused people to participate. Bob Geldof's story reminds us that sometimes it's necessary to broaden your search beyond the usual suspects in order to find the perfect Chief Disciple.

CEO AS CHIEF DISCIPLE

Evidence overwhelmingly suggests that we now apply the same basic criteria to culture shifts that are commercial in nature as we do to ones that are humanitarian or political. Once upon a time, most brands were wholly separate entities from their corporate parents by design, in the way that Head & Shoulders® and Tide® have little visible connection to

Procter & Gamble. From an image standpoint, this allowed the parent company to operate very different brands in different segments, creating niche appeal to select groups of people. Because of the Web and social media, however, today nothing can be hidden. In image terms, the brand and its parent company become joined at the hip unless, as in the case of Dove (which I discussed in the first chapter), consumers choose to employ a form of selective hearing.

So the corporate leader comes under tremendous scrutiny. Not only must the leader manage the company in a way that's compatible with the stand that the company's brand has taken, but also the leader's very persona must project the values that the customers embrace. More than that, today's political and corporate leader must be a living reflection of the company's brand, in much the same way as a corporate pitchman used to function in the past. This is something that the leaders of the International Monetary Fund (IMF), which recently has played such a crucial role in helping to avoid an economic meltdown in Europe in particular, were forced to reflect upon when the managing director of the organization, Dominique Strauss-Kahn, was arrested on sexual assault charges, after he was alleged to have forced a maid at the Sofitel Hotel in New York to perform a sexual act on him.[17] Although the criminal charges were subsequently dropped, the damage to his image and that of the IMF was done.

Following the inevitable resignation of Strauss-Kahn, who had been considered a leading contender in the forthcoming presidential elections in France prior to his arrest, the IMF had multiple considerations in choosing his replacement. Given the increasing importance of emerging economies like Brazil, India, and China, choosing a non-European to replace Strauss-Kahn might have been the most logical approach, and would have signaled a complete departure from the perceived nepotism of continually appointing a European to the position. However, given the nature of Strauss-Kahn's scandalous departure and the need to project an entirely different image of leadership at the IMF, the immediate front-runner was another European,

Christine Lagarde—who was talked about as much for her impressive economic credentials, having previously been the French finance minister, as for the fact that she is a woman, and would therefore project an entirely different persona for the tarnished image of the IMF. Therefore, perhaps it came as no surprise to anyone when Lagarde was confirmed as the new IMF chief in June 2011.[18]

When the public's relationship with a company or brand has elevated to form a social contract, the heightened degree of emotional connection puts an even greater emphasis on the leader, typically the CEO. He or she is no longer simply the head of the company that makes your particular brand of choice but the driving force behind a culture shift that you have aligned yourself with. Leaders today need to recognize that their personal profiles directly impact consumers' support of their company and brand, and that consumers expect to be part of an environment in which they can actively participate.

As well as being CEOs of progressive companies that have achieved extraordinary success by changing not only their business categories but in many ways the world, Howard Shultz and the late Steve Jobs each became an integral part of their organization's lore. Founders of Starbucks and Apple, respectively, Shultz and Jobs left or stepped back for a period of time during their reigns and saw the fortunes of their companies dip dramatically. Both later returned in triumph. Shareholders hung on their every word, as evidenced when Apple's share price took a downturn on both occasions after Steve Jobs announced he was taking a sabbatical due to health issues related to his ongoing battle with pancreatic cancer, a battle that he ultimately lost on October 5, 2011.[19]

Anyone who believes that the era of the CEO rock star is over has failed to understand the nature of the relationship that customers and shareholders have with these companies—and specifically with their leaders. There is a high likelihood that successful young executives walking down the street in Manhattan will have a Starbucks cup in one hand and an iPhone in the other. The social contract they have with each company states: *I define myself in part through these excep-*

tional and iconic products, and your company will embody my progressive values in the person of your charismatic CEO.

Of course it isn't logical that an iPhone owner should have personally held Steve Jobs to a certain level of "coolness" or that Apple shareholders should have rushed to sell their shares because he'd taken a medical leave. Logically, we all knew that Apple was a business with thousands of accomplished individuals—and that Steve Jobs was largely an inspirational figurehead. But as with any commercial culture shift—and Apple and the iPhone certainly rise to that level—we take our cues from the organization's leader.

When a Chief Disciple steps away from his or her respective role, at that time, in order to maintain the momentum of their commercial culture shift, the organization has two options: (1) It can seek to install an equally charismatic individual who is thought to personify similar values, as Hewlett-Packard attempted to do when Lew Platt stepped down to be replaced by Carly Fiorina, then Leo Apotheker, and most recently Meg Whitman, the former eBay CEO;[20] or (2) it can install an essentially gray individual in terms of image and continue to perpetuate the myth and legend of the former leader, keeping him or her present in people's minds—as Microsoft did when Bill Gates stepped down and Steve Ballmer replaced him as CEO. After all, it was Bill Gates and not Steve Ballmer who appeared in the iconic 2008 Microsoft television commercials, created by their agency Crispin Porter + Bogusky, and playing alongside Jerry Seinfeld—even though Gates had previously announced he would be stepping down from his position as CEO in order to focus more attention on the Bill & Melinda Gates Foundation.[21]

The more essential the CEO is to the founding or reinventing of the company and therefore the culture shift, the harder it is to find a charismatic replacement. Steve Ballmer's excellent stewardship of Microsoft has been done in the shadow of Bill Gates's continuing persona, rather than under Ballmer's own public spotlight. And although Steve Ballmer hasn't replaced Bill Gates as the iconic persona at the heart of Microsoft, the company's Disciples happily accept him as the leader. It is likely that the board of directors at Apple had this example in mind in August 2011 when they chose to announce that Tim Cook, the companies COO and a trusted deputy of Steve Jobs, would be replacing Jobs as CEO. The well-planned transition ensured that even posthumously, Steve Jobs would remain the company's iconic persona and the leader of Apple's culture shift, while Cook assumed the arduous duties of being the CEO.

When only the Zealots (and not the Disciples) accept your CEO, it's impossible to expand the social contract and perpetuate a culture shift, as Napster discovered in the late 1990s. The emergence of peer-to-peer sharing of music as MP3 files via the Web is illustrative of several important aspects of how social contracts form—and of the role of a leader within them. Shawn Fanning and Sean Parker founded Napster while attending Northeastern University in Boston. They envisioned an independent file-sharing service that offered music for free, using technology that allowed users to bypass the established market.[22]

Early Zealots of the technology found it easy to download copies of rare music from bootlegged recordings, and felt justified in doing so because they'd already purchased the music in other formats like CD or cassette tape. They felt empowered by the process of trading and downloading music for free and making their own compilation albums on recordable CDs. At the same time, these Zealots enjoyed thumbing their noses at the record companies that they felt had been making undue profits by controlling the availability of music. When Napster ran into legal troubles over copyright infringement, Fanning and Parker became folk heroes within the community, taking on the profile of outlaws who robbed from the rich to give to the poor.

Early Disciples of peer-to-peer music sharing and downloading were equally attracted to the benefits of the technology, but they had a different perspective on Fanning and Parker. For many, it was the artists who were suffering from copyright infringement, fueled by the fact that the likes of Metallica, Dr. Dre, and Madonna had filed lawsuits against Napster. To the Disciples, Fanning and Parker were less heroic outlaws than opportunistic thieves who were muddying the image of an important technology—an image which, in Parker's case, was reinforced by Justin Timberlake's portrayal of him as both opportunistic and hard partying in the acclaimed 2010 movie *The Social Network*, about the travails and intrigue related to the founding of Facebook.[23]

Ultimately, the US Court of Appeals for the Ninth Circuit ruled that Napster needed to block access to infringing material, and because it was unable to do so, Napster shut down the service in July 2001.[24] Beyond the legal barriers to Napster becoming the leader of the music-sharing and downloading culture shift, the profile of Fanning and Parker was such that the Disciples and the Congregation of music enthusiasts sought a less militant and controversial face for the new technology.

They found it in Steve Jobs after Apple acquired SoundJam MP in 2000, which later became the basis for iTunes®.[25] Apple had the profile of a pioneer of progressive technology, and Steve Jobs's vision and connections ensured that he had the perfect platform to take music sharing and downloading into the mainstream in a way that was acceptable to the Disciples—and the rest, as they say, is history.

If you ask whether another company or leader could have affected the mainstreaming of music sharing and downloading, the answer is yes—but beyond Apple's technology, Steve Jobs's unique persona (and connections) was a key ingredient. The Zealots may have relished outlaws who fought the record companies in court, but the Disciples preferred someone who could find a solution that was acceptable to all parties. The Congregation simply wanted music downloading and sharing to be made simpler and more accessible, and Apple obliged through iTunes, the iPod®, and later the iPhone.

Apple's domination of the music-sharing and downloading industry has strengthened the social contract it has with its Disciples and created a culture shift. It also heightened the importance of Steve Jobs as the Chief Disciple, making it essential that Apple's succession plan was handled flawlessly. Only time and Tim Cook's performance without the physical presence of Jobs in the background can truly answer that question. Napster's failure to extend its social contract into the Congregation is illustrative of the need to have a leader who can appeal beyond the early Zealots.

CEO: CHIEF EMOTION OFFICER

I experienced the emotional importance of the CEO firsthand when I was working with NASDAQ after the "Dot-Bomb" era in 2002. NASDAQ's image had suffered a major blow, and investors and prospective listed companies had lost confidence in the market. To be "NASDAQed" had become a commonly used negative verb, and companies were switching to the NYSE and other exchanges.

Research revealed that many executives didn't know where NASDAQ's best-known companies were listed, and as soon as they realized that Amazon, Apple, Cisco, Dell, Intel, Microsoft, Oracle, Starbucks, and the like had chosen to list and prosper on NASDAQ, their confidence and positive impression improved. And the simplest and most effective way to profile a successful company was through its charismatic leader and CEO.

So in partnership with its agency McKinney, NASDAQ developed a campaign featuring the iconic CEOs of NASDAQ's best-known listed companies.[26] Howard Shultz, Michael Dell, Steve Ballmer, Larry Ellison, John Chambers, Jeff Bezos, and many others appeared in the commercials, not to promote NASDAQ overtly so much as to talk about their vision as leaders. Of course, these CEOs weren't just figureheads, they were the living embodiment of their company's culture and its values, and the campaign offered a window into them—both in front of and behind the camera.

The campaign featured Howard Shultz reclining on a couch in the original Starbucks store in Seattle after he'd wandered in early for the shoot, unseen by the crew, and made himself a latte—his words, manner, and confidence wholly reflective of the vision he'd help set for Starbucks as the welcoming "third place" between home and work. Larry Ellison of Oracle was piloting his racing yacht through the choppy waters of the San Francisco Bay, personifying the bold and competitive nature of the company he had built. Michael Dell was recalling with a chuckle his parent's obvious alarm when he'd explained he was dropping out of college to start a computer business, with Steve Ballmer remembering his mother asking him why anyone would ever need a computer! It was an opportunity to see what made these great business leaders tick, to hear their stories, and to experience firsthand the Disciple persona that enabled them to inspire others.

The campaign took the conversation away from the rational world of where you wanted to list your company, and into the emotional world of which club you wanted to belong to. It helped NASDAQ rebound after the Dot-Bomb crisis, and set the company back on course where it now competes head-to-head with the NYSE for global dominance—indeed, such is NASDAQ's relative strength today that in 2011 it attempted to buy the NYSE only to see its bid squashed by the US Justice Department, citing multiple monopoly issues.[27] But during the five years that the campaign ran, NASDAQ saw no major switches to the NYSE and reestablished itself as the market where progressive companies and leaders listed, and the verb "NASDAQed" disappeared from common vernacular. As a result, NASDAQ's campaign received the AAAA (American Association of Advertising Agencies) Gold Effie Award, the advertising industry's top award for sustained effectiveness (meaning it was not only an outstanding creative campaign, but it helped the organization achieve its stated goals, year after year).

A further illustration of the importance of the CEO as an emotional barometer for his or her company can be seen in the insightful work of two professors at Duke University's Fuqua School of Business, whose research has shown that a CEO's voice inflection, tone, and attitude can predict his or her company's future stock performance. Associate Professor William Mayew and Professor Mohan

Venkatachalam analyzed the conference calls of seven hundred US corporations from various industries throughout 2007, using software to measure the emotions in the CEOs' voices versus their actual words. CEOs who resonated positive emotion saw their stock prices rise. Those who resonated negative emotions saw their stock prices drop, even if they'd met earnings expectations.[28] Aware of the importance of inflection, tone, and projecting a positive attitude, most CEOs of Fortune 500 companies go through extensive training to ensure they present the best possible picture and keep cool under analyst questioning, but clearly some degree of genuine emotion seeps through, as the results indicate.

If you are a fan of Whole Foods Market, chances are you lead a progressive lifestyle, are more likely to vote Democratic, exercise regularly, and are an advocate for Green policies and products. Whole Foods Market exists in that part of your psyche where other passionate beliefs and causes reside, strengthening the likelihood that if you enter into a social contract with Whole Foods and help drive their culture shift, you will hold the company and its leader John Mackey to a high standard. Whole Foods' social contract states: *Progressive values and Green politics are important to me, just as eating wholesome and all-natural foods are a key part of my personality. Since being progressive and eating naturally are inextricably linked in my mind, they should also be part of the values of my preferred grocer, Whole Foods, and its leader John Mackey.*

Of course, it's illogical to think that the CEO of a huge corporation should share the individual values of its customers, but in this instance John Mackey's public statements that "Whole Foods is a social system" and a "community of purpose" versus a corporate organization feed well (pun intended) into how progressive consumers think and feel.[29]

Whole Foods Market has a unique operating structure that the organization terms the "cell." Instead of mandating rules and procedures from the top down like many companies do, the cell structure puts power and responsibility in the hands of teams who are incentivized to pressure their team members to perform. If the team has a weak link, they fix it or get rid of the person who is slowing them down. This creates a culture of participation and empowerment that is essential for any company seeking to establish and perpetuate a movement from the inside out.

One fascinating aspect to Whole Foods' collaborative cell structure is that as a self-proclaimed fan of *Star Trek*, John Mackey's cell seems uncannily similar to *Star Trek*'s structure for the United Federation of Planets. Rather than raising an eyebrow that the operating structure of a major corporation is loosely based on a late 1960s television show, Disciples and shareholders of Whole Foods appear to be entirely comfortable with it, if not mildly amused by it. Perhaps this signals that a further aspect of their social contract with Whole Foods and with John Mackey is that they be somewhat unconventional. At the same time, Mackey needs to ensure that the unconventional doesn't tip into the bizarre, and his recent acknowledgment of having posted anonymously on Yahoo!® message boards in praise of himself could certainly be construed as just that.

Progressive companies and their CEOs must understand that because the category they operate in creates heightened emotional engagement with customers, the need to be completely pure in words and deeds is absolutely essential. Patagonia—the Ventura, California–based outdoor clothing company—is a major contributor to environmental groups, committing 1 percent of its sales or 10 percent of the profits, and encouraging other companies to do the same. From the company's inception, Yvon Chouinard has made it Patagonia's stated mission to "build and support a strong alliance of businesses financially committed to creating a healthy planet."[30] Of course, this sets a high bar for any organization, but these principles are the basis for the social contract that Patagonia's Disciples have entered into, and the culture shift that they feel part of.

Patagonia has stayed true to its commitment of helping the environment since its founding in 1972. In addition to larger initiatives like reducing toxic impact and ensuring that products cause no unnecessary harm, the company also sponsors and supports smaller programs like the World Trout Initiative, the Organic Exchange, and environmental internships. As a surfer, kayaker, falconer, rock climber, fly fisherman, and environmentalist, Yvon Chouinard isn't just the most successful outdoor industry businessman alive, he *is* the Patagonia brand in human form, and his purity of purpose gives Disciples the assurance that his company will never compromise their principles.

Yet it isn't just in the obviously emotive sectors of healthy eating and environmental protection where an organization and its leader must be perceived as remaining true to the principles of their Disciples. Even in the world of business software, passions flow, forming social contracts and creating culture shifts.

It's easy to forget that the software industry has been in existence for only about thirty years—Microsoft wasn't founded until 1975—and in that sense it has a relatively young business model. Companies like Microsoft and Oracle create software that they sell to consumers and businesses, and traditionally there hasn't been much opportunity to modify the software to suit your particular needs—companies simply have to wait for the next update of a brand like Windows® and then buy the new version. The inability to modify the software that these companies sold gave rise to the term *closed source.*

Red Hat was founded in 1993 and is largely responsible for the free and "open source" software sector. The company created a different model by providing business software for free and then charging for support services. Red Hat® business users, known as the Fedora Project community members, can add enhancements that are often incorporated into new Red Hat software releases, which explains why the category is known as *open source.*[31]

Open versus closed, free versus paid, small versus big—these polar distinctions ensured that battle lines were drawn between the two sides. Early community members had all the characteristics of Zealots in the earnest and vocal campaigns they waged through blogs and via social media against the enemies of open source—namely closed-source software monoliths like Oracle and Microsoft. As the commercial culture shift progressed, Disciples of open source (and therefore Red Hat) carried the message forward to the point where, today, Red Hat has seen overall revenue increases of 20 percent plus for the last several years, even as larger software companies have stalled.[32] Red Hat is no longer a challenger nipping at the heels of the big boys; it has become an emerging software titan in its own right.

Jim Whitehurst, the energetic young CEO of Red Hat—who joined the company in 2007 after having successfully stewarded Delta Air Lines out of bankruptcy—has some fascinating and revealing challenges as he moves the company toward mass acceptance among the global Congregation of business software users and further into the consumer market.[33] In becoming the CEO of Red Hat, Whitehurst inherited the mantle of the "leader of the open-source movement," revered by the Zealots whose social contract with Red Hat states: *I will be an evangelist for Red Hat—if you stay true to the principles of open source by empowering the user community, and if you continue to lead the charge against the evil of closed-source software and the companies that produce it.*

In reality, the world of business software is less black and white and more gray. There are products that Red Hat offers today that aren't open source in the purest sense, and there are closed-source competitors that sell their own variants of open-source software. So while open and closed source have begun to overlap in the logical world of business, for many open-source Zealots the divide is still absolute. It would be disingenuous and bad business for Red Hat to loudly preach against companies that in some cases they now partner with. As open source becomes increasingly universal and other competitors prosper in the category, it would be polarizing to be seen as simply the leader of the open-source movement—and not as a power player in the broader business-software category.

The organic transition that Red Hat and Jim Whitehurst have to make is classic in the natural evolution of any culture shift. Zealots are by nature uncompromising purists and the category landscape no longer allows for Red Hat to take such a militant stand. To ensure acceptance among the wider Congregation, Red Hat will need to leave some of the original Zealots behind, and in order to strengthen Red Hat's position in the expanding business-software category, it will need to make a distinction between being seen today as "the leader of open source" and being seen tomorrow as "the business software titan that's created a commercial movement."

This is illustrative of the principle that in leadership Zealots can afford to be purists in the beginning, but the Disciples who must later perpetuate the movement often need to take a more nuanced, though no-less-emotive stand.

A SIMPLE TEST OF LEADERSHIP

If reading this chapter has made you begin to think about the abilities of the leader of your organization, ask yourself these seven basic questions to better evaluate how effective your leader is likely to be in establishing a social contract and creating a movement:

1. Is there one single dominant leader in practice?
2. Does that individual inspire passion and emotional commitment?
3. Does that person match the profile of a Disciple?
4. Does his or her persona embody the vision, values, and culture of the organization?
5. Does he or she always act in accordance with the vision, values, and culture of the organization?
6. Does he or she enable and encourage participation and engagement in the organization, from within as well as from the outside?
7. Is the individual the best available choice to personify the company or brand?

If you find the answer to all these questions is an unequivocal yes, you almost certainly have the right leader in place to establish a social contract with the Disciples, and the broader Congregation, and potentially create a culture shift. If you have some nos scattered among your answers, ask yourself if there is a former leader whose spirit can be channeled for the good of the organization, or whether there is another leader waiting in the wings who better matches the criteria. As a leader yourself, if you take this simple test and find that you are lacking in any of these criteria, it can provide a focus for evolving your leadership style and persona to better match the required profile of a Chief Disciple.

Bill's Gates's quote at the beginning of the chapter is pertinent for any leader who aspires to create a culture shift: "As we look into the next century, leaders will be those who empower others." CEOs, politicians, and even celebrity leaders may not have created the social contract that their Disciples establish with them, yet these leaders must be seen to adhere rigidly to its terms and have the vision to create a movement.

A Chief Disciple is a living, breathing encapsulation of the organization and the standard-bearer for the terms of the social contract. He or she must inspire passion and commitment—and be proactive in causing participation. He or she must display appropriate behavior at all times and be an advocate for the organization's values as well as nurture the culture. He or she must be seen to lead and yet be happy to learn from the organization's Disciples at the same time. Therefore, Chief Disciples' rational actions are important, but no less so than the emotional manner in which they conduct themselves at work and at play.

If you are serious about establishing a social contract, having a Chief Disciple with these qualities in place is crucial, because nobody wants to be part of creating a movement without an inspirational leader.

CHAPTER 4

THE PSYCHOLOGY
OF ILLOGICAL LEAPS

*"Life forms Illogical Patterns. It is haphazard and full of
beauties which I try to catch as they fly by, for who knows
whether any of them will ever return."*
—Margot Fonteyn,
Margot Fonteyn: Autobiography, 1977

I llogical leaps shape our relationships—with people, with brands, and with just about everything else.

I've run hundreds of focus groups and observed thousands more. I've waded through copious amounts of brand-opinion research, political polling data, and advertising testing reports. And there is one inimitable truth that I've come to believe: most of us aren't in any way logical in the way we think, talk, and embrace political, cultural, or commercial movements. This is significant because many organizations still seem to think their consumers *are* logical, and consequently they develop marketing programs that they believe will lead consumers to a reasoned place of adoption. I continue to find this baffling because we marketing people are consumers and there is nothing logical about our perceptions and choices, so why would we expect the average person to be any different?

In this chapter I'm going to share examples of illogical leaps that people have made to justify supporting—or distancing themselves from—a cause, a brand, or a personality. The noted cognitive anthropologist Dr. Bob Deutsch provided one of the best examples I've heard regarding illogical leaps. In running one of his signature focus groups, which he calls "thinkering groups,"[1] that can last up to three hours (he believes that people are more likely to tell you what they truly think if they're socialized into a state of thinking and feeling that reflects the deep structure of their cognition), one woman said: "I love Paloma Picasso perfume. It reminds me of when I was in Rome. Actually I never was in Rome, so I guess it reminds me of what it will be like when I do visit Rome, if that makes sense!"

Of course it made absolutely no *logical* sense, but it made complete sense to the woman who said it. If anything, Paloma Picasso perfume should connote memories of Barcelona or perhaps Madrid, not Rome, even if one could be reminded of something one hadn't yet experienced. This is a perfect example of the type of illogical leap that we continuously make as we form impressions. It's how we create affinity by giving brands a place of value in our own lives. We create our own personal images and choose and mold facts to fit the story we want to tell about ourselves.

People are biased to think of their choices as being correct, despite all evidence to the contrary. It's this bias that gives cognitive-dissonance theory its predictive power, shedding light on otherwise puzzling behavior. The theory of cognitive dissonance suggests that people are motivated to reduce their dissonance—the conflicting thoughts they are carrying at the same time—by shifting their beliefs and actions, either through denial, apportioning blame, or self-justification.

Buyer's remorse is a common form of cognitive dissonance that most of us have experienced at one time or another. You do your taxes and find that you are owed money, and while you know you should use the refund to pay down your credit-card debt, instead you use it as a deposit on a new car. Every time you get in the car, you feel guilty. You don't like that feeling, so instead of acknowledging that you simply wanted the car more than you wanted to pay off your credit card, you provide self-justification by suggesting the new car has more safety features and the true motivation was to keep your kids safe—or that your boss had complained about how run-down your old car was, making this a career move rather than an indulgence. Cognitive-dissonance theory is central to social psychology, and social psychology is central to understanding culture shifts.

If we apply this theory to the strange dichotomy I mentioned earlier in the book in relation to the Dove brand, it helps to explain why highly engaged brand Zealots seem happy to overlook the fact that Dove's sibling brand Axe is one of the worst offenders when it comes to female stereotyping. Even though many consumers are aware that Unilever manufactures Dove, as well as ultramacho Axe, they choose to ignore this fact because Dove plays an important role in defining their own personal image. As a result, they deny the contradictory behavior of Dove's rogue sibling Axe, because it's convenient to do so.

There is nothing logical or linear about the way brands are shaped in people's minds, and organizations would do well to remember this as they try to establish a social contract as the basis for affecting a culture shift.

ILLOGICAL LEAPS SHAPE OUR PERSONAL RELATIONSHIPS

We apply this type of cognitive dissonance every day in our personal relationships when we choose to ignore hard facts about a friend or loved one because they conflict with our neatly packaged image of that person and their relationship to us. We do it with the people we are closest to, we do it with politicians and celebrities, and we do it with the brands that we use to define ourselves. Let's look at a few examples.

What parent isn't driven to see the best in his or her children? At times we are all guilty of overlooking our children's shortcomings. Lionel Dahmer, father of Jeffrey Dahmer—the serial killer and sex offender who killed seventeen men and boys before he was convicted in 1992—gave several interviews after his son was incarcerated.[2] During these interviews, he tried to offer guidance to other parents in the hope of avoiding another "Jeffrey."

Lionel Dahmer had a master's degree in analytical chemistry. He described Jeffrey's early life in Milwaukee as being extremely normal—Lionel shared his love of nature and wildlife with his son. Mr. Dahmer claimed to have been completely unaware of the fact that between the ages of twelve and fourteen, Jeffrey was taking his love of wildlife in a perverse direction by collecting roadkill, bringing it home and experimenting on it, sometimes sexually. Mr. Dahmer also claims to have been unaware of his son's drinking, drug use, and homosexuality, but ironically in his interviews he did encourage parents to *really* talk to their children.

When we hear this, our instincts as parents lead us to conclude that Lionel Dahmer was either lying about his complete lack of awareness, or he's the least perceptive analytical chemist (and parent) on the planet. In fact, it was probably neither. Mr. Dahmer was likely aware of Jeffrey's early fascination with roadkill—you tend to know pretty quickly if there are dead animals in the house—although not of Jeffrey's penchant for necrophilia, or he certainly would have acted. Because it conflicted with Lionel Dahmer's optimistic image of Jeffrey, he reframed Jeffrey's behavior as perhaps a bizarre hobby that he hoped was indicative of a future career in science or medicine, following in his own footsteps.

The parents of the Columbine High School killers Eric Harris and Dylan Klebold have similarly been portrayed as having tragically disengaged from their sons' dark lives. However, the extensive evidence taken from the boys' homes and cars—including a notebook kept by Eric's father, Wayne—indicates that the families were indeed aware of their sons' troubling behavior.[3] But while clearly bothered by the direction in which their sons were headed, their families didn't get help for the boys or police them more vigorously. If they had, the growing arsenal in their garages might have been discovered before twelve children and their brave teacher were murdered in 1999.

If Wayne Harris was engaged enough in his son's life to keep a notebook and call the parents of other children on several occasions, he was certainly aware of Eric's increasingly aggressive tendencies. In all probability Wayne Harris had convinced himself that these were the typical problems and growing pains of a teenage boy, and in a state of cognitive dissonance he took an illogical—and ultimately tragic—leap when he chose not to dig deeper.

Lionel Dahmer's and Wayne Harris's attitudes are extreme examples of the type of cognitive dissonance that causes people to ignore the most reasonable explanation in their personal relationships—in these instances, that both Jeffrey and Eric were seriously disturbed young men—and instead they took an illogical leap in order to justify their preexisting biases.

In the tragic events caused by another serial killer, it was instructive to listen to the words of a casual interviewee on the BBC World Service from Oslo, in the wake of the unspeakable events of July 22, 2011. In explaining the disappointment she felt in being unable to hear and see the murderer Anders Behring Breivik explain his actions in person, the interviewee stated, "I just want to have a chance . . . to glimpse the monster inside."[4]

It is perhaps natural to want to reach through the radio and explain to this traumatized citizen of one of the most peaceful nations on earth that there was no monster inside, only delusion and insanity. And in the case of the lunatic Breivik, his delusion apparently took the form of being inspired to reform the ancient order of the Knights Templar, in order to defeat an attempted takeover of Western Europe by Muslims. Not jihadists so much but doctors, scientists, and shopkeepers!

While each of us was born with the capacity to take illogical leaps, it's important to draw a distinction between mere illogic and the insanity of individuals such as Breivik. For the truly deranged mind, anything can act as a catalyst for lunatic behavior—whether it be an obsession with actress Jodie Foster, as was the case for John Hinckley Jr. when he tried to assassinate Ronald Reagan, or reading J. D. Salinger's *The Catcher in the Rye*, which prompted Mark Chapman to murder John Lennon.

Where we do perhaps share some responsibility as a society is in our tendency to rewrite history and romanticize groups or individuals, as in the case of the Knights Templar Order, which appears to have become somewhat of a pop-culture obsession of late. Regardless of the picture we may have in our minds of the kindly old knight protecting the Holy Grail at the end of *Indiana Jones and the Last Crusade*, the Knights Templar generally were not the congenial good guys they're portrayed as, and it is disingenuous to have them constantly celebrated as the poster children for modern morality in books and movies like *The Da Vinci Code, Ivanhoe,* and most recently, *Ironclad*.

In the twelfth and thirteenth centuries, this group—which was installed by the Catholic Church as a sort of global militia—imposed a radical form of cultural conservatism at the point of a sword. The Knights Templar became the power behind the throne in many European nations through their political, economic, and military influence, and instigated vicious and suicidal attempts to recapture the Holy Land. In effect they operated as "puritanical fighting religious zealots," which for many of us in the West is precisely how we might describe groups like al-Qaida today. And just because Hollywood likes to depict them as maiden-rescuing, strong and silent types, doesn't make it so! Indeed it would be preferable to get back to the late Graham Chapman's ludicrous depiction of the Knights Templar Order in *Monty Python and the Holy Grail,* providing lunatics like Breivik with one less thing to be inspired by.

ILLOGICAL LEAPS IMPACT THE WAY WE VIEW STRANGERS

Not all examples of cognitive dissonance have such tragic consequences. These types of illogical leaps also are present in the way we react to people whom we don't personally know, such as media celebrities. Consider Brad Pitt as one example. From the moment his career started to blossom and he came into the full public spotlight following his role as J. D. in *Thelma & Louise* (1991), Brad Pitt became a Hollywood icon and sex symbol—and his career has continued to go from strength to strength with movies like *A River Runs through It*, *Seven*, and *The Curious Case of Benjamin Button* on his illustrious résumé.[5]

Pitt had a series of glamorous and very public relationships with his costars, including Robin Givens, Juliette Lewis, and Gwyneth Paltrow (to whom he was eventually engaged). This ensured that the public was already emotionally engaged not just in Brad Pitt the movie star, but also in his glamorous love life even before he met Jennifer Aniston.

For almost ten years, from 1994 until 2004, *Friends* was the most popular show on television, not just in the United States but internationally—Jennifer Aniston was the show's most talked-about cast member. The nature of her role, her looks, and her reported manner off the set created a public image of a glamorous yet grounded person—the ultimate girl next door we all root for. To quote Aniston, "I don't get sent anything strange like underwear. I get sent cookies."[6]

Brad Pitt and Jennifer Aniston met in 1998 and married two years later. For many, they were *the* glamour couple of Hollywood—the closest thing the United States had to royalty. Enter Angelina Jolie, stage right: the archetypal villain in our story. Her look and public persona were the antithesis of Jennifer Aniston—she was the dark to Aniston's light. Jolie had a publicly strained relationship with her father, the actor Jon Voight, and had displayed a degree of affection toward her brother at the Oscars ceremony that made people uncomfortable. She had been briefly married to the perceptually wild Billy Bob Thornton, and she had won an Oscar playing a mental patient in *Girl, Interrupted*.[7] Many people had formed the impression that she was either weird, dangerous, or both.

Pitt and Jolie costarred in the film *Mr. and Mrs. Smith* (2005), in which they played a married couple that also happened to both be assassins. Their on-screen relationship and sexual chemistry fed on the danger that they routinely faced. In real life they allegedly began a relationship on the movie set that became public after pictures of the two vacationing together in Kenya were widely circulated.

As with all people we view from afar, we actually know nothing about the nature of Pitt and Aniston's relationship or their true personalities, just as we know nothing about Pitt and Jolie. However, our impressions of intertwined relationships become fixed in our minds—although based on an illogical leap fueled by gossip and innuendo—and feel as real to us as any relationship we have experienced firsthand. And so—in true fairytale fashion—the universal story that society adopted was as follows: evil temptress seduces handsome prince; handsome prince leaves beautiful princess distraught and betrayed.

The illogical leap toward Pitt and Jolie stated: *Brad and Jen were happy until crazy Angelina seduced him with dark magic. She has a weird relationship with her family, and she broke up with Billy Bob because she was too strange even for him. Therefore Brad and Angelina will never last; Brad will realize she's weird and dangerous, and he'll go back to Jen and they'll live happily ever after.*

In fairytales the handsome prince always ends up with the princess, which perhaps explains why an overwhelming majority of people believe that Brad Pitt and Jennifer Aniston will eventually get back together. The tabloids didn't plant this thought—they are simply feeding on a mass delusion we've created ourselves.

If you choose to look at their relationship objectively, Brad Pitt and Angelina Jolie are happy and settled with their six children. Despite being under an almost unbearable media spotlight and under constant pursuit by the paparazzi, both their careers and their relationship have blossomed. They have both done admirable humanitarian work, with Jolie being named a UNHCR goodwill ambassador in 2001. By any logical measure, their lives, careers, and relationship have been an unqualified success. And yet, go into any grocery store on most days of the week and you will likely find at least one tabloid or magazine cover speculating on the imminent reconciliation of Pitt and Aniston. Although it is based on our illogical leap, the fictional story of Brad Pitt, Jennifer Aniston, and Angelina Jolie feels so real to us that we cannot let go of it, even though all rational evidence points to the contrary.

Instead of celebrating the rare success of a Hollywood couple, we allow the tabloids to perpetuate our own myth, demonstrating the addictive nature of illogical leaps. Because we create them, we come to treasure them—and nothing can shift our perspective. This is hardly a new phenomenon—when the late, great Elizabeth Taylor reunited with her ex-husband Richard Burton for the third time, she is supposed to have said that she knew "people just expected it."

Because most of us choose to marry or live with a partner in a permanent relationship at one time or another, we feel somewhat expert and confident making judgments about other people's relationships—regardless of how well we know them. We meet a couple and quickly diagnose who is dominant and how their partnership seems to work. And in the event that their relationship breaks down, we draw on the impression we've formed about them to diagnose the root cause of the problem or to assign blame: *He took her for granted. She never let him hang out with his friends. She's just too outgoing for him. They never did anything together without their kids.*

Of course, no matter how close we may be to another couple, we still witness only a snapshot of their relationship, and we never see how they truly function when it's just the two of them alone, with their public guard down. Yet, with mere snippets of information, we form opinions, offer advice, pronounce judgments, choose sides— and take illogical leaps.

To operate this way with couples we actually know is presumptuous, but to do so with people we've never met is bordering on the delusional. Several high-profile murder cases in my state of North Carolina—not to mention the Casey Anthony trial in Florida in 2011—brought into question that age-old legal debate around what constitutes reasonable doubt. Although not a lawyer, I do have legal training, which makes me somewhat dangerous, and in layman's terms my understanding is that reasonable doubt means the case against the accused must be so convincing that "a reasonable person wouldn't hesitate to convict."

I suspect the above criteria goes a long way toward explaining the outrage at decisions that seem to have gone against public opinion. The myriad of social-media groups that emerged to decry not only these decisions but also the juries that reached them provides ample evidence that there are increasingly few "reasonable people" about today. So much so that the judge in the Casey Anthony trial decided against releasing the names of the jurors for their own safety! Of course these cases involving murdered children and spouses generate incredible emotion, and as parents and spouses ourselves, we think we understand what drove the behavior of the accused. We therefore become outraged when the jury disagrees with our assessment and rules in the other direction.

The truth is that no matter how closely we might have followed these cases, we don't know everything that the jury knew, we didn't have the physical in-court experiences that the jury did, and we certainly didn't have any firsthand knowledge surrounding the circumstances that led to the victim's death. We weren't there, either when the alleged murders took place or in the jury room during the trial. In these circumstances, any reasonable person would withhold judgment and give the long-suffering jurors—who already had to sacrifice months of their lives and wrestle with the incredibly unclear threshold of reasonable doubt—the benefit of the doubt themselves. But our instinct to project our feelings and beliefs is so great, and emotion is so charged in cases of this sort, that we are unable to give the benefit of the doubt. Hence we take an illogical leap, blame and abuse the jury, and yes, behave unreasonably, proving beyond doubt that we are the last ones who should have been sitting in judgment in these traumatic cases.

In the world of popular culture, did we really know anything about the underlying dynamics of Tom Cruise and Nicole Kidman's marriage before they broke up, other than what we could glean from their strained sexual chemistry in Stanley Kubrick's film *Eyes Wide Shut*?[8] The same is true today with Tom Cruise and his soon-to-be ex-wife, Katie Holmes—dubbed "TomKat" by the media. Rumors of Tom Cruise's dominating behavior in his previous marriage, a public spat with Brooke Shields over her use of antidepressants, a heated argument on the *TODAY Show* with Matt Lauer,[9] and Cruise's public advocacy for Scientology have convinced many that he is both strange as well as domineering in his treatment of women. And whatever the facts pertaining to Tom Cruise's latest marital breakup, it is certain to reinforce this negative public perception of him.

We apply the same illogic to artistic collaborations that we do to celebrity relationships, believing that we understand how the partnership works and where the real talent lies. Many believe that John Lennon was the true musical genius behind the Beatles, while Paul McCartney simply had the gift of writing extremely catchy and commercial songs. Yet after the breakup of the group, it was McCartney who proved to be not only the more prolific and commercial of the duo in his solo career, but also the more experimental in his various musical projects and collaborations—and perhaps his daughter, the fashion designer Stella McCartney, was justified in wearing her infamous T-shirt that read "It's about f—ing time," when in 1999 McCartney was finally inducted into the Rock and Roll Hall of Fame for his solo work, some five years after Lennon's induction.[10] In June 2011, when McCartney announced he would be performing in New York, the *New York Times* headline read "Aging Bassist from Liverpool to Play at Yankee Stadium," which, while clearly intended as a tongue-in-cheek attempt at humor, continues to suggest that McCartney isn't given the respect in some quarters that his extensive portfolio of solo work deserves.

Peter Cook and Dudley Moore were among England's most beloved comedy duos in the 1970s, and similarly, conventional wisdom had it that Cook was the comedic genius while Moore was effectively his sidekick and accompanying musician—and yet it was Moore who went on to achieve international stardom and acclaim as a film actor for his roles in *Arthur* and *10* in the 1980s,[11] while Cook struggled with alcoholism and was only seen occasionally as a guest on talk shows.

History has repeated itself as British fans of the 1990s comedic duo Stephen Fry and Hugh Laurie have been somewhat surprised to see

Laurie establishing a highly successful acting career in America, most notably for his lead role in the hit television show *House,* for which he's won two Golden Globe Awards[12]—while Fry, a talented writer and performer, has remained largely unknown outside the United Kingdom. And for those who don't know Stephen Fry, he appears in many ways to be this generation's embodiment of Oscar Wilde, and it's no surprise therefore that he was chosen to play the title role in the 1997 film *Wilde,*[13] alongside Jude Law who played Lord Alfred (Bosie) Douglas. Like Wilde, Fry is known in part for his caustic quips, of which my two personal favorites are: "We've all met people who are supposedly incredibly intelligent but don't know which way to sit on a lavatory," and "I don't watch television, I think it destroys the art of talking about oneself"—from his novel *Paperweight.*[14]

And few perhaps would have thought after the breakup of the 1980s pop band Eurythmics that it would be lead singer Annie Lennox alone who would go on to achieve critical and commercial success, including winning a Grammy Award for her first solo album, *Diva* (1992)[15]—while the band's perceived musical genius, Dave Stewart, would recede into relative obscurity. Each of these examples illustrates our tendency to boldly make uninformed and illogical judgments about the nature of pop-culture relationships that we experience only from a distance.

Whether it's Hollywood royalty, an artistic collaboration, or whether it relates to our own personal lives, we are wired to take illogical leaps. In Princess Diana's tragically shortened life, two distinct public personas were created around her. The first was of a fairytale princess, and the second was of a saintly campaigner for the rights of the downtrodden and the oppressed. The national outpouring of grief following her death was unprecedented for the traditionally stoic British public and took everyone, including Queen Elizabeth II, by surprise—as the insightful 2006 film *The Queen* dramatized.

But perhaps we shouldn't be surprised at the extent of the emotion expressed and the sense of loss. We were mourning someone whom our unconscious minds had come to believe we knew intimately—

someone who died in tragic circumstances, and someone whose troubles we felt partially responsible for—given that it was our obsessive interest in her that fueled the paparazzi's pursuit of her—right to the end. It was for this reason that Elton John's reworded rendition of the song "Candle in the Wind" struck such a chord when he sang it at her funeral—we saw Princess Diana as an icon like Marilyn Monroe, mercilessly and tragically hounded by the media.

The essential part of what we lost when Princess Diana died was the fairytale of her life that we had helped to create. Our sense of loss, combined with feelings of guilt over our perceived role in her unhappiness, helps to explain both the extent of public mourning and the ability of some to believe the enduring conspiracy theory that she was murdered. The most talked about film at the 2011 Cannes Film Festival was the documentary about the inquest into the death of Diana. Keith Allen's *Unlawful Killing*[16] was entirely funded by Mohamed Al-Fayed, the father of Diana's romantic companion Dodi who died in the accident with her—and contains no counterviews to its sensational implication that they were murdered by a conspiracy of the monarchy and British elite. And the conspiracy theories will continue in large measure because we created Diana's myth and became emotionally committed to it. We mourn the fact that she's been taken away from us and feel responsible at the same time. As a result, we look for someone or something to blame for that loss.

In a similar vein, amidst all the Tweets, blogs, and articles written after the passing of the late, great Steve Jobs on October 5, 2011, the question that lingers most after his death following a lengthy battle with pancreatic cancer, is, why has it affected so many people, so deeply? National grieving on this scale is usually reserved for beloved religious, political, or occasionally entertainment figures, Princess Diana being a case in point, but not for a deeply private person like Jobs from the world of technology and commerce.

Some have argued that Apple is less a consumer brand and more a cult with disciples who hold devices like the iPhone as sacred objects, and who had an almost spiritual reverence for Jobs himself as a visionary sage. Indeed after the initial heartfelt testimonials and recapping of his illustrious career, some of the dialogue has turned to his "teachings" and his future predictions as though he were the Silicon Valley equivalent of Nostradamus. So why did Steve Jobs's passing so affect our national psyche? As with Diana's death, on a rational level we understand that we didn't know him personally—and that sharing vicariously in his triumphs and failures at Apple and Pixar, and owning many of the ingenious devices that he conceived doesn't explain the sense of loss we felt at his passing.

Although Steve Jobs was by no means a tragic figure given the staggering success he had achieved in his life, perhaps what people were experiencing on some level was a feeling of guilt over his passing, similar to the guilt felt in Diana's case. We knew him to be a rare genius, a perfectionist who brought his heart and soul to his company and his craft. And over his last few years we watched him literally waste away before our eyes on stage, as the next great Apple invention was unveiled. It was almost as if the more he gave us of himself in the form of ingenious technology, the more he seemed to physically decline.

As a result we were being tricked by our subconscious into believing that we were partly responsible for his death. That somehow we asked too much of him, drew too much of his life force with our obsessive need for the next great device. And really, this isn't as far-fetched as it might sound. Our unique human capacity for empathy regularly convinces us that we have a level of intimacy with various celebrities and public figures.

Because we live vicariously through celebrities like Brad Pitt, Tom Cruise, Princess Diana, and Steve Jobs, we think we understand their lives and their relationships. We come to think that we inhabit their worlds and so we form opinions, offer advice, pronounce judgments, choose sides—and take illogical leaps.

ILLOGICAL LEAPS IMPACT HOW WE
JUDGE OTHER RACES AND CULTURES

Illogical leaps are equally present in the way we think about societies
and even entire races of people, as a further example from the work of
Dr. Deutsch illustrates. After more than a year of extensive interviews
with ordinary Americans, Dr. Deutsch's research revealed that in the
early 1990s, at a time when the Japanese economy was booming and
Japanese companies appeared to be taking over crucial segments of
American business, one woman epitomized American perceptions of
Japan more than any other—Yoko Ono.

Yoko Ono had experienced a relatively turbulent upbringing,
from the extremes of attending one of the most exclusive schools in
Japan to finding herself and her family destitute after the bombing
of Tokyo in 1945. Her early life experiences gave her the mind-set of
an outsider. When she moved to New York City with her family after
the war, she was drawn to individuals and groups that seemed to exist
on the edgier fringes of New York society. She visited galleries to
attend art happenings so she could hang out with artists and poets
who represented the bohemian freedom she was drawn to, eventually becoming an artist herself.

By the time Ono introduced herself to John Lennon at her
Indica Gallery exhibition in 1966, when she passed him a card that
simply read "breathe," she'd been twice married and divorced, was
estranged from her daughter, had attempted suicide and been insti-
tutionalized, and could claim to be an artist, experimental musician,
and filmmaker. But to the average American who came to know
her by association with Lennon, she was simply weird, impossible to
understand, and a key reason that the Beatles broke up.

For people in the late 1960s who remember her animal-type
screaming on the Yoko Ono/Plastic Ono Band album, the increasingly bizarre custody battle over her daughter, Kyoko, and public
spectacles like spending her honeymoon with Lennon in bed for a
week,[17] the illogical leap went something like this: *I don't trust Yoko*

Ono. She's a weirdo. She seduced John Lennon and made him nuts, so he left the Beatles. She's Japanese and they are all like that. They are weird and they want to take our stuff away, just like Yoko Ono did.

Based on this outwardly odd behavior—even in the 1960s when the bar for strangeness was very high—it is entirely understandable that people would brand her as "weird." It's also understandable that Beatles fans would continue to look for a scapegoat to blame for the loss of an extraordinary musical collaboration. There is little doubt that John Lennon's fixation with Ono was in part the catalyst for him to finally part ways with the Beatles. But twenty years later, after living in relative obscurity after the murder of Lennon, for people to personify Ono as the symbol of Japan's takeover of significant parts of American industry is nothing short of bizarre.

As is still the case today, most people in the early 1990s understood very little about the underlying conditions that cause economic downturns and recessions, let alone the nature of global commerce—they only saw how events affected them in terms of jobs lost, inflation, and foreclosures. Our instinct in any circumstance, especially when emotions are running high, is to create meaning out of chaos. We do that by pulling together tidbits of information, both real and imagined, past and present, and in our unconscious minds we construct scenarios and stories that feel true to us, largely because we gave birth to them.

In associating Yoko Ono with the Japanese takeover of parts of American industry and commerce, many people weren't even sure whether she was in fact Japanese, making the connection all the more illogical. But this particular mental jambalaya had many disparate ingredients for the average American, including:

- Images of kamikaze (suicide) pilots in World War II preferring to commit suicide rather than face the disgrace of defeat
- Japanese game shows like *Endurance,* in which contestants appeared to be willingly tortured
- Godzilla rampaging through Tokyo's metropolis

- The unprovoked bombing of Pearl Harbor
- Conflicted feelings over the bombing of Hiroshima and the end of World War II

This was the complicated picture that shaped the emotions that the average American felt toward Japan—fear, amusement, guilt, revenge, anger, and above all, mistrust. As the Japanese rebuilt their infrastructure and their economy to become world leaders and a trade and industry powerhouse, Americans carried or inherited this baggage as the basis for shaping their opinions. But the unconscious mind prefers a single persona to crystallize beliefs, and with logic set aside, Yoko Ono was perfect for the role.

Ono was "weird" like the Japanese, looked Japanese so probably was, brainwashed John Lennon into leaving the Beatles just as the Japanese sought to do with American businesses, and ultimately stole from us something meaningful, probably as an act of revenge for Japan's defeat and destruction in World War II. Our perceptions of Yoko Ono and Japan are illustrative of the fact that we are constrained only by our emotions when taking illogical leaps.

Today, history has the potential to repeat itself. To most Americans, China is an even greater unknown than was Japan in the 1990s. To many, the spectacle of the Beijing Olympics in 2010 saw the emergence of an illogical leap that stated: *The Chinese are strange and there are millions and millions of them. They have an incredible knack for organization and militarylike discipline as shown by the Olympics opening ceremony. They are getting richer and stronger and we are in debt to them up to our necks. They plan to bankrupt and overrun us.*

Perhaps this helps to explain the appearance of a revealing commercial sponsored by the Chinese government that started running on cable stations in late 2010, in tandem with a large billboard in New York's Times Square. It wasn't an ad that encouraged people to vacation in China; it was seemingly intended to humanize the Chinese people. The commercial cut from images of Chinese athletes to scholars to artists to ordinary and extraordinary people.

The commercial arguably then took a misstep in its attempt to create a warm and friendly image of China when it showed a member of the Chinese military followed by a series of stern-looking Chinese astronauts. These images, combined with the rather staged and formal nature of the commercial, may have actually achieved the opposite effect by reminding people of China's differences, their emerging military might, and worse—their intention to dominate us from space.

The Chinese illogical leap is still forming in the psyche of the average American, and doesn't yet have a single persona attached to it as Japan had in the 1990s with Ono. As part of creating its social contract, if China wants to shape its image in the United States by seeding a single persona before people do so for themselves, the affable and unthreatening Hong Kong–born actor Jackie Chan might offer a better persona than the imposing and unnervingly tall, recently retired basketball player, Yao Ming.

We saw the same tendency to stereotype an entire nation after Libyan rebels cemented their victory by securing Tripoli and bringing the tyrant Colonel Gadhafi to brutal justice. Apart from the ongoing dilemma of how to spell his name, even after his death, the primary question posed by news pundits was what was next for Libya—as various politicos somewhat patronizingly cautioned that Libya (unlike Egypt) had no democratic history and no institutions outside of the Gadhafi regime, and therefore was more likely to fall into chaos and anarchy.

I was reminded, however, of the central role that Libyans played in perhaps the greatest military campaign in history under the leadership of the extraordinary Hannibal Barca. In 218 BCE, nearly a couple of thousand years before the United States existed and while the Britons liked to paint themselves blue and were ruled by the Druids, Hannibal led an extraordinary coalition that included his own Carthaginians, Numidians, Tunisians, and Libyans. They passed through the Straits of Gibraltar, into Spain, through the Gallic territory, across the Alps, and into Italy with a few hundred elephants.

Nothing like this had been attempted before or since, and almost a third of Hannibal's force of around forty-six thousand perished on the journey.

Having arrived in Italy after this most grueling of marches, with a dramatically diminished force of men and elephants, and against vastly superior numbers, Hannibal's army twice defeated the Romans with superior tactics at the Battle of the Trebia and then at Lake Trasimene. But Hannibal's greatest triumph was at the Battle of Cannae in 216 BCE, where his army of thirty thousand out-thought and out-fought one hundred thousand Romans. Hannibal managed to encircle the core of the Roman force with his Libyan heavy infantry, who played the decisive role in Rome's greatest military defeat. With the help of his Libyan militia, Hannibal occupied a large swathe of Italy for sixteen years before he was forced to return to Carthage to repel a Roman attack on his homeland.

Libyans therefore have a proud history, and in time the Gadhafi regime will seem like an unfortunate blip as they use their natural resources and perhaps invoke the spirit of Hannibal in rebuilding. They'll welcome help from the West but they'll do it their own way, and it would be unwise and illogical to underestimate what they are capable of achieving. After all, their ancestors made it across the Alps with elephants in tow and thrice defeated Rome, so the present generation can likely figure out how to establish a modern democracy, if they so choose.

ILLOGICAL LEAPS CAN EVEN LEAD US INTO WAR

The beginning of the Iraq War represents another significant case in examining whether we as a country entered into a military conflict based on a mass illogical leap, or whether we did the logical thing in attacking Iraq. The logical argument at the time stated: *We must attack Saddam Hussein's Iraq because in all probability he has weapons of mass destruction that he will use against us, our allies, and his people, as he has done previously. 9/11 taught us that we need to act preemptively rather than waiting to be attacked.*

It's impossible to overstate the degree of emotional fervor that existed in the period after September 11, 2001, and to some extent still exists. The American public has gone through various emotional stages including grief, denial, anger, and fear. The terrorists had succeeded inasmuch as we felt truly terrorized.

There was almost unanimous public support for the invasion of Afghanistan, in part because evidence indicated it was where the September 11 attacks had been planned and coordinated— even though the majority of the terrorists were Saudi nationals. The Taliban had supported and helped to finance the late Osama bin Laden and his al-Qaida terrorist group and were continuing to shelter them, and we had almost universal international support.

After the successful and rapid invasion of Afghanistan,[18] al-Qaida and many Taliban fighters were driven into the mountainous region between Afghanistan and Pakistan, and it seemed just a matter of time before they would be captured or killed. Effectively the military heavy lifting had been done and we'd acted righteously in removing a global threat and avenging an unprovoked attack on innocent civilians.

Future generations will likely be told that the national mood of fear and anger continued unabated between the successful overrunning of Afghanistan and the invasion of Iraq—in reality the mood had evolved. There wasn't the same singularity of purpose or the same overwhelming sense of righteousness in the case for war with Iraq. There was a degree of uncertainty caused in part by the fact that UN inspectors were finding no evidence of weapons of mass destruction, and leading voices in the world community were urging caution or actively rejecting the notion of attacking Iraq.

In the end, the key emotional element in justifying the invasion of Iraq was fear—fear that we would be attacked again. But that fear could be justified only if there was a clear link between what happened on September 11, 2001, and what *could* happen if we didn't dismantle Saddam Hussein's regime.

It has been suggested, particularly by those on the political left, that the Bush administration used half-truths and fear-mongering to fabricate the case for war. But arguably they could not have sold the war in Iraq if the link with Afghanistan and September 11 didn't already exist in the minds of the American people. The link did exist in the form of an illogical leap that roughly stated: *Crazy Arabs attacked us without provocation for reasons we don't fully understand. We've already fought one war against Saddam Hussein, who is [was] the craziest Arab of them all, so we should invade Iraq and remove him because if he doesn't have weapons of mass destruction, he will soon, and it's better to be safe than sorry.*

In reality, any number of logical arguments against invading Iraq could have been persuasive at the time. For instance, there was no proven link between Saddam Hussein's regime and al-Qaida. Iraq and Afghanistan were two completely separate sovereign nations with entirely different political dynamics and challenges. Removing Hussein could create a power vacuum in Iraq that would be exploited by neighboring countries in the region. Attacking Iraq at this [that] time could prevent us from successfully completing the mission in Afghanistan. In other words, the UN inspectors hadn't finished their work before we invaded Iraq.

Because people had taken an illogical leap in relation to the need to deal with Saddam Hussein, the conditions for attacking Iraq were created, requiring very little convincing by the Bush administration to justify its invasion.

REVEALING THE ILLOGIC AT THE HEART OF YOUR SOCIAL CONTRACT

What does all of this have to do with you or your organization? Reading this, you might conclude that if people are prone to build a completely illogical picture of an entire race or take an illogical leap into war, what hope do you have of shaping their perception of your company or your brand? You might as well save the time and money, right?

To some extent I would agree that the linear and reasoned approach most companies take to establish and maintain their brand image is essentially flawed, but that doesn't mean it isn't possible to influence perception. The first step is accepting that the image people hold isn't fair or logical. The second step is to try to reveal the true nature of their illogic and begin creating a culture shift from there, rather than from a corporate strategy or political program developed by a group of suits during countless hours of naval gazing.

So how do you begin to unlock what people may feel unconsciously about a brand, an idea, a politician, or a celebrity? By using projective techniques to reveal the nature of people's illogical leaps. Projective techniques adopted from psychotherapy enable you to unlock the unconscious or hidden motivations that are shaping people's belief systems and therefore the basis of their illogical leaps.

One of the simplest and most common techniques used in progressive qualitative research is personification. Ask a group of men why they chose their Mercedes, BMW, Cadillac®, or Audi, and you'll get hit with a highly rational menu of features and performance attributes intended to justify their expensive purchases. In fact, the purchase of a luxury vehicle in particular is a highly emotional decision, driven by many layers of ego. It's unlikely you'll get a bunch of guys to tell you about these motivations, in part because these thoughts reside in the men's unconscious and aren't available to access, even if they wanted to tell you.

Instead, you have to put these men in an altered state, one in which they are free to play and project and can access their emotion chips. You might ask them to imagine if their brand of car were an animal or a famous celebrity, what or who would it be? After some grumbling and uncomfortable shifting, they'll start to tell you that their new Audi TT® is a cheetah, or their new Cadillac CTS® is George Clooney, and when you push them to explain why, it becomes clear how these men are defining themselves through their choice of car.

Consumer insights of this type that get at how people think and feel unconsciously about your brand are invaluable in deciding how to frame your advertising and PR messages, and should be the basis of how you begin to create a commercial culture shift. Even the most utilitarian of purchases has an emotional basis to it—from the toilet tissue you prefer to the brand of gas to buy for your car. As we are first and foremost emotional beings, it is only natural that our decision making should be emotion-based. But when it comes to parting with money, we hate to acknowledge that we made an emotional decision, so we mask our true motivation with logical answers and post-rationalization— and it's only by utilizing projective research techniques that you can hope to access the unconscious minds of consumers.

Ask someone how he or she would feel if their favorite brand of beer ceased to exist, and they'll probably tell you they'd just go out and buy another brand without giving it much thought. But ask them to imagine they had to give a eulogy at the funeral of their favorite brand, and—by putting them in a state that naturally creates an emotional response—you'll likely hear the true affinity that they have for Corona® or Miller Lite® (or in my case, Newcastle Brown Ale®). At the same time you need to be prepared for tempers to become frayed or even for open hostility, as I once experienced by suggesting to a group of guys that they consider life without Budweiser®.

Another fascinating technique to observe in attempting to draw out the unconscious mind that people are using to make decisions is the "alter ego." Several years ago, I ran a series of focus groups with people who had run up significant credit-card debt. It's no secret that credit-card companies make money off our personal debt. It's a simple model—the more in debt we are, the more money they make. It's logical to assume that when you talk to a group of people who have significant credit-card debt, they will feel pretty angry toward the credit-card companies.

However, the people I spoke didn't at first appear to be at all angry with credit-card companies because they didn't acknowledge they were actually in debt, even though that was the very criteria for which they'd been recruited for the focus groups. Their comments, manner, and body language all projected that they were the most prudent and careful of spenders. They weren't intentionally setting out to lie—they had simply rationalized their own behavior and didn't see themselves as having a debt problem, even though they continued to accrue interest month after month.

I wasn't getting anywhere in understanding the unconscious motivations driving their spending, so I asked them to imagine that a friend or a family member whom they knew to be less prudent and more inclined to spend recklessly had now come into the room. I told them to turn their name cards around and write the person's name on the card, and to then answer the questions I'd been asking on behalf of that person—I forced them to alter their persona (or ego), and become that other person. As a result, their alter ego emerged—body language changed and they appeared to transform. Suddenly they were spending money liberally, indulging themselves without a second thought, piling up debt with the same intensity as a compulsive gambler. They'd been unable to consciously reveal their attitude to credit-card spending and needed to be in an altered state in order to do so.

In this example, whether you represent a credit counseling service helping to get people out of debt, or a credit-card company happy to see them continuing to spend, you have to be able to glimpse people's true unconscious motivations. It is these motivations that drive people's actions and provide the foundation for creating culture shifts.

Conducting qualitative research of this sort is time consuming, expensive, and frustrating for many companies that typically have a long menu of rational questions to wade through. I'd hazard a guess that 95 percent of all focus groups that are run by companies and political groups—supposedly to better understand the attitudes and motivations of their consumers—are run as Q&A sessions instead of being designed to draw out the unconscious perceptions of the people they hope to influence. It's for that reason that the focus group as a research medium has become so devalued. On the other hand, if you take the time and a projective approach to understanding the unconscious root of the illogical leaps your customers are taking, they will reveal powerful insights into how they view your organization and your brand.

I've never been one for New Year's resolutions. Perhaps it's because you see so many people making a commitment and then falling short a few weeks later. I've worked out three days a week pretty much religiously for almost thirty years and I dread going to the gym in early January because I know it will be overrun with people who've made New Year's resolutions to get in shape. You see them either overexerting themselves or simply sitting on the machines looking forlorn and miserable. And every year you can observe the fall-off with monotonous regularity as about a third disappear after a couple of weeks, half by the end of January, and by mid-February things are pretty much back to normal.

Since most of us have experienced breaking resolutions within days or even hours, why do we imagine that this is a good time of year to make such commitments? There's nothing magical about January 1—after all, the first day of the year used to vary annually before Julius Caesar charged Sosigenes of Alexandria with changing the calendar to match the Egyptian calendar—inserting three extra months (which is almost identical to the calendar we use today). Yet we make these resolutions every year, and the health, fitness, and diet industries bombard us with advertising accordingly. We do this not because we are eternally optimistic, or because we are simply sheep, but because we as a species are wired to take illogical leaps, which explains our enduring commitment to making significant changes on this one day. But since we are committed to making New Year's resolutions, can we perhaps at least change the nature of the motivation to affect a more positive outcome?

To that end I was fascinated by the launch of online fitness company GymPact®'s app, in January 2011. GymPact users had to set a goal for the number of visits they'd make to the gym each week and then agree to an amount they'd pay if they failed to meet that commitment. If they failed to reach their goal, they'd lose the cash, and if they succeeded they'd get back a portion of the cash collected from those who fell short. Yifan Zhang, co-founder of GymPact and a product of Harvard behavioral economics, noted that "Everyone else is giving out points or badges or cash, but nobody's really thinking about ways we can use negative motivation to help people meet their goals."[19] Of course that isn't strictly true, as books like professor Dan Ariely's *Predictably Irrational* have addressed this idea extensively; but Zhang's reasoning was sound. At least initially, GymPact's initiative proved to be a success, which raises the question whether negative motivation would work with other common resolutions.

Certainly weight loss could employ a "cash penalty for gained pounds" system, but what about other things like curbing spending and saving money? The notion of making a commitment to save a specific amount every month and paying a cash penalty for failure is intriguing. Particularly if you had the added incentive of receiving extra cash from other people in the pool who failed to meet their commitments, per the GymPact model.

Back to the credit-card companies: it would seem logical that one of them would have employed something similar for their most indebted customers. Of course they make money by people continuing to overspend, but for those customers who are so indebted that the company will likely end up having to write off their debt anyway, a "penalty card" based on negative motivation would seem like an interesting solution. An indebted customer would roll their debt onto a "penalty card" and if they paid off an agreed amount monthly they perhaps would incur no interest that month and also receive a portion of the interest charge that other card members who'd failed to make their payments had incurred. And the credit-card companies, instead of making their money on the interest payments that in this model would go to the more responsible cardholders, could collect a percentage transaction fee as GymPact does.

In reality, something with this type of incentive would likely drive too many regular cardholders to switch, which wouldn't be good business for the big credit-card companies. But perhaps some entrepreneurial financial-services company will launch a "penalty card" to apply negative motivation to saving and spending!

Whatever your New Year's resolutions, if you can't be talked out of making them at this most challenging time of year, you could try taking a leaf out of GymPact's book and see if there is a way to add a dimension of negative motivation. Some negative motivation may considerably improve the chances of success. If nothing else it probably will illustrate how serious you really are about sticking to your resolutions!

In another striking example of people taking illogical leaps, if you've ever eaten a White Castle® burger you know they have a very distinct look and taste relative to a traditional fast-food burger. White Castle burgers are smaller so instead of eating a single burger, you tend to buy several. They have a distinctive taste, one where the onion, mustard, and pickles are more dominant. There is also something about the taste and texture that encourages you to eat more than you planned, which can be problematic later in the day.

A conventional Q&A session will reveal little about the true motivations of a White Castle lover, but if you apply some of the projective techniques I referenced earlier, a myth will likely be revealed. A number of people genuinely believe there is something addictive in the burgers, resulting in an almost unnatural craving for them (often at about two in the morning after consuming alcohol). They also believe that the craving compels you to consume far more of the little burgers than you'd planned, resulting in an uncomfortable bloating effect—hence their sometime nickname, "gut busters."

An illogical leap such as the one that White Castle lovers have taken in creating this myth would make many companies extremely uncomfortable, and they'd likely focus their advertising on something safer and more generic, such as wholesome ingredients. But White Castle chose to accept the notion of an uncontrollable craving and made it the focus of their advertising message and tagline. They even went one stage further in embracing the irreverent cult movie

Harold & Kumar Go to White Castle, rather than attempting to put a corporate gag on it. As a result, White Castle has gone from being a little-known regional brand to one with a cult following with mass distribution of its products in the freezer section of most national grocery chains.

A lot of what people say and believe about you or your brand can be uncomfortable, and we've come to believe in our litigious society that using the courts to attempt to silence people is a smart strategy. But with the influence of social media, it's unrealistic to think that if a large swathe of society believes something about you that it won't be shared and perpetuated. The smart thing is to embrace the conversation—leverage it when it makes sense—and have a sense of humor about it, as White Castle did.

So whether it's the intimate relationship we have with our spouse or children, the detached relationship we have with a celebrity or other famous person, the picture we paint of a particular group, or the way we connect with a favorite brand, people use very little logic when forming perceptions and making choices. But it's possible to understand the nature of these illogical leaps that are essential ingredients in the creation of movements, if the will exists to do so.

Whether we are attempting to shape our own image or that of a candidate, a company, or a brand in creating a culture shift, we need to accept that the image people have created isn't logical, and then commit to decoding the true nature of the illogical leap they have taken.

CHAPTER 5

SOCIAL MEDIA'S EMOTION BEACON

"All emotion is involuntary when genuine."
—Mark Twain, *Letters from the Earth*, 1909

Emotion is the cure for information overload.

Microsoft aired a TV commercial for its Bing® search engine in 2010 (developed by its agency at that time, JWT[1]) that featured a man in a grocery store asking a random question that immediately sparked chaos—as everyone else in the store started at once to add their loosely related thoughts. The purpose of the commercial was to illustrate how Bing can simplify your online searches by providing greater focus. But the entertainment came from seeing the random and illogical nature of how information travels around a group, and it spoke to the insight we all recognize—that in the online world we are forced to process an avalanche of information to find anything meaningful.

It is not coincidental that in tandem with the rise of social media and gaming, which teenagers absorb more readily than any other group in society, we've seen the emergence of an epidemic in Attention Deficit Disorder (ADD) and Attention Deficit Hyperactivity Disorder (ADHD) in the United States. Our genetic makeup and basic chemistry hasn't changed, and yet our brains are required to absorb and process an overwhelming amount of information relative to the past. There is as much information in a weekend edition of the *New York Times* as the average seventeenth-century person would have absorbed in a lifetime, and the number of advertising messages of various kinds that an ordinary person is exposed to in a *single day* in the United States is now estimated to be two hundred and forty-five. If you include all the available advertising messages that we pass or glance at in the course of a day but don't necessarily absorb, according to the research group Yankelovich Partners, the number can be as high as five thousand for a person living in a major city![2]

Although neurologists tell us that we use on average only 30 percent of our brain's capacity—as the 2011 film *Limitless*[3] recently dramatized—clearly, as a species, we are experiencing some "mental teething trouble" in dealing with the information overload. Turn on CNN or ESPN television channels and count the number of individual messages available to process at any given moment, on a single screen. I typically count somewhere between four and eight separate pieces of visual, written, and auditory information. While we are waiting for our species to evolve, in the meantime we have developed coping mechanisms to deal with the overload.

Unconsciously we have trained our brains to become selective and filter out 90 percent of what we are exposed to. But in the process we don't simply delete information. Our natural instinct is to create meaning, and so we add to our edited version of events by imagining and inventing. In essence, we take illogical leaps and reframe the stories in terms that make sense to us.

It's also in our nature, when being bombarded by an avalanche of stimuli, to let our emotional compass take over, which, since it relates to our survival instinct, we therefore do unconsciously. We naturally gravitate toward the story or event that has the greatest emotional resonance. Stand in the middle of Grand Central Station during morning rush hour with your eyes closed, and when you open them see what events you immediately take in. It will inevitably be those where some kind of human drama is unfolding: lovers quarreling or a mother scolding a child—versus the mundane acts of people going about their day-to-day business en route to work.

Emotion is central to creating culture shifts because it provides us with an involuntary light beacon to follow through the noise and intrusion of today's media overload—and the more information we are forced to process, the more that emotion becomes the only thing that can cut through.

SOCIAL MEDIA CAN UNLEASH EMOTION

The uprisings in the Middle East in early 2011 unleashed a cauldron of emotion and gripped our attention, as we intuitively recognized that some seismic shift was taking place. As events unfolded in Tunisia, Egypt, and Libya, journalists were quick to point out the importance of social media in enabling people to communicate, adapt, and organize. Some went so far as to call these uprisings "social media revolutions."[4] Tweets, however, while allowing protesters to convey the immediacy of events and enable them to organize on the fly, didn't capture the emotional core of the protest movement. If you weren't there on the streets to feel it in person, you needed to rely on the physical images and sounds from television or on your laptop or smartphone to truly empathize and engage.

While it was a Facebook page posted in tribute to a murdered businessman that created a focal point for protestors, to suggest that Facebook somehow caused the uprising is erroneously crediting the medium with being the message. It was the sense of emotional injustice that Khaled Said's murder generated that created a tipping point for protestors in their struggle against the Mubarak regime, whether it had been posted on Facebook or written as graffiti on a wall.

Similarly, on May 2, 2011, a day after the news broke that Navy Seals had killed Osama bin Laden in an attack on the compound where he'd been living in relative public view in Abbottabad, Pakistan, although the story first appeared on Twitter, people immediately sought out more emotive means to connect with the enormity of bin Laden's death, or in many cases chose to physically visit Ground Zero in New York.[5]

This isn't to suggest that social media cannot generate emotion around a given topic—it can and it does. Where social media most often creates emotional resonance is in terms of the experience of hundreds of thousands of people contributing to a conversation. Mass participation, in itself, generates emotion—and the greater the participation, the more it becomes a beacon for others and serves to perpetuate any culture shift. As might be expected, NASA has been ahead of many organizations in embracing the opportunity that social media allows to create emotional engagement in its programs and missions. The contrast between a previous generation gathered around a blurred black-and-white television screen to watch the moon-landing, while this generation received live Tweets from *Endeavour* space shuttle captain Mark E. Kelly, couldn't be more stark. As for the nature of Captain "KillerKelly's" Tweets—"Houston, we have a problem . . . haha, just playin'" and "I'm on a space shuttle; I'm on a space shuttle. Take a good, hard look at the mother-f—ing space shuttle"[6]—that's something that the pioneers of the space program in the 1960s might be shaking their heads at!

Social media is central to the creation of culture shifts, not just because it allows people to share information and organize—but also because it enables the mass participation that serves as an emotional beacon for engagement with politicians, celebrities, and brands alike.

In the political realm, Governor Howard Dean's 2004 presidential campaign was ignited by its formative use of social media, which helped to marshal support from his youthful body of Zealots. A Yale graduate and a practicing physician, Dean was elected to the Vermont House of Representatives in 1982, having first come to prominence while spearheading an environmental campaign to build a bicycle trail instead of a proposed lakeside development. In 1991, while treating a patient, he was informed that then Vermont governor Richard Snelling had died of a heart attack, and Dean assumed the office and went on to serve until 2003.[7]

In his own state, and from his position of chairman of the National Governors Association, which he held in 1994–95, Dean was considered a moderate Democrat—fiscally conservative and socially liberal in the mold of a "Rockefeller Republican." And when he announced his presidential candidacy, he was considered a long shot in a broad field of twelve Democrats who each sought to challenge then president George W. Bush in 2004.[8]

Although Dean gained traction initially with a series of strong speeches attacking Democrats for their support of the Iraq war, his real momentum came from his progressive use of social media both to locate supporters and to enable participation in the campaign. Through Meetup.com he changed political campaigning during the 2004 primaries, receiving the bulk of his considerable donations from individuals, and unleashing an army of young Zealots that became known as the Deaniacs to create content and share materials.[9] Governor Dean's social contract with the Deaniacs stated: *You are a Washington outsider with extensive legislative experience. You're a doctor who has shown you care about the environment as well as ordinary people, and you're a progressive, as your use of social media to empower young people proves. You also have a passion and a refreshing energy that many of the other primary candidates seem to lack.*

After his campaign ultimately failed, many of the Deaniacs remained actively engaged in politics through social-media platforms aligned to Democracy for America and other locally centered organizations. These groups provided the platform for then senator Obama's 2008 social-media-centered campaign. With fundraising efforts and organic participation driven by the Zealot-like Deaniacs, Governor Dean became the front-runner during the primaries, was able to forego federal campaign funding, and received key endorsements from former vice president Al Gore and celebrities like Martin Sheen—which felt like a presidential endorsement, given Sheen's popular role as President Bartlett in the television show *The West Wing*. Coming from relative obscurity, Governor Dean looked as though he had a real opportunity to become the Democratic presidential nominee—but then came the Iowa caucuses and "the Scream" on January 19, 2004.

After a last-minute surge by his opponents and a disappointing third-place finish in the Iowa caucuses behind Senators John Kerry and John Edwards—and suffering from a bout of flu—Governor Dean gave a concession speech that literally sunk his campaign. Shouting to be heard above a raucous crowd of supporters, he gave a full-throated scream into his microphone, unaware that to television viewers and listeners the crowd noise was being filtered out. He finished his speech with, "We're going to Washington, DC, to take back the White House! *Yeeeeaaaaaaah*!!!" The scream sounded primal, and paired with his rolled up sleeves, his red face, and slightly crazed expression, it created the impression of someone who wasn't fully in control of himself.[10]

David Letterman referred to the incident as a "crazy, red-faced rant" and the political media went into a feeding frenzy. Over a four-day period, the Scream was replayed more than six hundred times on network and cable channels, but in many ways that was the least of it. With Governor Dean's greatest support coming from young social-media-active Zealots, the Scream was shared and swapped endlessly—creating the enduring perception for many potential Disciples and the broader Congregation of a candidate who lacked the temperament to be president.[11] At this writing seven years later, if you run a Google® search for "Dean Scream" today, you will still receive almost nine million hits.

The Dean '04 campaign demonstrated the growing power of social media and the Web as a way to organize and create engagement that could act as a positive emotional driver—but Governor Dean was undone by the digital forces he'd unleashed, as the Scream created a torrent of negative publicity.

Without doubt, the greatest illustration to date of the emotive power of social media in politics came in the 2008 presidential primary campaigns of Representative Ron Paul and then senator Obama. As I discussed earlier in detailing the lessons learned from the viral launch of *The Blair Witch Project*, as well as from Governor Dean's 2004 campaign—these programs created a social media *how to*, in terms of perpetuating a viral message organically at minimal cost. But while the Obama '08 campaign was able to apply these best practices, there was no equivalent template to study the aftereffects of having unleashed this unprecedented level of engagement and emotion via social media.

If you were a supporter of the Obama '08 campaign, or if you simply engaged with the campaign in some capacity via the Web or social media, you were immediately made to feel like an important player in the culture shift—receiving regular updates on various social networks, as well as e-mails from Michelle and Barack Obama themselves.[12]

The campaign did a masterful job of using social media and e-mail to maintain engagement, drive fundraising, and fuel passion around Senator Obama's candidacy—but it also established an intimate relationship with his Disciples that couldn't simply be switched off once the senator became president. Social media was conceived as a way to enable people to connect with one another in order to continuously share and discuss topics they care about. If you engaged in the Obama campaign, your interest and passion was hardly likely to have abated once the senator was elected!

But instead of seeding new social-media content for this young army of Disciples to continue their advocacy, the campaign went into relative "radio silence" after the election. The website offered little that was fresh, there was minimal new stimulus made available via social media, and after the mandatory thank-you e-mail from the Obamas, the digital airwaves went quiet. For Disciples of the campaign, in a heartbeat they went from feeling like they were part of the culture shift to losing their sense of connectedness to the Obamas. This must have been how Frank Sinatra felt after he'd allegedly used his influence with Carlo Gambino to help John F. Kennedy secure union backing in 1960. Sinatra was effectively shunned after the election, on one occasion building an extension to his Los Angeles home for Kennedy's promised visit—only to have the president, who was now understandably sensitive about Sinatra's Mafia connections, fail to show up.[13]

President Obama's social contract with his Disciples was rooted in participation and stated: *Since your speech at the 2004 Democratic*

Party convention it's been evident that you had the talent, charm, vision, and global appeal to be president—and for progressives it helps that you are the antithesis of the current president. But this has been a social-media movement driven by young people, and as long as you stay true to your progressive principles and continue to engage and empower us, we'll support you through this election and the next—but become a prototypical politician, or fail to allow us to participate, and we'll find someone else who will.

During the 2008 election, the Obama campaign did everything right in terms of its use of social media but failed to maintain the same level of digital engagement among its loyal Disciples afterward. This may have left a bitter taste in the mouth of both Zealots and Disciples, especially when a few months later they began receiving fundraising requests from other Democratic candidates—evidence that their contact information had been passed along—as if they were names on a catalog mailing list! Of course it's difficult and time consuming to run a continuous campaign, but the nature of social media is such that while it allows you to generate heightened emotion through mass participation, once achieved, you can't simply turn off the faucet!

So while social media can play a huge role in unleashing the emotion that is the lifeblood of a culture shift, it's important to recognize and monitor what you've unleashed—because if you fail to continuously feed and nurture your Disciples, it could come back to haunt you, as President Obama may discover in 2012 if he struggles to reactivate his social-media machine.

SOCIAL MEDIA CAN FERMENT ILLOGICAL LEAPS

The Obama '08 campaign and the aftereffects demonstrate both social media's emotive power as well as some potential pitfalls. But back in 2001—when social media was just emerging as a new means of sharing information and organizing—its power was almost immediately evident in terms of the ability to relay information organically.

From its inception, social media's impact in driving illogical leaps and helping to fuel emotional fervor was in evidence in the tragic case of Chandra Levy. Chandra Levy was an intern at the Federal Bureau of Prisons in Washington, DC, who disappeared in May 2001.[14] Soon after her disappearance, allegations surfaced in the media that she had been having an extramarital affair with US Representative Gary Condit from the Eighteenth Congressional District in California.

Representative Condit, a married man, denied the allegations, refused to submit to a polygraph test by the police, and avoided answering questions during a televised interview with Connie Chung of ABC.[15] It subsequently came to light that Representative Condit had also been engaged in an affair with a flight attendant—and it was suggested by unidentified police sources that he had admitted to the affair with Chandra Levy during an interview with law-enforcement officers in July 2001.[16]

Through the launch of the campaign to "bring Chandra home" by the Levy family, the story went viral across various fledgling social networks, including Myspace, the leader at that time. Representative Condit wasn't talking, which created a vacuum of hard information, and everyone felt an emotional connection to the story as both parents and friends saw the events as their own worst nightmare. As a result, in July 2001 a FOX News/Opinion Dynamics poll found that 44 percent of American respondents—fueled by a mistrust of politicians, armed with a new means of participation, and driven by an emotional fervor—took an illogical leap, and determined that Representative Condit was probably an abductor and possibly a murderer![17]

In March 2002, less than ten months after Chandra Levy's disappearance, Representative Condit's three decades in politics ended when his former protégé Dennis Cardoza unseated him, winning the Democratic nomination to represent California's Central Valley in Congress.[18] In February 2011, almost a decade after Levy's disappearance, Ingmar Guandique—who was a suspected member of the Latin American criminal gang Mara Slavatrucha and was already serving a ten-year prison sentence for attacking two other women in Washington's Rock Creek Park where Levy had disappeared—was convicted of kidnapping and murdering Chandra Levy.[19]

Social-media-centered campaigns of this nature designed to facilitate a movement when emotions are running high are, of course, the norm today—so it's no surprise that the families of the six young girls who were abducted, raped, and in four of the cases murdered by Belgian pedophile Marc Dutroux turned to Facebook to wage their campaign against the release of his ex-wife, Michele Martin. Martin was released for good behavior in June 2011 after serving less than half of her thirty-year sentence,[20] but the feelings generated in large measure through the Facebook campaign ensured she had to leave Belgium after being freed—and she was ultimately moved to a convent in France, out of reach of those seeking revenge for her part in these monstrous crimes.

But it isn't only in the highly emotive context of an abduction or a murder that the role of social media in perpetuating illogical leaps is apparent, as the example of Zicam® and the FDA illustrates. Zicam is a homeopathic remedy that claims to reduce the duration of the common cold and lessen the severity of cold symptoms. Zicam is basically zinc delivered in a tablet or nasal swab, and as an herbal supplement it can be marketed with limited government oversight.[21] The history of zinc being used as a remedy for tackling cold symptoms in the United States dates back to the early 1800s when physicians in Connecticut and Massachusetts regularly prescribed it. When it comes to herbal remedies and dietary supplements, I'm as cynical as the next person, but I used to suffer from a number of heavy colds dating back to my days in rainy England, until I starting using Zicam. For me at least, Zicam actually did what it claimed by limiting the length and severity of my colds.

In 2009, the FDA attempted to ban Zicam, citing more than one hundred and thirty reports it had received that Zicam caused temporary or permanent loss of smell, known as anosmia.[22] There was little data used to support the FDA's ban, and perhaps the true reason for the ban wasn't so much the one hundred and thirty complaints received but a combination of pressure from the pharmaceutical industry—as well as an explosion of commentary across the Web and various social networks linking Zicam with anosmia. At its peak in 2009 you could run a Google search for "Zicam and loss of smell" and receive more than fifty thousand hits—not quite at the level of Governor Dean's Scream, but not bad for an obscure homeopathic remedy. Perform a Google search for the same today and you'll still get over ten thousand hits.

Perhaps we shouldn't be surprised at the frenzy of social-media dialogue that this caused. The cure for the common cold remains an undiscovered country for the pharmaceutical industry—and everyone has a stake in it, as we all get colds from time to time. But the illogical nature of the debate as well as the ultimate ban by the FDA is illustrative of social media's ability to generate illogical leaps—because the greatest cause of anosmia or loss of smell *is and always has been* the common cold—and with limited data to prove that Zicam was the cause rather than just the cold itself, the FDA's ban represented a social-media-driven illogical leap.

So it isn't simply the ability that social media allows Zealots and Disciples to engage and organize—it's the emotional impact of mass participation, coupled with social media's capacity to generate illogical leaps, that makes it so formative to the creation of social contracts and to creating (or inhibiting) culture shifts.

SOCIAL MEDIA ENGAGEMENT DOESN'T GUARANTEE SALES

Many companies are learning the lessons of social media—that it's a powerful emotional force to unleash and must be nurtured, that it can ferment the illogical leaps that drive culture shifts—but also that just because you've managed to engage people doesn't mean they'll take the action that you intended! To that end, it's worth contrasting two social-media-driven campaigns that have both been lauded in the marketing and advertising communities, but that achieved very different results in terms of meeting their sales goals. Pixar and Disney's 2010 campaign to promote *Toy Story 3*, and Pepsi's ambitious experiment in social media through its global Refresh Project campaign, have each proved to be illuminating.

The original *Toy Story* launched in 1995 and was the first full-length feature film created using digital animation in its entirety, and it has become a modern classic for parents and their children alike—as well as creating a new genre of animated films that have followed ever since. *Toy Story 2* was released relatively close on the heels of the original film—in 1999—and rode the wave of the original movie to achieve box-office success, although like most sequels, it was less well received by the critics: *Godfather Part II, Terminator 2,* and *Shrek 2* being several notable exceptions.

For the promotion of *Toy Story 3*, Pixar and Disney understood the value of playing on the nostalgia of both parents and their kids.[23] They created and released a barrage of viral videos made to look like vintage-style ads, featuring both the original as well as the new films' characters. Pixar and Disney also created an iAd® featured on the new iPhone 4,[24] as well as a Facebook page that contained a built-in ticket-purchasing app. The premise was brilliant, directly linked to the movie itself, and blindingly simple—and they provided support for these initiatives with traditional banner ads as well as billboards. The viral videos prompted the parents to reminisce about their own childhood toys, while their kids simply enjoyed the fake toy commercials at face value—and the opportunity for bonding and creating common ground between parents and kids went straight to the heart of the original *Toy Story*'s universal appeal.

The Facebook app was connected to news streams in such a way that it was possible to share with friends when you purchased tickets for the movie, and this prompted extensive social-media-based word of mouth and in-stream recommendations. Disney described the entire initiative as being designed to ensure that "no friend gets left behind," which, if you haven't seen *Toy Story 3*, is the underlying narrative of the film.

A few critics have suggested that Pixar and Disney's efforts were solid but not spectacular, in that they didn't introduce an especially new approach to social media or new digital technology in the campaign. This fails to recognize the essential point—that a social media campaign, like any traditional advertising campaign before it, needs to be creative in the way that it establishes a simple and immediate link to the product it's driving—and in this case that meant pre-engagement in the *Toy Story 3* movie narrative, as well as a nostalgic connection to the *Toy Story* franchise. In any event, results speak louder than words, and *Toy Story 3* has gone on to become the highest-grossing animated movie of all time worldwide, eclipsing *Shrek 2*.[25]

Contrast the experience of *Toy Story 3* with that of Pepsi, which has become the poster child for many social-media Zealots, with its Pepsi Refresh initiative launched in January 2010. In 2009, Pepsi decided to shift its focus away from traditional advertising (television, print, outdoor) and emphasize social media.[26] This was probably the first example of a major advertiser making social media the centerpiece of its advertising and marketing efforts and had been the largest (paid) social-media initiative attempted to date.

Pepsi Refresh Project® was designed to allow altruistic consumers to engage with Pepsi via Facebook, Twitter, YouTube, and other social-media platforms by voting for the Refresh projects that they considered most worthy. Some of the projects funded included a program to make ten thousand schools safer, one to educate future civic leaders, and another to fund gene therapy to find a cure for the genetic disorder Sanfilippo Syndrome. At this writing, Pepsi has donated around $20 million to causes as part of the Refresh campaign, voted on by its consumers through social networks. Social-media advocates point to the degree of engagement that Pepsi has achieved through this initiative, especially with younger consumers, as evidence that Pepsi Refresh Project has been an unqualified success. More than eighty million voters registered—the Pepsi Facebook page received nearly 3.5 million "Likes"—and there were sixty thousand Twitter followers.

However, on March 2010, Diet Coke® became the number two soda brand in the world behind Coke®, eclipsing Pepsi for the first time.[27] Also in March 2010, the *Wall Street Journal* reported that Pepsi® and Diet Pepsi® each lost about 5 percent of their market share in 2009. By some other estimates Pepsi's market share had decreased by a factor of eight in the previous year. This led to a chorus of advertising traditionalists claiming that social media *is*, as they'd always suspected, the emperor's new clothes of marketing. Their opinion appeared to be reinforced by the fact that archrival Coke, which had been the beneficiary of Pepsi's market share woes, had remained on a more traditional advertising path, running television ads in the Super Bowl and during the Academy Awards in 2010.[28]

So what can the apparent contradiction in how Pepsi Refresh Project performed tell us about the role of social media and how it impacts commercial culture shifts? Clearly, the program created mass participation, particularly among younger people. It also made people feel good about the Pepsi brand because of its altruistic focus—and undoubtedly drove people to get involved in many of the causes and programs that Refresh sponsored.

However, it doesn't seem to have prompted people to buy more Pepsi, and assuming that that was the main purpose of the Refresh initiative in the first place, it would have to be considered a failure.[29] But it would be a mistake to conclude from this that social media doesn't have a key role to play in generating the emotional fervor that social contracts thrive on. Examples like the Egyptian uprising demonstrate that the mere fact of people coming together en masse is inherently emotive. Also, Pepsi's own results indicate the level of passionate engagement that it has achieved.

Perhaps the real learning, as it relates to the role that social media can play, is that the emotion generated around a topic like school safety or curing a genetic disorder won't necessarily lead directly to people buying the products of companies that sponsor these programs. Pepsi no doubt intended that its social contract with the average consumer who engaged in Refresh would state: *As a younger person I care about worthwhile social causes and I'm going to be more inclined to buy soda from a company that also cares about them.*

In reality, the social contract that the average consumer who engaged in Refresh now has with the company states: *I applaud Pepsi for this altruistic program, and it's encouraged me to get involved in some of the worthy causes it has sponsored. But I don't see what any of this has to do with whether I like Coke better than Pepsi, and I'm still more likely to drink Coke if I prefer the taste. Also, I'll admit that I saw a cute Coke commercial with a polar bear, which prompted me to buy some.*

In essence, while consumers applaud Pepsi for being altruistic, just as they applaud Bill Gates for giving his billions away through his foundation, there is no direct link made in their mind to the products Pepsi sells—which perhaps explains why every positive brand and engagement measure went up, while sales of Pepsi's soda went down. If you want to create a culture shift among Disciples, social media has a huge role to play in allowing people to engage, and the experience of mass participation will generate emotion, particularly if you highlight altruistic initiatives. And while that's extremely valuable in strengthening your social contract, don't assume that people will take the linear step of buying your product if it isn't directly linked to the cause you are sponsoring! As a rule of thumb, if success is ultimately measured in sales of your product, then taking a more direct, but no less creative approach to the application of social media, as Pixar and Disney did with their launch of *Toy Story 3*, is the smarter way to go.

However, a social contract, like any relationship we enter into, is layered, complex, and often illogical. It's wrong to suggest that the Pepsi Refresh Project program hurt the Pepsi brand—indeed it has likely added a conscious or unconscious association with altruism for many Disciples, which can only strengthen the Pepsi brand in the long term. Pepsi's mistake was to believe it could allow itself to be outspent so dramatically by Coke in relation to traditional media like television, which still generally does a better job of creating emotional prompts to purchase.

So just as it was an overstatement for journalists to call the uprisings in Egypt and Tunisia social-media uprisings, it's a mistake for marketers to think that social media's greatest use is to play a linear role in making people buy their products. With the right idea social media can achieve that, as the *Toy Story 3* example demonstrates, but that was never social media's primary purpose. Social media, like every social forum ever invented, was designed to allow people to engage with one another and share things that are important and meaningful to them. Simply put, curing a genetic disorder is more important to most people than which brand of soda they buy. If you prompt important topics in a social forum, then relatively trivial ones will inevitably get pushed to the side. You'll score points for having raised them, but your real purpose—in this case, selling your brand of soda—may get lost in the mix if the link isn't made blindingly obvious.

As social-media sites like Facebook continue to try to find ways to monetize all the commercial traffic that users send them, they risk diluting their original purpose—and people may look to new networks where they can focus on simply engaging with friends on topics that matter to them, without being interrupted by marketers. Facebooks' social contract with its Disciples states: *You have provided an environment where I can connect and share things that are important to me with friends. And as long as you ensure it's a safe and secure environment where I can choose what to engage in and whom to invite, without distraction, you'll be my social network of choice.*

The fact that in a recent national customer-satisfaction survey Facebook ranked below several airlines[30] should be a wakeup call for Facebook to return to its original purpose before it undermines the foundation of its social contract, particularly as users are presented with new alternatives, including Google+® and Pinterest®.

DECODING SOCIAL-MEDIA PERCEPTIONS

Accepting the importance of social media in creating and driving culture shifts, increasingly it can also play a key role in allowing you to monitor how the relationship is maturing with Zealots, Disciples, and the Congregation. Today there are a myriad of fast, free, or relatively inexpensive online research tools available that make it easier than ever to understand how your candidate, your company, or your brand are perceived, enabling you to recognize a culture shift as it's developing. In fact, for many companies, social media's greatest value now lies in its ability to conduct real-time interactive research among hard-to-reach younger consumers.

If you need to field research among a broad group conducting what's often called *open* social ethnography, tools like Radian6® and NetBase® operate on the basis of key-word searches, allowing you to monitor the most discussed theme against a particular topic. For example, during the 2008 campaign, if you'd been monitoring the online discussion around the McCain campaign you could have learned what specific policy or personal issue people were focusing on, on any given day. Twitter mining similarly offers the ability to conduct online monitoring using key-word searches, while Google Zeitgeist™ lets you measure key trends via Google.[31]

Other great online tools and services available for conducting social ethnographic research include BrainJuicer®, which allows you to compile virtual brand archetypes or profile portraits based on key-word searches[32]—and the ShareThis® widget, which helps you monitor what people are sharing across various social-media platforms. You can also conduct photo searches via Flickr® or video searches through Visible Measures® and YouTube to see what relevant images and videos people are sharing across social networks. All these tools allow you to better understand where the Congregation's attention is broadly focused—before putting a narrower spotlight on the Zealots and Disciples.

With a more targeted group of Zealots and Disciples, you can conduct what's often called *closed* digital qualitative research to build a real-time portrait of your most influential group. Tools like Evernote® let people build a virtual scrapbook via their laptop or smartphone, allowing you to see how they are processing information or thinking about a particular topic[33]—while foursquare® captures their location when they check in.[34] A tool like WeePlaces then lets you visualize the places where they checked in from.[35]

So for example, if a chain of restaurants wanted to understand more about the healthy eating habits of people who eat there regularly, they could ask their Disciples to keep a virtual scrapbook on the topic. When the Disciples checked in they could record where they were and what that environment looked like—enabling the restaurant chain to get a real-time sense of how healthy eating fits into people's lifestyle as part of their normal day, as well as their meal choices.

If the restaurant chain wanted to have several of these healthy-eating Disciples from different parts of the country meet to discuss the topic, both Ning® and Facebook enable people to create their own virtual discussion groups.[36] And if restaurants then wanted to know more about customers' viewing habits, online tools like Miso could enable them to record that—or they could discover what consumers were reading with tools like Delicious® and Instapaper®.[37]

With these progressive digital and social-media research tools at our instant disposal, and armed with knowledge from the kind of projective research I referenced earlier in the book, it is possible to monitor the actions and behaviors that fuel illogical leaps, create culture shifts, and ultimately drive purchasing. If you want to know how people feel, think, and act toward you, your candidate, or your brand, social media has ensured that the answers are within easier reach today than ever before.

But in the future, perhaps the real opportunity and true realization of social media's potential will be to take all of this rich and virtually instantaneous consumer data and pair it with advanced technology—in order to communicate brand or political messages in real time as we go about our busy lives. Great science fiction has always been somewhat predictive of future technological advancement, and ever the visionary, Steven Spielberg's 2002 film *Minority Report*, starring Tom Cruise, was centered on a vision of a world where crime could be predicted and therefore prevented.

Minority Report painted a picture of an urban environment where, as we walked into shops, restaurants, or travel terminals, immersive ads would engage directly with us and serve up pertinent personal information based on our previous visits and brand preferences. With advances like Wiji software from Immersive Labs already allowing for relatively advanced interaction between consumers and billboards, it's only a matter of time before Spielberg's vision becomes reality, and perhaps signals that the next frontier that social media will conquer will in fact be terrestrial versus virtual.

It isn't so hard to imagine a scenario in the near future in which you are shopping for a car through an airport terminal billboard, with a virtual salesperson advising you about various features and benefits tailored to your preloaded personal preferences and interests, while you collectively converse with friends and advisors via a social-media portal on the same billboard about the merits of the car you are thinking about buying. Indeed, the only unlikely aspect of this futuristic scenario is that you would be in an airport terminal at all, as it will be increasingly unnecessary for you to have to physically travel anywhere.

The car of the future is already here in the form of the Toyota Fun-Vii®, which was unveiled at the 2011 Tokyo Motor Show and takes the notion of an automotive service avatar to a new level and closer to reality. The most striking thing about the concept is how tangible and imminent this technology truly is. Once inside the thirteen-foot seat capsule, you consult your personal holographic "navigation attendant" to confirm the route and destination and guide you through the journey. A click of your smartphone can design the look of the car's exterior and interior for the day, while on your commute you can drive it or have it drive you. You can use it as a gaming consul, an entertainment hub, or as a virtual office to conduct business while speaking with extraordinary image clarity to your clients and colleagues.

This machine isn't the car of the future, it's what's next, and its genealogy owes as much to the iPhone as it does to the automotive industry. When this vehicle launches and becomes mainstream it will do what the iPhone claimed it would do and "change everything." You only have to revisit movies like *Demolition Man* (1993) with Sylvester Stallone and *The Fifth Element* (1997) with Bruce Willis to see the inspiration for Toyota's Fun-Vii.

And when this car finally does become reality—and happily extends our ability to drive beyond the point at which we can see or react properly—the debate about whether it's removing the "joy of driving" will no doubt be raised. But in truth, on most people's average car journey today there is very little joy and a great number of distracted people who would rather be talking, texting, reading, playing, or otherwise entertained. The Toyota Fun-Vii has everything the post-digital generation already wants in a car.

As for crime prevention, IBM already has a predictive technology model in place, which in partnership with the Memphis Police Department has helped to reduce crime in Memphis by as much as 30 percent—while in the Merseyside district of the United Kingdom, drones that have been adapted from military technology are already being tested to help police in areas where violent crime is most prevalent. It's a shame this technology was not put to use in Tottenham, North London, during the riots of August 2011!

UNDERSTANDING SOCIAL MEDIA'S TRUE VALUE

Future gazing aside, today social media isn't a silver bullet in itself, as so many people seem to believe, or at least not yet anyway. Social media is a powerful medium, but still just one medium. It is dramatically less expensive to see your message carried organically via social media sites than it is to invest in traditional media like television, but it's easy to both overstate and mischaracterize social media's true value and purpose.

When companies and organizations get it right the results can be extraordinary, as the case of *Toy Story 3* illustrates. Sometimes the sheer creativity of the digital application is such that the organic buzz and word of mouth via social media can propel you to new heights, as was the case with the band Arcade Fire's 2010 "The Wilderness Downtown" online project—which enabled viewers to take a tour of their hometown using Google Maps™ and Google Street View™. It's perhaps no surprise that, based in part on their creative use of digital and social media, Arcade Fire's *The Suburbs* won the 2010 Grammy Award for Best Album of the Year, and was one of the top-selling albums of the year.

As the Mark Twain quote at the beginning of this chapter states, "All emotion is involuntary when genuine," and emotion is the irresistible driver that causes Disciples to create a culture shift. The experience of mass participation via social media can serve to generate that emotion, but social media's primary role is still to allow people to organize, engage, and increasingly to provide companies with rich insights. The way information is shared is such that any message disseminated via social media will naturally be modified and reframed in the manner of the "telephone game," which may run counter to your original intent or wishes.

Social media can encourage the digital equivalent of Attention Deficit Disorder, so it should be used judiciously—and while it can help people organize support for you or spark an idea, once that has happened, you must be prepared to step back and see what transpires organically. Nevertheless, social media is central to the creation of a social contract because it helps to fuel the invention of illogical leaps and serves as an emotion beacon. And as technology continues to allow for more personalized real-time interaction from any location, social media's potential for generating the heightened emotion, which is the lifeblood of any culture shift, will only continue to increase.

CHAPTER 6

THE SANCTUARY OF CERTAINTY

"Certainty? In this world nothing is certain but death and taxes."

—Benjamin Franklin, from a 1789 letter
reprinted in 1817 in a volume of his works

W e strive for certainty in our political, cultural, and commercial relationships as a basis for creating culture shifts. It is, and always will be, an uncertain world. And never more so than as we find ourselves battling a great recession, two wars, the ongoing threat of global terrorism, and seismic changes in the Middle East—not to mention global warming, population growth, and spikes in global commodities. But even during the best of political and economic times, we are wired to instinctively look for certainty in order to maintain the illusion that we are in control of the events around us. The power of social contracts stems in part from the certainty they offer people in their choices and affiliations, whether those contracts relate to a favorite movie star, a sports team, a politician, or a particular brand. This helps to explain why there is such anger and resentment when a social contract is perceived to have been broken, because it removes the emotional sanctuary that the feeling of certainty provides. And once the social contract has been broken, the basis of our affinity to a related culture shift is also destroyed.

Outside of our personal relationships with family and friends, one of the most powerful and enduring relationships people establish is with a favorite sports team. Team affiliations, and the sense of community and belonging that they provide, often generate intense emotions, and no more so than the relationship that an English football (soccer) fan has with his or her favorite club. England has a storied history as a global power, yet geographically it's a relatively small country with a landmass roughly half the size of the state of Texas.[1] But whereas Texas has a grand total of two National Football League teams, the Dallas Cowboys and the Houston Texans, England's Premier League and Football League have a combined *ninety* teams spread across four divisions! London alone has nineteen clubs, including five in the 2011 Premier League: Arsenal, Chelsea, Fulham, Tottenham, and West Ham—and while West Ham was relegated after the 2011 season, Queens Park Rangers, another London-based team, was promoted, keeping London's contingent in the top flight at five in 2012.

In many cases, intercity team rivalries are the most passion filled, as they are in most parts of the world, and the intensity that these encounters generate is based on a form of tribal passion that is often passed on from one generation to another. Tottenham Hotspur versus Arsenal establishes North London bragging rights until the next encounter. Liverpool versus Everton has consistently torn Merseyside households apart. And the passion-filled Manchester City versus Manchester United match that always generates incredible emotion is likely to hit the boiling point in the 2012 season when Manchester City, the Football Association Cup holders battle Manchester United, the English Premier League champions, in the Football Association Community Shield (formerly Charity Shield) match that traditionally kicks off the new football season.[2]

But of the historic rivalries in English football, few over the years have been able to match the traditional intensity of Manchester United versus Leeds United.[3] The enmity between the two clubs dates back to the fifteenth century and the War of the Roses, when the House of York and the House of Lancaster fought over the throne of England. The battles were some of the bloodiest and most gruesome in England's history, and at the Battle of Towton—only a few miles from Leeds—Edward IV of York displaced Henry VI as king, as fifty thousand men at arms took to the field and twenty-eight thousand casualties were recorded. Attending Leeds–Manchester matches over the years, you get the distinct impression that the various supporters knew many of the victims personally—and still hold a grudge. Although it might be hard for some to imagine, given the outwardly sedate and gentlemanly nature of the game itself, even Yorkshire versus Lancashire cricket matches tend to get rather heated.

Although Leeds is currently languishing outside the English Premier League, occasional cup matches between Leeds and Manchester United still serve to continue the rivalry, with Leeds wearing their white jerseys, in honor of the white rose of the House of York, and Manchester United wearing the red of the House of Lancaster. However, the War of the Roses isn't the only point in history to add fire to a modern-day soccer match between the two teams. In the late eighteenth century and early nineteenth century during the Industrial Revolution in England, Manchester's cotton industry challenged and ultimately overtook Leeds's woolen industry, sending many Yorkshire weavers into poverty. It's not surprising therefore that the first football match played between the two teams in January 1906 was, to say the least, a spirited affair. It has continued in that vein through the years under their storied managers, Sir Matt Busby and Don Revie, right up to the modern day where Manchester United remains one of the world's great football clubs under Sir Alex Ferguson—narrowly losing in the 2011 UEFA Champions League final to Barcelona for the title of Europe's top club.[4] Indeed, Manchester United was named the world's most valuable sports franchise by *Forbes* in July 2011.[5]

Although thankfully the violence and hooliganism that marred English football in the 1970s has largely disappeared, the intense allegiance that Leeds "Service Crew" supporters and Manchester United's "Red Army" feel is both loud and visceral at every match played. From the sea of supporters' colors, which act as a virtual military uniform, to the continuous chanting and singing that can go on for hours, both before, during, and after the game, to the bragging rights that endure until the next encounter—the social contract that these fans have established with their teams allows them to feel they are part of a popular culture shift that transcends sport, and offers them a sense of purpose and certainty in an uncertain world.

The social contract that a Manchester United fan has with his team states: *Before anything, I am a Man U supporter. And when we play Leeds, the rivalry reminds me of my roots and my heritage. No matter what's going on in my life or in the wider world, the one thing that is certain is that Man U will always be there, and as long as I'm a fan I'll feel part of something bigger than myself.*

The illogical leap in this case is to define yourself through a football club based on an ancient rivalry against a team that's located less than forty miles away—particularly when Manchester United was actually founded in 1878 in Newton Heath by railway employees from *both* the counties of Yorkshire and Lancashire. But the nature of a social contract, particularly one that carries this much history and passion, is anything but logical. And the level of emotion isn't limited to Leeds and Manchester United, or even to fans who are actually based in England. Fans of all sports teams, but particularly football teams with storied histories, can be equally passionate, whether or not they have a physical connection to their favorite club—and sometimes with tragic consequences. In Nairobi, on May 7, 2009, Suleiman Omondi, a Kenyan man who was a passionate supporter of Arsenal, the North London–based English Premier League team—committed suicide after his team lost to Manchester United in a UEFA Champions League match.[6] Omondi had told his neighbors repeatedly that he intended to hang himself if Arsenal lost, but sadly no one took him seriously.

Although similar rivalries rooted in passionate social contracts and based on illogical leaps exist all over the world—such as Duke versus Carolina, the Yankees versus the Red Sox, and Barcelona versus Real Madrid, thankfully sanity usually prevails when fans experience painful defeats, and events sometimes conspire to remind fans that what unites them is greater than what divides them.

The tragic abduction and murder of the University of North Carolina's student president Eve Carson in 2008 was one of those moments, as two schools came together poignantly at the Dean Dome in Chapel Hill before the start of the Duke–Carolina men's basketball game to observe a shared moment of remembrance.[7] Unless you've actually been to a Duke–Carolina basketball game it's difficult to express the degree of excitement and the local bragging rights at stake—particularly, it has to be said, when the game is held at Duke's Cameron Indoor Stadium when the temperature dial is allegedly turned way up.

Although the schools are literally eight miles apart, whether you support the Tar Heels or the Blue Devils is the first allegiance many people coming to the North Carolina Triangle area often need to pledge. But in the period around Eve Carson's death and on the night of the game, the sense of tribalism and competitive animosity viscerally fell away, as one community stood together in grief and remembrance for a young woman with limitless potential who had died far too soon. Then the game began and the natural order of things began to be restored—and with it a healing sense of certainty—as the young athletes of Duke and Carolina went at one another again as they have since 1920.[8]

In relation to the social contracts we establish with our favorite sports team and players, much of the allure *is* that sense of certainty and comfort that comes from an enduring rivalry. Ask most sports fans and they will tell you that they want to see healthy competition in sports, but at the same time the emotional sanctuary that sports offers, particularly in troubled times, is somehow weakened when old rivalries become less meaningful, or when great players appear to be waning. The National Football League has created a situation of relative parity in the last few years, where any one of the thirty-two teams can conceivably win the Super Bowl each year. In the past decade only Coach Bill Belichick's New England Patriots, led by Tom Brady at quarterback, have been able to repeat their Super Bowl victory.[9] And it's become increasingly common in the NFL for a team that finishes at or near the bottom one year to win their division the next year.

When the New York Yankees or the Dallas Cowboys don't make the post season, as neutral fans we might applaud the Arizona Diamondbacks or the Jacksonville Jaguars who took their place; but there is also a sense that the natural order of things has shifted out of balance, and that creates a degree of uncertainty. For most of a decade we knew who the greatest golfer in the world was, until that fateful evening of November 27, 2009, when Tiger Woods drove his Cadillac Escalade® into a fire hydrant outside his Florida home, and his life and golfing career began to unravel.[10] Today the golf world appears to be struggling on some level, with the absence of Tiger as the game's unquestioned dominant player. And while it's interesting to see who the world's number one golfer will be on any given week— perhaps the brilliant young German player and 2010 PGA Champion Martin Kaymer, or the charismatic Englishman Luke Donald—the lack of certainty can also feel strangely disquieting.[11] In giving twenty-two-year-old Irish phenom Rory McIlroy a thunderous reception for his runaway victory at the 2011 US Open—after he led but ultimately fell short in the Masters—perhaps the audience were reacting in part to the possible return of certainty, as a new force emerged with the talent and temperament to dominate the game in years to come.

It was fascinating to contrast the public reaction of McIlroy's win with Darren Clarke's victory at the 2011 British Open at Royal St. George's in the same year. Clarke, the amiable Northern Irishman, whom I had the privilege of meeting a dozen years ago—and who dominated the Open at Royal St. George's through the weekend with his tee to green ball striking in swirling winds and with his beaming personality—is perhaps the quintessential example of a "big lug." In watching him give interviews in the lead-up to his amazing victory, it was evident that here was someone who was now entirely comfortable in his own skin. In a live televised interview with the BBC the day before he won the British Open, Clarke was asked why he thought people loved him, and his attempt at self-analysis was worthy of any therapist, as he stated "Well, I'm not your normal athlete, I'm a bit on the heavy side and I like a drink, and I've had to deal with some stuff over the years, so I guess people see me as being just like them."

While we felt particular empathy with Clarke in large part because he had lost his wife to cancer five years previously and had shown plenty of emotion on the path to recovery from this tragedy, the crowd's aura surrounding Clarke's victory was quite different from the aura surrounding McIlroy's win. The fans cheered for Clarke in celebration of one man's reward for enduring the hardships of life with a beaming smile and receiving his just rewards. By contrast, they cheered for McIlroy in part because of the promise of certainty that an emerging young champion with the potential to dominate for years to come had provided the game of golf.

Do people really prefer parity and the opportunity for anyone to win, or does it make things too complicated and take away from their sense of certainty? It's never hurt tennis having an undisputed number one world champion, as long as there was at least one credible rival who could keep things interesting. Indeed, the height of tennis's popularity as an international sport has always been at those moments where there is a young prince battling to unseat a king, as in the eras of Björn Borg versus John McEnroe and more recently, Roger Federer versus Rafael Nadal, and Nadal versus Novak Djokovic.[12]

The NCAA March Madness college basketball tournament provides an interesting case in point. In contrast to the BCS (Bowl Championship Series) college football bowl system[13]—which seems to have a myriad of bowls provoking constant criticism from everyone including President Obama for its inability to crown an undisputed national champion—the NCAA tournament appears to give every team that makes the tournament the chance to be champion. And yet the actual winners since the late 1990s tell a different story. It is the powerhouse college basketball programs that have consistently dominated, with the likes of Duke, Carolina, Florida, Kansas, Kentucky, and Connecticut collectively winning thirteen of the last seventeen tournaments played. Although fairytale teams with lower tournament seeds like Davidson led by Stephen Curry's pinpoint shooting in 2008,[14] and VCU in 2011,[15] have threatened to upset the natural order of college basketball by winning the tournament, at the last hurdle they always seem to fall to the usual suspects.

March Madness enthralls us because it offers both the excitement of a completely open competition and at the same time a sense of certainty, as the winner is almost always one of college basketball's titans. The power of a social contract with a player, a team, or a tournament lies partly in its ability to provide certainty—yet it's impossible to have certainty in an environment where absolute parity causes a sea of competitive sameness. So, perhaps counterintuitively, certainty is a central element in the creation of a culture shift—or at least the illusion of certainty—because it provides the confidence that Disciples and the Congregation need to move beyond the status quo.

"GRASP-ABILITY"

Just as leading teams and players provide a feeling of certainty when they dominate the competition, so too do simple ideas—whether those ideas are proposed by a politician, a celebrity, or a company. In order to provide that sense of certainty and cut through, an idea must be able to be grasped instantly—and must instinctively feel true, regardless of whether or not it is based on illogical beliefs. Proposed by several Republican presidential candidates in the 2008 election, in recent history the "flat tax" is most closely identified with Steve Forbes during his 1996 and 2000 Republican presidential primary campaigns.

A true flat-rate tax is a system of taxation in which one tax rate is applied to all income levels with absolutely no exceptions. In an article from April 2005 titled "The Flat-Tax Revolution," the *Economist* succinctly summed up the argument in favor of a true flat tax as follows:

If the goals are to reduce corporate welfare and instead, to enable household tax returns to fit on a postcard, then a true flat tax best achieves those goals. The flat rate would then be applied to the entire taxable income and profits, without any exception or exemption. Under such a tax, it could be argued that nobody gets to enjoy a preferential or unfair tax treatment, no industry receives any special treatment, large households are not advantaged at the expense of small ones, etc. Moreover, the cost of tax filing for citizens and the cost of tax administration for the government would be drastically reduced, as under a true flat tax only businesses and the self-employed would need to actively interact with the tax authorities.[16]

In arguing for a true flat rate of taxation, Steve Forbes gained enormous traction, at one point becoming the front-runner in the 1996 Republican primaries, largely by campaigning on this single issue. And on the face of it, the flat tax is hard to argue against. It appears to offer simplicity, certainty, less bureaucracy, smaller government, and is a true expression of equality and democracy in practice. But critics of a flat tax have argued that if everyone pays the same, the marginal dollar for people with lower incomes is vastly more important than it is to people with high incomes, and that this is especially true for those at or below the poverty level.[17] True flat-tax proponents contest the notion that a marginal dollar should be taxed differently, and so the debate inevitably continues.

Yet at every presidential election, including in 2012, candidates have run largely on a platform of instigating a flat-tax rate and have gained traction in the polls because of it. Indeed, in the Republican primary most of the leading candidates put a spotlight on tax reform including Ron Paul, Rick Perry, Hermann Cain, Newt Gingrich, and Mitt Romney.[18] That's because the basic premise of a flat tax has almost universal appeal due to the certainty and simplicity it appears to offer. Who wouldn't want to be able to calculate their taxes in about one minute and send in their return on a postcard, or not even be required to file at all? Advocates can also point to successes in the former Communist states of Eastern Europe such as Lithuania, Estonia, and Hungary, which claim to have benefited from instituting a version of the flat-tax-based system.

So it's evident why the flat tax continues to hold mass appeal, particularly for those on the conservative right of politics in the United States, and for a period of time it seemed as though Steve Forbes had successfully established a social contract, as the basis for a culture shift with supporters, driven by his flat-tax advocacy. Forbes's social contract stated: *You are the owner of* Forbes *magazine and a respected businessman and financier, so you must know what you're talking about when it comes to tax systems. We all pay the same, we can basically file our returns on a postcard, and the government and its bureaucracy shrinks. Brilliant! Some of the poorest folks may have to go without a few government services, but we'll have more money to give to charities, so what's the problem? It seems like a win-win and you have my support if you keep it this simple.*

Perhaps if the debate had stayed at that level, Steve Forbes would have become the Republican candidate in 1996. But while the overwhelming majority of voters find the basic idea appealing, as soon as the debate becomes more granular, as it did in 1996—and some of the nuances for and against are presented and the real impact on public services become apparent—most people tend to simply tune out. As an "elevator speech" the flat tax passes the grasp-ability test and also carries the requisite amount of passion for a culture shift to occur. But the moment the debate expands, all but the most engaged and impassioned Zealots switch off. As a result, the flat tax will likely always threaten to be a dominant vote-winning issue for one presidential candidate or another, but will never be able to sustain the passion required to fuel a culture shift.

The iPhone and iPad® each passed the grasp-ability test with flying colors, not only because of their intuitive technology and simple user interface, but also because of the system they created for downloading applications (apps).[19] But for the Disciples of these products, choosing the right app is less simple and can create uncertainty, particularly when there are more than six hundred thousand available apps for the iPhone today, and one hundred thousand for the iPad, with the number constantly growing![20] Users rely heavily on their peers to select the best apps and weed out the weaker ones, particularly as it relates to the myriad of gaming apps. But while the iPhone and iPad had the power of the Apple brand behind them and the support of its many Disciples worldwide, one of the most successful iPhone apps was developed by a previously unknown company from Finland, with limited funds and almost no traditional advertising support.

Rovio Entertainment's Angry Birds® takes Albert Einstein's definition of insanity—"doing the same thing over and over again and expecting different results"[21]—and turns it on its head. As someone who started playing arcade video games in the late 1970s, I find that Angry Birds has the same addictive qualities that the original Space Invaders® had, and if you keep repeating your actions and persevere, you will eventually beat each puzzle and graduate to get those magical three stars!

For the uninitiated, Angry Birds is the world's most successful mobile app to date and has managed to captivate both avid gamers and bored travelers alike.[22] It has the same appeal whether you are in your teens or whether you're a grandparent. A variety of different birds use each other as slingshot ammunition to crush smiling pigs, or monkeys in some later versions. Peter Vesterbacka, founder and CEO of Rovio has said, "Angry Birds is going to be bigger than Mickey Mouse and Mario."[23] With new-version releases, a tie-in with the 2011 Disney movie *Rio,* board games, and soft toys building the franchise, Angry Birds may be just scratching the surface.[24] Originally developed for about one hundred thousand euros and currently bringing in revenue of more than one million euros a month, Rovio, through Angry Birds, has created a pop-culture shift with an army of global Disciples and attracted twenty million followers. But of the six hundred thousand apps available to download on the iPhone, why has this simple game, which doesn't feature breakthrough technology or particularly distinctive graphics, been the one to break through?

Like Space Invaders and Tetris® before it, Angry Birds is both simple and addictive—you can attempt the same level again and again without success, and then suddenly complete the level or move your score from two to three stars. The effect of successfully completing a puzzle is emotive and tangible, as you survey the absolute devastation you've wrought on the enemy pig encampment or the monkeys' tree houses. When you complete a game it creates a tremendous feeling of satisfaction and draws you hungrily back for more. And like so many other cultural phenomena, the game passes the grasp-ability test in that you can almost immediately tackle the easiest games by simply playing without having to learn a complex set of rules. While Angry Birds is often frustrating, particularly the final game of the *Rio* app that introduces a moving target for the first time (which took three days away from writing this book for me to finally complete), the certain knowledge that you will eventually triumph is both addictive and satis-fying, and also provides a feeling of being in control.[25]

Angry Birds has also created a pop-culture shift, because many of its Disciples are celebrities whose addiction has been made public. The occasionally accurate *National Enquirer* reported that Angelina Jolie and Jack Black had become addicted to playing the game during the making of the movie *Kung Fu Panda 2* in April 2011, and that the rest of the staff and crew were afraid to play Jolie in partic-ular because of her tendency to scream and make bird screeches—that and the fact that she wouldn't allow them to stop until she'd beaten them![26] For Angelina Jolie and the game's many Disciples, Angry Birds has been able to create a pop-culture shift, because it offers an addictive sanctuary from your busy life while providing the certainty that you will eventually prevail.

The same mind-set that drives our desire for certainty explains why Hollywood churns out essentially the same movies again and again, but with different casts. In Hugh Grant's genre of romantic comedies, the plots are often entirely interchangeable with only his leading lady costars switching out to create a degree of variety. Increasingly in Hollywood, as with the 2011 release of *The Hangover Part II*, the producers effectively made the same movie twice, in this instance simply changing the location from Las Vegas to Bangkok.[27] The desire for familiarity that breeds certainty also causes studios to remake classic films with little more than an updated cast and a modicum of refinement in keeping with the political nuances of the day—and advances in special effects. But the desire for the certainty that familiarity and repetition offers has limits, as the 2011 release of *Arthur* demonstrates.[28] Even given the hilarious performance of Russell Brand as the title character in this remake of the 1981 original, which made the late Dudley Moore an unlikely international sex symbol, the nuanced changes in characters and plot are so discreet as to leave you wondering why they even bothered to remake the film at all.

The publishing industry is also not immune from the desire for certainty, as any writer discovers when they begin to receive advice to modify their work to be more in line with a particular genre of books, or even to mirror the approach of another author. The genius of Angry Birds is in offering just enough variation in the birds themselves, the settings, and the protagonist pigs and monkeys to provide the nuanced changes in each puzzle that keep us coming back for more without changing the essential game in such a way as to create unfamiliarity and the resulting uncertainty.

MINIMIZING CHOICE TO EASE SELECTION

In creating a pop-culture shift, Angry Birds had to rely on the compulsive nature of the game and on the endorsement of celebrities and Apple Disciples to simplify selection for its two hundred million followers. Other companies and brands have had to take it upon themselves to find inventive ways to simplify choice in order to make selection of their products easier.

In 1988, United Distillers (which is now owned by Diageo) decided that the best way to sell more single-malt whiskey was to simplify selection for drinkers, by rebranding as well as limiting the number of whiskeys they offered. Instead of giving equal attention to the numerous single malts from distilleries they owned in the various regions of Scotland, they decided to create a Classic Malts of Scotland® collection—selecting a single high-quality and representative malt from each of the six key Scottish whiskey-producing regions. Dalwhinnie represented the Highlands, Glenkinchie the Lowlands, Cragganmore represented Speyside, while Oban stood for the western coastal area of the Highlands. From the Islands of Scotland, Talisker represented Orkney, while Lagavulin captured the distinct characteristics of Islay.[29] Apparently I'm not alone in having a particular fondness for Lagavulin, as Johnny Depp also is reportedly a Disciple of its unique taste and above all its distinctive aroma. Initially there was an outcry from single-malt aficionados—who in the typical mode of Zealots saw this as an attempt to "dumb down" single-malt whiskey—and the various distilleries themselves who saw the focus shift to just six representative brands also were not pleased initially.

But in partnership with its design agency Lewis Moberly, United Distillers understood the importance of simplifying selection in order to create greater certainty for single-malt whiskey buyers. Through award-winning packaging they told the engaging story of each distillery on every box and label and enhanced the overall quality appearance at the same time. At a stroke they took the confusion out of single-malt whiskey selection and created heightened appeal for their brands—as well as for the product itself—by allowing a broader, yet still-discerning group of drinkers, who had previously felt intimidated choosing single malts, to feel confident in making their selections.

One description of Lagavulin as "a smoke bomb with a silky texture and a strong marine influence, and a note of brine and peat" captures the taste and aroma perfectly. And by limiting selection and allowing drinkers to feel more confident, United Distillers saw sales of its Scottish single-malt whiskeys increase by more than 200 percent in the first year after the relaunch.[30] United Distillers established a social contract with discerning single-malt Disciples that continues to make the Classic Malts of Scotland among the most sought-after whiskeys today. The company ensured the livelihoods of many remote distilleries and also created a template that many other spirits brands have proceeded to follow. Admittedly, Scottish single-malt whiskey hasn't yet been able to create a commercial culture shift in the United States, but like the product itself, it just takes a little time for it to reach its peak!

Contrast the story of the Classic Malts with the experience of selecting wine, and it's fairly apparent that the wine industry needs to affect a revolution in how wine is categorized and branded. Perhaps this is because so many wine manufacturers still appear to maintain an elitist air that almost seems to enjoy having knowledgeable insiders looking down on the occasional wine drinker. The snobbery associated with wine tasting and selection was perfectly captured by Paul Giamatti's character Miles in the breakout 2004 hit movie *Sideways*—for which Thomas Haden Church deservedly won the Academy Award for Best Supporting Actor, playing Jack, Giamatti's reprobate "wine-luddite" sidekick.[31] Who can forget Miles's heroic dash into the disheveled home of the waitress that Jack had spent the night with, in order to retrieve his friend's wedding bands—or his hysterical retreat while being pursued by her terrifying and naked husband?

Wine has its own vernacular and its own unfathomable nomenclature, as well as a seemingly arbitrary price scale that feels almost akin to a fine-art auction. It's as if the entire category has conspired to intentionally alienate the Congregation of prospective wine drinkers, driving the average American back into the safe haven of beer drinking, where brand and product distinctions are far clearer—at least so far as it relates to domestic light beers, as the microbrew category can also get quite confusing. Whereas most product sectors seek to invite customers in, the wine category asks you to knock on its door and prove you are worthy of their products, not unlike *Seinfeld*'s intimidating "Soup Nazi."[32]

Ask the occasional wine drinkers how they go about selecting wine and they'll demonstrate that they understand the basic varieties: Cabernet Sauvignon, Chardonnay, Pinot Grigio, and so on. But beyond that they tend to be flummoxed and generally buy according to price—and more often than not it will be the mid-priced wine, as Duke Professor Dan Ariely explains in his enlightening book,

Predictably Irrational.[33] These occasional wine drinkers may move to a higher-priced wine if the bottle has to be taken to a social event, or they may drop to a lower price if they plan to consume several bottles at home. When asked to select between several wine brands of the same variety, such as Chardonnays for example, they will seldom choose the cheapest bottle—yet in blind taste tests they often pull out the cheapest wine because it's typically the sweetest, which tends to better suit many Americans' taste palates.

Because wine manufacturers and brands are unwilling or unable to make the process of selection any easier, it's fallen to the wine retailers and restaurants to try to demystify wine selection. The Grape Restaurant is an example of a chain of wine-oriented restaurants in the southeastern United States that actually tries to help its customers select wine by using a simple color-coding system within each variety, organized on the basis of taste and price. This simple and logical system doesn't dumb down selection, but rather gives average wine drinkers a sporting chance of actually choosing a wine they'll like at a suitable price point—and serves to avoid the often-seen dining-out ritual where the wine list is passed around the table like a hot potato until one anointed "expert" begrudgingly makes a selection for the table.

Wine specialty stores like Total Wine & More, as well as some grocery stores, have followed suit in attempting to create simplified coding systems to aid selection, although they lack the taste-testing advantage that restaurants enjoy. Indeed, many prospective wine buyers find the process of selection so difficult that they'll turn to the most unlikely of sources for guidance. In my own neighborhood, Taylors', a local gas station that sells wine, has become a virtual "wine oracle" for the community—as the discerning owners are on hand to offer recommendations, provide certainty of choice, and help demystify selection.

The example of Classic Malts and the impact that its launch had on sales of single-malt whiskey in the United Kingdom gives an indication of the degree to which wine sales in the United States could multiply if wine manufacturers committed to making selection simpler. In doing so, manufacturers would provide the sanctuary that Disciples feel when they are certain about their choices, and could move heavy wine consumption beyond just the elitist Zealots. The contrasting examples of single-malt whiskey and wine showcase the importance of certainty as a key component in creating a culture shift. Many of my wine-drinking friends on both sides of the Atlantic suggest that the greatest barrier to wine rivaling beer as America's favorite adult drink is the lack of a wine-drinking culture in the United States—but it seems equally likely that it is the wine industry itself that is preventing wine from creating a culture shift.

A RISING CERTAINTY

If any experience is likely to create a sense of uncertainty today, it's US commercial air travel. From the indignity, hassle, and seemingly arbitrary nature of TSA inspections at overcrowded airports, to delays for reasons that vary from genuine weather issues to embarrassing shortages of seat-belt extensions (as NFL player Tony Gonzalez recently Tweeted about), air travel in our society has gone from being something that, if it can be believed, we once looked forward to, to an experience akin to a colonoscopy. Commercial air travel today often causes a traveler to pass through several emotional phases including confusion, hope, anger, and, ultimately, resignation. Resignation can actually be the most debilitating state as air travelers come to realize that they have no power over the fact that their flight is four hours late, no ability to gain a meaningful explanation for the delay, and no recourse after the event—other than to write a strongly worded letter that will sit atop a mountainous pile for six months until, if you are lucky, you might receive a standard apology. No wonder that passengers, and occasionally flight attendants, as in the famous case of JetBlue's Steven Slater, occasionally freak out at the experience and simply lose control.[34]

The overwhelming emotion that the air traveler seeks today is certainty. Certainty that the flight will take off within half an hour of its scheduled departure time, that the plane has gone through its mechanical maintenance and checks, and that a cabin crew is actually available with an adequate amount of seat-belt extensions to hand out. Certainty that the seat will have enough leg room for you to at least vary the position of your knees, and enough width for you to be able to joust for the armrest with your seatmate, while of course avoiding eye contact. If you are a nervous flyer, you also seek certainty that the plane is both large enough and new enough for you to avoid the feeling that you're hurtling through the air in a 1959 Ford Edsel®.

So it's little wonder that, for the business traveler in particular, an inordinate amount of time is spent trying to find ways to avoid commercial air travel whenever and wherever possible, in the manner of Macon Leary, the travel writer in Anne Tyler's near-perfect novel *The Accidental Tourist.*[35] As virtual tools like video-conferencing and "go to meeting" software have become increasingly mainstream, it's little wonder that most of the traditional so-called "hub and spoke" airlines continue to struggle—not simply because of high fuel prices and recessionary factors, but because their customers would rather have a root canal than fly their domestic services.

There is the once-tiny but now-dominant exception to the rule, Southwest Airlines. From its humble beginnings as Air Southwest Company, when it was founded by Rollin King and Herb Kelleher in 1967—with four planes providing service within the state of Texas—to its current position as the largest airline in the United States, Southwest Airlines now operates 3,400 flights a day with a fleet of 552 aircraft[36] and provides something different—but perhaps not in the obvious way that people might think.

Southwest Airlines has successfully established a social contract with an army of air-travel Disciples that states: *Since September 11, air travel in the United States has generally become a hassle-filled nightmare, but Southwest Airlines has made the experience much more bearable by offering cheaper flights, characterful service, planes that are generally larger and newer, allowing me to choose my own seat and a model that runs efficiently and doesn't try to nickel-and-dime me at every turn. Flying Southwest may not be luxurious, but its better and cheaper and more consistent than the rest, and for that I'll fly them whenever I can versus the competition.*

While on the face of it the commercial culture shift that Southwest Airlines has created and continues to perpetuate is based on a series of rational benefits that the airline offers over its competitors, the real distinguishing factor is emotional. Within what it is able to control, Southwest Airlines has brought a degree of certainty back into an uncertain experience and has been rewarded by becoming America's largest airline in the last decade. Fixed, low prices without additional fees for bags or changing tickets creates certainty. Running only two types of aircraft, predominantly the Boeing 737, provides certainty that you won't be crammed into a regional jet—or worse, something with propellers—as well as certainty that the maintenance crew were expert in servicing your type of aircraft. Certainty that you'll be able to choose your own seat, confident in the knowledge that you won't have to be separated from a loved one—and that the flight attendant won't scowl at you when you make an innocent request. Certainty is the secret weapon in Southwest Airlines's success and the emotional currency that has fueled its culture shift.

LOSS OF CERTAINTY MEANS LOSS OF MOMENTUM

The famous Benjamin Franklin quote at the beginning of this chapter, "Certainty? In this world nothing is certain but death and taxes," while true in a logical world, doesn't stop us from striving for certainty in our choice of sports teams, brands, games, or airlines! The allure of certainty is central to the establishment of social contracts and the resulting culture shifts, because by helping people decide, individuals and organizations generate both trust and credibility.

It isn't a lack of imagination or intelligence that causes us to look for simplicity in making our choices, it's the feeling of self-affirmation that we are smart and knowledgeable enough to make informed selections. When we feel confident in our choice of airline, or when a sporting competition feels conclusive, it fuels the illusion of certainty that we seek from the world around us—and we inevitably feel connected to the organizations that try to give us this peace of mind.

If the NCAA dramatically widened its tournament schedule to include additional college teams, and the result was that the perennial winners in playing more games were knocked out more often, resulting in a new champion every year—the NCAA could justifiably claim to have done so in the spirit of open competition. But it's doubtful on an emotional level that the fans would thank the NCAA for it. In changing the natural order of things it would have created a sense of uncertainty, which has the potential to undermine the basis of the culture shift that Disciples of March Madness have created with the NCAA.

If Southwest Airlines decided to move beyond priority boarding and establish a business-class section, or if it chose to broadly expand the variety of its airline fleet, not only would it undermine its competitive difference but it would add a layer of complexity to its service and potentially undermine the sense of certainty that its Disciples currently feel. Similarly, as Rovio Entertainment expands its Angry Birds franchise, if the essential premise of birds methodically and cumulatively creating destruction were to change in favor of, say, the birds being used to actually construct an environment, it would risk undermining the sense of certainty about the gaming experience that its addicted Disciples enjoy.

Seeking emotional certainty is by its very nature illogical, in a world in which we can never really be certain of *anything* but death and taxes. Nevertheless, we continue to strive for it, which explains why upward of seventy million Americans read their horoscopes every day. So when Parke Kunkle, a board member of the Minnesota Planetarium Society, was quoted in the Minneapolis–St. Paul *StarTribune* in January 2011 as saying that there ought to be a thirteenth sign of the zodiac due to the process of *precession,* it caused an incredible uproar.[37]

Precession means that the particular constellation the sun is in front of had shifted at least one month from the way it looked three thousand years ago when the zodiacal constellations were set. The implication is that seventy million Americans have been looking for daily insight and emotional certainty while reading the wrong star sign! It would be particularly tough if you were born between November 29 and December 17, as you would now be assigned an entirely new thirteenth sign called Ophiuchus—which in ancient Greece was commonly represented by the troubling image of a man grasping a big snake!

Considering that astrology is a multimillion-dollar industry, with more than 25 percent of Americans *admitting* they believe in astrology (therefore the real number is likely much higher), it's not surprising that astrologers quickly struck back with various attempts to debunk Kunkle's assertions in an attempt to assuage the concerns of millions of Americans who had been thrown into a state of "zodiac-induced paralysis." Noted astrologer Rob Brezny sought to clarify by explaining, not altogether simply, that precession is irrelevant to modern Western astrologers because, "their data has to do with movements of the planets in our own solar system within a zone of influence defined by the relationship between the Earth and Sun."[38] While New York–based astrologer Eric Francis noted that "there are two zodiacs in common use. Kunkle is describing what is called the *sidereal zodiac*: the backdrop of the stars. It's not the zodiac used by most Western astrologers; it's the one used by Vedic astrologers in India. The two zodiacs are offset by about 23 degrees."[39]

While to the uninitiated this might all seem to be the most outrageous load of bunkum, these attempts at debunking Kunkle's assertions were largely unnecessary. Most people understand rationally that astrology is at best fuzzy and at worst delusional, but their desire for insight in order to create the illusion of certainty is at the same time irresistible—and so it's no surprise that after a small blip, the number of Americans reading their *original* daily horoscope, and ignoring the creepy Ophiuchus, has remained virtually unchanged.

Parke Kunkle acknowledged being astonished at the degree of

fervor and vitriol that his interview unleashed, but when certainty is lost we feel enormous resentment toward whomever has taken it away from us, whether it be an innocent astronomer, a politician, a celebrity, an organization, or a brand. Certainty is a central currency in the establishment of any social contract and therefore of any related culture shift, and once the illusion of certainty is lost, all momentum is also lost.

CHAPTER 7

SIGNS, SYMBOLS, AND ICONS

"Symbolism is no mere idle fancy . . . it is inherent in the very texture of human life."
— Alfred North Whitehead,
Harvard Lecture, 1927

S igns, symbolism, and iconography are pivotal to the formation of social contracts and to creating movements.

THE EAGLE

Rome's Ninth Legion (Legio IX Hispana) was assembled in 65 BCE and came under Julius Caesar's command four years later in his position as governor of Spain.[1] The Ninth became the bulwark of Caesar's army, staffed by many of his most tried and trusted veterans, and served under him both throughout his campaigns in Gaul from 58 to 51 BCE—as well as in the civil war against Pompey and the Senate two years later. In 46 BCE, the Ninth Legion also fought in Caesar's Africa campaign until it was disbanded after the Battle of Thapsus, when, in gratitude for their loyal service, many of the veterans were given land and settled in Histria (which lies within the territory of Romania today).[2] After Caesar's assassination, the Ninth was recalled to serve with Octavian, Caesar's nephew and adopted son, who later became Rome's first emperor, Augustus—and again fought against fellow Romans, this time under the rebel command of Sextus, Pompey's younger son. And the Ninth Legion also played a pivotal role in the center of the fray at the Battle of Actium, as Octavian defeated Marc Antony and Queen Cleopatra to reunify the empire.

Tracking the history of the Ninth, therefore, is a journey through some of the most storied events in the formation of the Roman Empire, and their service continued after the Battle of Actium through campaigns in Spain (where they acquired their title Hispana), as well as in Germania, and finally Britannia around 65 CE. That is where the recorded history of the Ninth Legion becomes cloudy and myth takes over. After having suffered severe casualties in the uprising led by Queen Boudica in Britannia five years earlier, the Ninth was sent to guard the northern fringes of the empire, where it helped build the Eboracum fortress near York—and this was the Ninth's last known stationed posting. With the support of some historians, legend then suggests that the Ninth led an expedition farther north against the wild and rebellious Picts, a mix of tribes from the eastern and northern regions of modern-day Scotland, and were never heard from again.[3]

The myth of the disappearance of the Ninth Legion—apparently slaughtered by the Picts north of where Emperor Hadrian built his famous wall to mark the edge of the empire, and of the civilized world[4]—was the basis for Rosemary Sutcliff's compelling 1954 novel *The Eagle of the Ninth.* The book recently was turned into the 2011 film *The Eagle,* starring Channing Tatum and Donald Sutherland.[5] Both the book and the film play on the legend that the Ninth had marched north to root out the main force of the Picts, which had been raiding villages and sowing unrest, and had then been ambushed, resulting in the loss of the entire legion—and with them the symbol of Rome's power and might, the legion's eagle. Sutcliff's novel was also inspired by the fact that in 1866, while excavating the Roman town of Calleva, near Silchester in modern Britain, a wingless Roman eagle was unearthed—which today resides in the Museum of Reading.

The *aquila* was the eagle ensign, or standard, that every legion carried, and it was handled by a higher-grade legionary called the *aquilifer* (or standard-bearer).[6] The eagle itself typically was made of bronze or silver, and not gold as it's usually depicted. It was General Gaius Marius, during his second consulship in 104 BCE, who formalized the eagle as the standard for all legions,[7] as a symbolic way of bringing unity to the army, whereas previously there had been five common icons in use: the wolf, the Minotaur (from Greek mythology), the horse, and the boar, as well as the eagle. Ever the pragmatist, Caesar supposedly had the eagles made smaller in size so that an aquilifer could remove it from the staff to conceal within the folds of his girdle, in the event that the eagle was in danger of being taken by the enemy. The loss of an eagle was a disgrace from which no general or legion could recover, and a wounded and dying aquilifer understood that his last duty was to deliver the eagle into the hands of his general or else see his name and his family shamed. Such was the myth surrounding the symbolic significance of the eagle that enemies of Rome believed that if they could take the eagle, in the manner of cutting the head off a snake, both the legion and eventually Rome itself would fall.

The drama in *The Eagle of the Ninth* is centered around the valiant attempt and ultimate success of a young Roman officer, the aptly named Marcus Flavius Aquila, to retrieve the Ninth Legion's lost eagle from the Picts. And in the process restore both the legion's and his family's honor—his father having been a senior officer with the Ninth. Indeed, the loss of an eagle meant that a legion would be disbanded and could only be reformed after the retrieval of the eagle standard. The returning members of a legion that had lost their eagle could expect far worse than mere disgrace and vilification, including, in rare cases, decimation. Decimation, from which the modern word *decimate* derives, involved every tenth soldier being pulled out and systematically beaten to death by his fellow soldiers—which understandably served as the ultimate motivation to retain the eagle.

Given their powerful symbolism, the loss of any Roman eagle was very well documented by Roman historians, and perhaps the most notable event was the loss of three eagles at the Battle of the Teutoburg Forest—where three legions under the command of the Publius

Quinctilius Varus were defeated by an alliance of Germanic tribes led by Arminius (also known as Hermann).[8] The ripple effect throughout the empire at the loss of the eagles was such that the new Emperor Tiberius realized that his ultimate survival might rest on their retrieval. He therefore assigned his nephew Germanicus (the renowned general, brother of Claudius, and father of Caligula) the task of defeating Hermann and the Germanic coalition and reclaiming the eagles. Germanicus's two-year campaign concluded at the Battle of the Angivarian Wall (close to modern Hanover), where he routed and splintered the Germanic tribes, resulting in the retrieval of two of the three eagles. The return of the eagles served to reaffirm the myth of Rome's military might and paved the way for the Romans' expansion into northern Europe.

Fast-forward about two thousand years, and the most powerful nation on earth again has an eagle as its national symbol, to signify both its political reach and its military might! And before the bald eagle became America's national symbol embedded in the Great Seal of the United States, eagles were featured as the symbols for some of the most powerful nations in history, including the Napoleonic Eagle in France, and the coat of arms for both Egypt and the Russian Federation.

Figure 7.1. The Great Seal of the United States.
Reprinted by permission from iStockphoto/Thinkstock.

Legend has it that during one of the early battles in the Revolutionary War, the sound of the British and American armies fighting woke a group of nesting eagles that then soared and encircled the troops while giving loud cries—and that this then rallied the patriots to shout, "They are shrieking for freedom." In any event, the eagle became America's national emblem in 1782 and the centerpiece of the Great Seal, and was intended to convey "supreme power and authority."[9] At the second Continental Congress six years earlier, where the original thirteen colonies had declared independence from Great Britain, Benjamin Franklin, John Adams, and Thomas Jefferson had prepared a design for the Seal of the new United States, but the committee had rejected it—proving what every creative agency person knows intuitively, that it's never a good idea to mix a strategy meeting with a creative meeting! In any event, there is little doubt that the eagle has been and remains the symbol of choice in signaling the most powerful nations on earth.

Professor Umberto Eco of the University of Bologna is one of the world's foremost experts on signs and symbols and the author of the formative 1978 book *A Theory of Semiotics.* He has also found time to write several novels, including *The Name of the Rose,* published in 1980,[10] which in many ways was a forerunner to Dan Brown's massively popular novel *The Da Vinci Code,* and the subsequent film of the same name, which starred Tom Hanks as Professor Robert Langdon.[11] Both novels use a central character to demonstrate the power of deductive reasoning and especially syllogisms, harkening back to the popular scholastic method of the fourteenth century.

In *The Name of the Rose,* Eco's hero, Friar William of Baskerville, portrayed in the film by Sean Connery, refuses to accept that the sinister events at the monastery are driven by demonic possession related to the coming of the Antichrist—but rather uses the deductive power of his logical mind to decode the various signs and happenings, concluding that the murders are entirely human in nature, though no less sinister.[12] The success of both books—and particularly the international phenomena that Brown's *The Da Vinci Code* and its forerunner *Angels & Demons* have become—demonstrate our enduring fascination with the power of symbolism and our compulsive need to decode and understand symbols.

It's this gravitational pull that signs and symbols have that makes symbolism such a central part of any culture shift. Indeed, in order to establish a social contract, there almost always has to be some form of graphic or pictorial symbolism, which serves to encapsulate the movement we are part of—whether that shift is religious, nationalistic, or political, or whether it relates to sports, music, or commerce.

In explaining semiotics—the study of signs—Eco observes that "A sign is everything that can be taken as significantly substituting for something else. This something else does not necessarily have to exist or to actually be somewhere at the moment in which a sign stands in for it."[13] A relevant interpretation is that the mere appearance of the sign or symbol that we've come to associate with a particular movement can connote all the associated experiences that we feel by being part of it—in exactly the way that the eagle encapsulated all that was Rome, for citizens and enemies alike. It speaks to our unique projective ability as humans to store the sum of our emotional affinity in one powerful symbol. A sign also speaks to the overwhelming significance of creating or adopting the correct symbol for anyone seeking to establish a social contract as the basis for creating a culture shift.

THE SWASTIKA

In the twentieth century, if the mere sight of one symbol was able to connote the sum of experiences related to the political movement it represented, it was the Nazi swastika. However, before it became associated with Nazism, the swastika had a rich and ancient tradition in many parts of the world. Some of the earliest examples of the swastika found in archaeology date back to neolithic Europe where it can be found in "Vinca script" from the region of the Balkans from

6000 BCE. It also appears in archaeology from ancient Mesopotamia as seen on the famous Samarra bowl dated 4000 BCE. And swastikas have been found from archaeological digs in places as diverse as modern Africa, India, Iran, Greece, as well as in Germany. It is also prominent as a religious symbol in Hinduism, Buddhism, and Jainism. The construction of the swastika is thought to relate to an equilateral cross with its arms bent at right angles, and one theory of its origin links it to the cross symbols on a sun wheel connoting the four seasons, where each of the ninety-degree sections corresponds to the solstices and the equinoxes. Given our twentieth-century Western association of the swastika with the evil of Nazism, perhaps the greatest irony can be found in the origins of the word itself, from Sanskrit—where the literal translation is "that which is associated with well-being," or more commonly a "lucky charm"![14]

Ever the aspiring artist, Hitler's final rendering of the swastika-centered flag for the Nazi Party in 1920 was a derivation of one created for the Thule Society[15] by his confidante Dr. Friedrich Krohn—a dentist from Sternberg whom Hitler refers to in *Mein Kampf*.[16] Hitler describes the design development process in the book as follows: "I myself, meanwhile, after innumerable attempts had laid down a final form: a flag with a red background, a white disk, and a black swastika in the middle." He went on to explain "those revered colors expressive of our homage to the glorious past and which once brought so much honor to the German nation"—in reference to the red, white, and black of the old German Empire. Hitler conceived that the red would also symbolize the social idea of movement, while white would represent the nationalistic idea, and the swastika itself would stand for the struggle for victory of the Aryan race. Again with terrible irony, given the genocide committed against the Jewish race in Europe, the swastika was also understood to be "the symbol of the creating, acting life!"[17]

Figure 7.2. The Nazi Swastika.
Reprinted by permission from Hemera/Thinkstock.

But of course, the mere creation of a powerful and meaningful symbol in the form of the Nazi swastika cannot explain away the rise of Hitler and the Nazi Party in Germany of the 1920s and 1930s. As with every powerful culture shift, the conditions had to exist for the formation of a social contract, in terms of the desire for fundamental societal change driven by passionate Zealots and committed Disciples—with effective propaganda providing the spark. Nevertheless, it was the German people who created the terms for the social contract with the Nazis, based on thinking that they knew logically to be flawed. They chose to enter into the contract with the Nazis, they perpetuated it, and the world suffered for it.

The Treaty of Versailles, signed between Germany and the Allied Powers in 1919, effectively created the conditions for societal change and the rise of Nazism in Europe, as Hitler blamed the German Republic for accepting the treaty's draconian terms. The national stigma of the "War Guilt Clause" in the treaty; the stripping away of Germany's prior colonies, which reduced its territories by more than 13 percent; and the effective blockade of Germany that continued after the signing of the treaty limited the amount of imported goods and therefore priced them out of the reach of most ordinary Germans.[18] Germans were already starving and in despair after four years of war, and they were disenchanted with their leaders and institutions—and at a time of crisis they sought change and a new era, enabling Hitler and the Nazis to begin their unlikely rise to power. As Hitler once stated, ironically, "How fortunate for leaders that men do not think!"[19]

In an environment conducive to extreme change, and with the German people looking for a convenient scapegoat for their suffering and shame, the Nazis' highly advanced and progressive propaganda machine was able to fuel a nationalist spark and offer up the Jews as a vessel for their anger. Of course, personifying the Jews as the source of their suffering, and not their own leaders or the conquering allies, was one of history's most tragic illogical leaps; but as Hitler commented, "Make the lie big, make it simple, keep saying it, and eventually they will believe it."[20] And perhaps the only thing that can be said to have been progressive about the Nazis was their use of propaganda and symbolism, as directed by Joseph Goebbels, the Reich minister for propaganda, as well as by Hitler himself. They realized that they didn't need to make the Disciples and the Congregation in Germany hate the Jews in the way that Nazi Zealots had come to—the Nazis simply needed for the Disciples and the Congregation to remain indifferent to their persecution of the Jews.

Hitler and the Nazis' extensive and highly effective use of graphic symbolism was a central factor in their ability to create a sense of unity and belonging among their party members and the wider German public—as well as being crucial to their ability to strike fear into the hearts of their enemies. Nazism was very effectively branded beyond the iconic and consistent use of the swastika, and included the twin "SS" bolts of the Schutzstaffel (meaning "protection squadron"), the black uniforms of the SS (Gestapo), the brown uniform of Sturmabteilung (meaning "storm troopers"), and of course the formal (versus the main) symbol of the Nazi Party—the inevitable *eagle* on top of the swastika. And grotesquely, they even had an insignia for the SS-Totenkopfverbände (concentration camp unit) in the form of the harrowing death-head symbol.[21]

While it remains inconceivable for most of us today how a majority of Germans in the late 1930s and 1940s, were able to stand to one side while more than six million Jews were murdered in the Holocaust—understanding the dynamics of how a social contract is formed, the underlying societal drivers, and the illogical beliefs around which people willingly coalesce—it can at least provide a new lens through which to view the rise of Nazism. It's also instructive in being able to grasp the absolute significance of symbolism in the creation of any political culture shift, however abhorrent that shift may be.

The enduring power of the Nazi swastika still draws in Nazi apologists and sympathizers, fascists, and white supremacists today—and in more recent history the extremist Afrikaner Weerstandsbeweging (AWB, or Afrikaner Resistance Movement) in South Africa and the Russian National Unity Party have both adopted stylized swastika symbols.[22] For that reason and because of the persuasive power of symbolism, it's entirely justified that the swastika is today banned in Germany, and that German politicians have called for it to be banned throughout Europe—most recently after the British Prince Harry was photographed wearing a swastika armband to a costume party in 2005![23]

POLITICAL SYMBOLISM

Thankfully, not all political symbols are quite as sinister as the swastika, but at the same time they aren't necessarily as effective either. Take the accepted symbols of the Democratic (DNC) and Republican (GOP) Parties in the United States, for example. For someone like myself brought up in the United Kingdom, who was used to the main political parties having relevant and evocative symbols—the flaming blue torch of the Conservative Party evoking liberty, and the (socialist) red rose of the Labour Party—I was somewhat surprised to see the historic DNC and GOP symbolized by a donkey and an elephant, respectively.[24] Not that there is anything wrong with either creature. The donkey is understood in Western culture to be an enduring and harmless beast of burden, but not, however, blessed with great intellect or any especially mercurial qualities.

Figure 7.3. American Republican and Democratic Party animal symbols. *Reprinted by permission from Comstock Images/Comstock/Thinkstock, © Getty Images.*

When we think of a donkey, an ass, or a mule, we imagine it trudging along, unaffected and unthinking, carrying its burden with good grace until it can carry it no more—a mindless beast of burden, if you will. The words *dynamic, inventive, powerful, energetic,* and *intelligent* are not words that would ever naturally come to mind when talking about a donkey—and yet they certainly would be desirable associations for a major political party. Then there is the issue of the male donkey or ass being named a jack, and of course in the United States, to call someone a *jackass* is to suggest that he or she is essentially a complete idiot, as well as potentially obnoxious. Indeed, calling someone a donkey in most parts of the world is similarly intended to offend. In Arabic, to suggest someone is a *himar* (a donkey) is to call him or her a "dumbass;" in Greek, *gaidouri* (donkey) connotes extreme rudeness; while in Portuguese, *burro* implies stupidity. Not then, by any means, the kind of associations you would think the DNC would be going for!

While the elephant fairs somewhat better in popular culture as a creature that is thought to be sensitive, powerful, exotic, and intelligent (their brains are larger than any other land animals), it too carries certain negative baggage as a symbol for a political party. An elephant is also thought to be stubborn, slow moving, and lumbering (not actually the case if you've ever been charged by one), somewhat prehistoric and certainly lacking in agility. Elephants also have no origin in the Americas, deriving from Africa and Asia. Whether it's "The Elephant's Child" from Rudyard Kipling's *Just So Stories,* or Disney's *Dumbo,* or Laurent de Brunhoff's *Babar,* we see elephants as endearing creatures to which we can easily attribute human qualities—but these attributes are typically passive rather than dynamic.

Harper's Weekly cartoonist Thomas Nast is credited with having created—almost by accident—both the GOP association with the elephant as well as the DNC association with the donkey. In his November 1884 cartoon, inspired by a *New York Herald* hoax known as the Central Park (Zoo) Menagerie Scare, Nast symbolized the *Herald* as an ass. Drawing on another *Herald* story at the time, in which the paper had decried President Grant's desire for a third term as being "Caesarism," which had helped to deflate Republican voters in the leadup to midterm elections, in the same cartoon Nast depicted these voters as elephants—one of the escaped New York (Central Park) Zoo animals.[25] As for how this depiction of the *Herald* as an ass morphed into the DNC being symbolized as a donkey—or how the Republican voter elephant came to symbolize the GOP—is somewhat of a mystery. Clearly, the associations made sense to his readers in the late nineteenth century, or the symbolism never would have stuck.

As for whether these symbols have any relevance—or play a role in strengthening the social contracts with the DNC and GOP—that seems extremely unlikely. They appear to be brought out at political rallies, more for reasons of tradition and a sense of obligation rather than to create a feeling of unity, or belonging, for party members. Indeed, the DNC has never officially adopted the donkey as its symbol, although it seems content to simply drag it behind the proverbial party wagon—rather than proactively creating a symbol that speaks to the values and emotional core of the Democratic Party movement. While the GOP has at least adopted the elephant, one has to wonder why a party that is often accused by its critics as being moored to tradition, lumbering, and slow to change would continue to tolerate a symbol that reinforces that perception.

Perhaps it was the entirely unhelpful DNC donkey symbol that, in part, inspired the Obama campaign to introduce more powerful graphic iconography into the 2008 presidential election, providing the senator's fledgling movement with a branding advantage over their Republican rivals. Designer Sol Sender developed the "Obama '08" logo idea, which, on the face of it, is a very simple mark; but if you probe a little deeper it is clear how it communicates on several levels. The red, white, and blue, along with the stripes, signal patriotism. The graphic interpretation of the sun rising into a blue sky over fields creates a feeling of new beginnings and possibility. The circular shape and embedded *O* signal Obama without the actual words *Obama '08* even being necessary—and, indeed, that's how many people first saw the logo, without the written name underneath, creating further intrigue for those not yet engaged in the election. Sol Sender was quoted as saying, "The strongest logos tell simple stories," and the Obama '08 logo certainly passed that test.[26] It became a way for people to physically express their support for the senator and to feel part of the political culture shift, as they put the logo on windows, on driveway posters, and most of all on bumper stickers.

Figure 7.4. The Obama '08 Logo, Democratic Campaign Button.
Reprinted by permission from Hemera/Thinkstock.

The Obama '08 logo was following in the tradition of other great political logos that have been able to transcend the dynamics of a particular campaign—and signify a broader and more timeless culture shift. The "Solidarnosc" logo, designed by Jerzy Janiszewski in 1980, became a similar beacon for supporters of Lech Walesa's Solidarity movement, initially in Poland and then throughout the world.[27] The logo, which was designed to represent united individuals, managed to communicate the essential truth of the movement in a single mark, passing Sol Sender's test—as to the uninitiated, the static red logo instantly created a feeling of ordinary workers marching for freedom against the rigid constraints of communism.

Figure 7.5. The Solidarity Logo.

As with any powerful design that is central to a culture shift, the Obama '08 logo served to inspire Zealots and Disciples to offer their own creative contributions. Although today you can find more than four hundred examples of Obama '08 posters, one in particular designed by the artist Shepard Fairey instantly became associated with the movement. The Obama "Hope" poster, which later had variants with the words *change* and *progress* as alternates, featured a stylized stark graphic portrait of Barack Obama in solid red, beige, and two tones of blue in the style of a classic screen print.[28] As well as being a powerful and iconic artistic rendering, the poster had a revolutionary quality to it in the manner of Jim Fitzpatrick's famous Che Guevara poster—which continues to adorn countless T-shirts worn by teenagers today, who in many cases aren't even familiar with Guevara's politics and personal story.[29]

Figure 7.6. Che Guevara Poster by Jim Fitzpatrick

The Obama "Hope" poster became an instant beacon for youth support of the campaign, and a symbol of coolness that transcended the campaign—and even politics—and served to perpetuate the culture shift. And as further evidence that Fairey's poster, designed from an original photograph by Associated Press freelance photographer Mannie Garcia, had become an instant classic, the Smithsonian Institution acquired it for its National Portrait Gallery in January 2009, after Senator Obama became president.

A powerful political graphic symbol doesn't have to be a logo or a poster—sometimes it can simply be a flag. After apartheid crumbled and Nelson Mandela was released, and recognizing the pivotal importance of having a flag that could symbolize the new South Africa, the African National Congress (ANC) and the South African Government gave their chief negotiators, Cyril Ramaphosa and Roelf Meyer, the task of resolving the new flag design. Such were the emotions the flag generated that the negotiations went down to the wire, with the new design being agreed to and published only on April 20, 1994—less than three weeks before Nelson Mandela's inauguration on May 10—and allowing precious little time for manufacturers to produce enough flags for the historic event.

The new flag—based on a *Y* shape to symbolize the convergence of different societal groups, and the multitude of colors including the black, green, and yellow of the ANC—encapsulates the "rainbow nation" that South Africa has become and is now enshrined in the country's constitution.[30] The flag's importance—as a symbol both of freedom and of the movement for national unity that Mandela was able to engineer against all odds—was dramatized in the 2009 movie *Invictus*. Directed by Clint Eastwood, the film tells the story of South Africa's unlikely victory in the 1995 Rugby World Cup—where Matt Damon plays Francois Pienaar, the captain of the South African rugby team, and Morgan Freeman is almost indistinguishable from the real Nelson Mandela.[31] The film's most poignant moments revolve around Mandela's drive and ultimate success in bringing the country together, which is symbolized by the multicultural support of the rugby team through the waving of the new national emblem.

The South African flag, like the Obama '08 logo and the related "Hope" poster, is a further example of the pivotal importance of graphic symbolism in the formation of social contracts and as a pivotal means to perpetuate dynamic political culture shifts.

COMMERCIAL SYMBOLISM

Founded in 1777, the Bass Ale Brewery's "red triangle" logo was the world's first registered commercial trademark, listed number one under the British Trademark Act of 1875[32]—and a chilled pint of Bass Ale remains just as smooth and appealing today as it did two centuries ago. However, the practice of commercial branding goes back centuries to pre-Dynastic Egypt, around 3000 BCE, where a *serekh* emblem of your family would be carved on ivory labels, which were then attached to goods you wished to trade. And through the Late Middle Ages and the Renaissance in Europe, the art and practice of heraldry was refined as early brands (in the form of coats of arms), which were applied to everything from wax seals to house banners, as well as to family tombs. Today there are thousands of brand-related trademarks registered on a daily basis worldwide, while Coca-Cola remains the world's most recognized trademark.[33]

While most commercial logos do a somewhat effective job of creating recognition and even differentiation for their brands, only a few become an integral part of the formation of a social contract and serve to perpetuate a commercial culture shift. *Rolling Stone* magazine recently listed what it considered to be the top eight logos of the last thirty-five years, and each of the ones it selected has played a pivotal role in creating and perpetuating commercial culture shifts—whether their respective audiences are primarily business- or consumer-focused in nature. The logos they selected were for Apple, Coca-Cola, FedEx, IBM, McDonald's, Nike, Playboy, and Starbucks, and exploring how several of these became icons is instructive in understanding the power of commercial symbolism.

Created in 1973, the original Federal Express logo was designed by Richard Runyan and was intended to show affinity with the US government from which the firm planned to secure contracts. Two decades later, however, as its logistics services grew in size and importance, the company commissioned designer Lindon Leader to create a more dynamic, distinctive, and accessible logo—and in 1994, the FedEx mark with its embedded arrow was born.[34] On the face of it, the FedEx logo connotes efficiency and movement, and the embedded arrow offers an extra surprise when you recognize it or when it's pointed out to you. But like any great mark, the FedEx logo has come to embody more than just the literal corporate values of the world's largest courier company—and has established a place in pop culture, thereby strengthening the social contract that its many Disciples have formed with the brand.

Great brands have always had stories told about them, and the 2000 Robert Zemeckis film *Cast Away*, featuring an inspired and largely solo performance by Tom Hanks, both dramatized and humanized FedEx. Hanks's character Chuck Noland is the quintessential FedEx employee, obsessed with the timely arrival of his packages around the world, until his plane is brought down in a storm and he finds himself stranded on a deserted island. Away from any of the trappings of Western civilization, the FedEx parcels that wash ashore act as a reminder of a way of life that Chuck has been severed from. There is little need to draw the contrast between his past life and current plight, in part because the ever-present FedEx logo handles that aspect of the narrative. Ironically it's another symbol—the stylized wings from an artist's ranch that have been rendered on one package—that inspires Chuck to make the sail that ultimately results in his rescue.[35]

The FedEx logo encapsulates more than just a way of doing business; it stands for the globalization of commerce and a shrinking world, and when you glimpse that hidden arrow as a truck speeds by, you feel part of this global culture shift. On a trip I made to London, intended as a way to give my children a taste of the "old country," my son—still an infant at that time—largely ignored attractions like Big Ben and only became animated at the sight of a FedEx truck, signaling a familiar reminder of home!

The Nike "Swoosh" is another logo that has transcended the boundaries of its brand and category and become lodged in our cultural psyche. In 1971, Carolyn Davidson, a graphic-design student at Portland State University where Nike founder Phil Knight was teaching, designed the Swoosh logo. Davidson charged Nike a grand total of $35 for what was to become one of the most recognizable symbols on earth.[36] A decade later, Knight gave an astonished Davidson a diamond Swoosh ring and a generous amount of Nike stock in gratitude. When Phil Knight and Bill Bowerman founded Blue Ribbon Sports in 1966, they initially imported running shoes but quickly decided to launch their own brand, and in 1978 Nike was born. Bill Bowerman coached the track team at the University of Oregon, and his star athlete was the hard-running, highly charismatic Steve ("Pre") Prefontaine. The Swoosh was first glimpsed on Pre's Nike running shoes in June 1972 at the US Track and Field Olympic Trials, and for both runner and brand, history was made— as Pre went on to set a new American record in the 5,000 meters and represent his country at the Summer Olympics in Munich.

Two films and a documentary have been made about Steve Prefontaine's tragically short life—he died in an automobile accident in 1975—and in the 1998 movie *Without Limits,* in which Billy Crudup portrays him,[37] the spirit of Nike's famous "Just Do It" mantra is viscerally on display. Prefontaine liked to run from the front and wear down his opponents, but in the Olympics Final in Munich, this approach finally caught up with him when he was passed on the final lap and pushed out of a medal position by Lasse Viren (the Flying Finn), who took the gold medal. But the legend of Pre became etched in the American psyche as the story has been passed down. Nike has grown over the years to become the most recognized and admired sporting-equipment and apparel brand in the world, in part through its successful sponsorship of athletes like Michael Jordan and Tiger Woods—and the Swoosh logo has become a badge of honor for Nike's global Disciples and the beacon at the center of its culture shift.

Shifting from one male obsession to another, for any teenage boy growing up in the late 1970s who thought of *Playboy* magazine (and therefore the brand) as nothing more than a way to look at naked women in the age before the Web, for *Playboy* to be included as one of the most significant logos of the past thirty-five years[38] seems like rather exalted company! But to appreciate the long and intimate relationship that a revered figure like the late William F. Buckley had with *Playboy*—beginning in 1963 with a verbatim transcript of his famous "swinishness" debate with Norman Mailer—encourages one to look more closely at the cultural movement that founder Hugh Hefner spearheaded. Buckley is considered the architect of the modern American Conservative movement, and writing in the *National Review,* the magazine that he founded, he referred to *Playboy* as "the great publishing success of the decade."[39]

An attack by Buckley on *Playboy*'s decision to publish an interview with George Lincoln Rockwell, the leader of the American Nazi Party—in which Buckley described the magazine and Hefner's decision to publish as "inexplicable to anyone save possibly those who subscribe to the *Playboy* philosophy"—ultimately led to a revealing debate between the two on Buckley's *Firing Line* program. Through the exchanges, Hefner crystallized the essence of *Playboy*'s purpose as well as the foundation of the social contract that its numerous Disciples had established with the magazine and its "spiritual leader." Hefner described *Playboy* as a response to the "Puritan part of our culture" and "what the American sexual revolution's really all about."[40]

Two weeks later in his syndicated column, Buckley acknowledged that *Playboy* was a movement "of sorts," and wrote thoughtfully and provocatively about Hefner's philosophy: that "a man's morality, like his religion, is a personal affair best left to his own conscience."[41] After the exchange on *Firing Line*, these two pillars of the 1970s cultural landscape, who represented opposite sides in the "sexual revolution" debate, seemed to have established an unlikely friendship, or at the very least, a begrudging respect for each other.

To the uninitiated, this snapshot of *Playboy*'s rich history demonstrates the cultural significance that the magazine had, and that the brand continues to have, in the central debate around sexual morality and individual freedom in America. *Playboy* deserves its place in the top tier of influential logos, and as with all influential cultural symbols, it represented an encapsulating beacon for a generation of Disciples who saw it as being central to the culture shift they were part of.

PHYSICAL ICONOGRAPHY

Perhaps the greatest omission from *Rolling Stone*'s list of the top logos of the last thirty-five years is the Harley-Davidson badge. And the place to best experience the culture shift that the brand represents is in Washington, DC, on Memorial Day, when close to four hundred thousand motorcycles, most of which are Harleys, take part in "Rolling Thunder" in honor of those who died in the Vietnam War.[42] The noise is akin to a six-hour continuous growl of manmade thunder, as riders from across the United States make their journeys to the Vietnam Veterans Memorial. For those like myself who have never fought in a war, the powerful symbolism of the Vietnam Memorial Wall, especially when this site is populated by thousands of these outlier American heroes, makes Memorial Day eminently more emotional and meaningful.

Architect Maya Lin designed the Vietnam Veterans Memorial when she won the memorial design contest while still a twenty-one-year-old student at Yale University.[43] Initial reaction to it from veterans was polarizing, to say the least, as men like former presidential candidate H. Ross Perot and future Senator Jim Webb withdrew their support for the project after seeing the design. And one can imagine the conversation, since the premise was introduced as a plain, angled wall buried into the ground with the names of all of the fallen etched into it! And yet when it was put in place, almost all of the opposition fell away as people experienced the elegant simplicity of the design and its ability to act as an emotional beacon for those who felt part of the culture shift that the Vietnam War has created. The Wall receives more than three million visitors every year and in 2007 was ranked tenth in the top ten list of "America's Favorite Architecture," by the American Institute of Architects.

As of June 2010, the names of 58,195 killed or missing servicemen (including eight women) were etched on the Wall.[44] The stone came from Bangalore, India, and was chosen for its reflective quality. When you gaze into the Wall to see the name of a fallen friend or family member, you can see your own reflection, which was intended to represent a union of the past and the present. The strange solemnity you feel when you walk along the Wall, particularly on Memorial Day as you're surrounded by so many who served, is hard to fully convey. It has become both a cultural shrine and a meeting place for those who feel part of the Vietnam War experience, and which today unites them ever more powerfully in remembrance.

Figure 7.7. The Vietnam Veterans Memorial.
Reprinted by permission from Hemera/Thinkstock.

In a similar vein, I was reminded of the inspiring words of Frederick Douglass, the famed abolitionist and former slave, after the cancellation of the Martin Luther King National Memorial dedication due to Hurricane Irene in late August 2011. For someone who committed his life to ease the burden of others, King no doubt would have wanted to delay the pomp and ceremony in order to focus our attention on the victims of the storm. As for the debate over one of the fourteen inscriptions, while I understand Maya Angelou's dislike for the arrogant-sounding, "I was a drum major for justice, peace, and righteousness,"[45] overall there are few things more difficult than trying to encapsulate a great leader and a movement in a single physical icon.

As with the most evocative graphic symbols, a few physical icons enable us to store in them the sum of our emotional affinity. It also speaks to the overwhelming significance of creating or adopting the correct physical icon for anyone seeking to perpetuate a culture shift—whether that shift is historical, political, populist, or commercial in nature.

Every monument builder and architect hopes that his or her creation will rise to the level of an emotional beacon for the culture shift that it represents—but most fall short.[46] On the drawing board it's almost impossible to grasp the emotional impact of a structure, and the more passion associated with the event, inevitably the greater the controversy before it is built—the National September 11 Memorial & Museum at Ground Zero in New York being a case in point. But whatever the emotional impact of the 9/11 memorial, it will undoubtedly compete with what has become the unofficial symbol for the attack on the World Trade Center that day in 2001, notably an immensely powerful photograph.

American photographer Thomas E. Franklin's "flag-raising photograph" was taken a little after 5 p.m. on September 11, 2001, while he was about one hundred and fifty feet away from where the firefighters were raising the US flag atop a pile of debris from the fallen towers. The image was chosen by *Life* magazine as one of the "100 Photographs

That Changed the World"⁴⁷—and it resonated in much the same way as Louis Lowery's original flag-raising photograph of American troops had with the previous WWII generation after the Battle of Iwo Jima.

Figure 7.8. The Iwo Jima Monument, United States Marine Corps War Memorial. *Reprinted by permission from Fuse/Fuse/Getty Images.*

As Franklin's 9/11 flag-raising photograph demonstrates, iconography that comes to encapsulate the emotional core of a culture shift—and stand as its enduring memorial—can come in many forms. In Prague it's a stroll through the New Jewish Cemetery surrounded by more than one hundred thousand graves packed together like sardines in a tin, after viewing the harrowing drawings of the children who were interned there. In London it's the photograph of St. Paul's Cathedral during the Blitz, caught in an unnatural glow of sunlight as smoke rises all around. In Berlin it's the video image of East and West Germans sitting together astride the Berlin Wall as they hammer away at almost thirty years of enforced segregation. In Beijing it's the image of the young man refusing to move out of the way as the tanks rolled into Tiananmen Square. In Bagdad it's the image of residents pulling down the statue of Saddam Hussein in Firdos Square, with the help of liberating American troops.

Powerful iconography—whether experienced in person at a memorial site or seen in a photograph or on video—can transcend the events it symbolizes and become ingrained in our psyche. It can act as a point of visual reference in the formation of a social contract—as the second flag-raising photograph did for so many young Americans after September 11—and it can operate as a constant incentive to perpetuate a culture shift. And this is also true of powerful commercial icons that serve to strengthen our connection to a particular organization or brand. A sports arena can be illustrative of this phenomenon, as a fan may only feel a complete sense of belonging to his team when he is in attendance at an important home game—with one hundred thousand people wearing the team colors and waving flags, towels, or scarves in rapturous support—as the leader implores his team to "protect this house."

With only a *virtual* connection to the culture shift we feel part of, and without a physical manifestation of the brand or company we have built a social contract with, we find it hard to maintain our allegiance. NASDAQ's MarketSite Tower in New York is more than mere office space for company executives and listed partners, and more than an iconic digital billboard. It's a physical manifestation of NASDAQ's stature at the heart of the largest financial center in the world and a tangible beacon for a brand that people otherwise interact with only electronically. In the same vein, the consistently swarming Apple stores are more than just a cool place to sit at the "Genius Bar" or to check out the latest iPhone or iPad models—they are places where Apple Disciples can feel physical kinship with fellow Disciples, and touch the brand (and not just the products) that they revere.

TO SYMBOLIZE IS TO BE HUMAN

The Alfred North Whitehead quotation "Symbolism is no mere idle fancy . . . it is inherent in the very texture of human life"[48] speaks to our unique projective ability as humans to store the sum of our emotional affinity in one powerful symbol.

And whatever tangible form a symbol takes—whether it is bricks and mortar or a graphic logo or any other form of iconography—it can become an encapsulating beacon for a movement, as well as an emotional conduit for its goals and beliefs. Without symbolism, organizations and brands can see a gradual erosion of their social contract, thus the creation or adoption of an appropriate icon is absolutely pivotal to perpetuating a culture shift.

Playing a similar role to the Chief Disciple, a political, cultural, or brand symbol is the standard-bearer for the terms of a social contract. It can inspire passion and commitment, and drive affinity and participation. Although many symbols are passive, when one rises to this level it becomes integral to a culture shift's lore and its continued progress. And to that end, its use and application must be fiercely protected and monitored to ensure that it doesn't become associated with anything that runs counter to the culture shift's key drivers. Just as a movement's Chief Disciple must display appropriate behavior at all times, its principle symbol must not become polluted, or the movement's momentum may be halted.

In the competitive and fast-moving world of advertising and marketing, a principal symbol can often be forgotten or relegated to make way for something that is thought to tie more directly into a topical campaign. In most cases, however, after the campaign cycle has ended, it becomes necessary to revive the original symbol in order to reconnect with the Disciples. In the process, the culture shift's organic momentum can begin to stall—and all for the sake of short-term gain.

Just as Zealots, Disciples, and the Congregation create the terms of a social contract and perpetuate a movement, they also determine its principal symbolism. If you are seen to remove a symbol with which they've established a personal relationship, it can feel to them as though you've interfered with something deeply personal in their lives—and that is something they won't easily forgive.

CHAPTER 8

BREAKING A SOCIAL CONTRACT
CAN BE TERMINAL

"Heaven has no rage like love to hatred turned."
—William Congreve,
The Mourning Bride, 1697

Be careful what you unleash.

Getting customers to be loyal to your particular brand of gasoline has long been one of the toughest things that any oil company can do. To the average driver, gas is simply gas—wherever you buy it—and most of us choose where to fill up based on location and price, versus a particular sense of brand affinity. Over the past decade, on a global basis, BP had invested literally hundreds of millions of dollars in an attempt to position itself as the greenest energy company on the planet. It spent heavily in traditional advertising and PR with the "Beyond Petroleum" campaign[1] and in "greening up" the look of its gas stations worldwide[2]—which in itself was a massive financial and logistical operation. It created the Helios House in Los Angeles as an illustration of the eco-friendly gas station of the future. BP also created social forums to encourage people to fight our addiction to oil and to support their efforts to develop alternative energy solutions.

BP had begun to reap some of the benefits from these initiatives as customers became more loyal to the company for the first time. Then, on April 20, 2010, the Deepwater Horizon oil spill occurred in the Gulf,[3] and BP learned the true price of breaking a social contract. The political consequences of reliance on foreign oil, global warming, and the drive for alternate sources of fuel meant there was a heightened state of emotional engagement in the category for many—and allowed BP to begin to establish a social contract and create a culture shift. The Green movement had given rise to eco-Zealots who were extremely well organized and vocal through various social-media sites and blogs—and BP had begun to tap into them as an organic source of propaganda when the spill occurred.

But BP quickly discovered that the powerful force they had unleashed could turn against them with ruthless force, as the Web was used to marshal global outrage against BP. In the worst way imaginable, BP had broken the essential terms of a social contract that had promised to bring green energy solutions to the planet, and the eco-Zealots took their revenge. From the "Boycott BP" campaign on Facebook[4] to the BP coffee spill video on YouTube,[5] the eco-Zealots used the digital airwaves to savage BP.

Because of blogs and social media, brand and company become joined at the hip in the minds of consumers. The leader of the company becomes the leader of the culture shift, and when the tide turns, he or she also becomes the focal point of attacks and derision. His persona, perceived values, and every utterance receive heightened scrutiny and are taken as a direct reflection of the company's pulse.

Tony Hayward, then CEO of BP, discovered this when he was forced to step down in July 2010, after his now famously insensitive comment, "I'd like my life back."[6] In truth, his position was always likely to be untenable, but in their heightened emotional state, people concluded from the comment that whatever BP was doing to fix the problem and repair the damage, it was still self-serving, callous, and didn't care about anything but profits. Logically they knew this was a throwaway remark made under intense pressure, but because they had already made the leap in framing their image of BP, it provided the reinforcing sound bite needed to confirm their impression of the company.

In April 2011, BP agreed to spend $1 billion that year alone on projects related to the cleanup of the Gulf of Mexico,[7] and by some estimates the total cost when all is said and done could exceed \$20 billion.[8] BP has also spent in excess of \$100 million on advertising to begin to improve its tattered brand image since the spill[9]—and additional millions paying lobbyists to rebuild bridges with the Obama administration. BP also announced that it would be paying a multimillion-dollar dividend to its shareholders,[10] and at its first major shareholders meeting in London in May 2011, representatives from the Gulf fishing communities tried to enter the event in order to lodge a protest about the slow progress of the cleanup—and how certain groups and communities had been unable to get financial relief. However, BP proceeded to undo the goodwill they'd paid millions of dollars in advertising, lobbying, and cleanup efforts to restore by barring the Gulf fishermen from the event—unleashing another wave of damaging negative publicity that quickly went around the world.

BP had once offered *hope* of a better way to tackle our energy needs, and people saw their hopes dashed with the Deepwater Horizon disaster and its subsequent missteps. BP is considered the worst company operating in the United States today, according to Consumerist.com,[11] and it will likely pay the price for its perceived betrayal for a generation, particularly if it continues to shoot itself in the foot as it did recently in London. Hope is an incredibly powerful force to unleash, because it's essential to our human condition and generates unending emotion. If you provide hope and then take it away or fail to deliver on its promise, people may never forgive you for the letdown.

The story of Senator Obama's promise of change, and the audacity of hope that he wrote about in the eponymous book[12] and spoke to in the 2008 presidential campaign, is still being written on a daily basis, and will no doubt be scrutinized in minute detail after he has left office. Of all the emotions a public figure can stir up, hope is among the most powerful and sets a high bar that, once promised, that leader must deliver against or deal with the consequences. Ultimately, whether President Obama ends up serving one term or two, the newspaper headline writers will begin with "Obama offered hope and delivered . . ." and the way they conclude the sentence will define his legacy. But perhaps the most notorious example of a politician offering hope and then failing to deliver can be seen in the person of Neville Chamberlain, the former prime minister of Great Britain from 1937 until 1940.

Chamberlain had served as chancellor of the exchequer in Prime Minister Stanley Baldwin's Conservative Party government from 1931 until 1937, when he became prime minister himself at one of the most difficult times in British and world history. Chamberlain was thought of as a caretaker leader by many, with younger and more colorful men like Sir Anthony Eden and polarizing figures like Sir Winston Churchill waiting in the wings. Chamberlain had been best known for his stewardship of domestic policy from his period as chancellor (treasury secretary) and his prior experience as minister of health. Faced with an increasingly hostile Germany under Hitler—history has largely forgotten how wildly popular Chamberlain was with the British public in the leadup to Germany's invasion of Czechoslovakia that ultimately led to Britain and France's declaring war on Germany on September 1, 1939.[13]

In March 1938, Hitler succeeded in forcing Austria to accept "Anschluss," a union between Germany and Austria, which amounted to the annexation of Austria[14]—where Hitler had spent much of his youth and where he'd cultivated his hatred of Jews while attempting to make a living as a struggling artist in Vienna. Hitler then turned his attention toward Czechoslovakia, when in May 1938 two Sudeten German farmers were shot by Czech border guards.[15] Germany used the incident as a pretext to move troops across the border; Sudetenland was a region of Czechoslovakia bordering Germany and today lies within the Czech Republic.[16] Chamberlain stopped short of overtly threatening war against Germany if Czechoslovakia was invaded, but hinted overtly that in tandem with France, "Britain might not stand aside" if Germany did so. As Hitler appeared to stand down, Chamberlain was applauded in Parliament, by the public, and in the media for his masterful handling of the crisis and for his skilled diplomacy.

But Hitler continued to press Germany's claim over the Sudetenland, and Chamberlain attempted to broker an accord, which became known as the Munich Agreement. He worked tirelessly for peace although he was neither a young man nor was he in the best of health. Chamberlain continued to reach out to Hitler, and on his third visit to Germany on September 29, 1938, they met privately to sign the now-infamous "piece of paper," which stated that the Munich Agreement was "symbolic of the desire of our two peoples never to go to war again."[17] News of the Anglo-German agreement leaked out before Chamberlain arrived back in England, and he was met with wild scenes and jubilant crowds. On arrival back in London he received a letter from King George VI— skillfully portrayed by Colin Firth in the 2010 Academy Award–winning film *The King's Speech*[18]—assuring him of the empire's lasting gratitude.

The British writer and actor Peter Ustinov was quoted as saying, "Courage is often lack of insight, whereas cowardice in many cases is based on good information."[19] History considers Chamberlain at best an appeaser and at worst a coward, but this fails to take account of the mood and circumstances of the period before the outbreak of World War II. Chamberlain was not a coward, although he was certainly guilty of a lack of foresight, as were a vast majority of the leaders in Britain and in Europe. With the horrors of World War I still fresh in the minds of that generation, they believed that no one other than a megalomaniac and a lunatic could want another war—and they failed to understand, as Churchill had, that Hitler was precisely that.

It's in our nature to hope for the best in people and to imagine positive outcomes—particularly when the alternative is too horrible to contemplate—and when Chamberlain waved his infamous piece of paper signaling "peace in our time," despair was replaced with hope, as people's greatest desire of averting war seemed possible. The British people had established a social contract with Chamberlain that stated: *We know that Hitler is a warmonger but he's not a fool, and we trust you to handle him correctly with both stick and carrot. You have given us hope that a war that all of Europe and the world wants to avoid can now be averted.*

When Hitler then proceeded to invade first Czechoslovakia and then Poland, causing Britain and France to declare war on Germany, Chamberlain's popularity was still such that he could have remained in power, even after some initial military setbacks including the Allied troop deployment and subsequent withdrawal from Norway in April 1940. The failure in Norway led directly to Chamberlain's resignation, yet on his departure from office on May 9, 1940, his approval ratings were still above 60 percent. Political leaders and institutions that were seen as having worked tirelessly for peace remained overwhelmingly popular during that period. And it's worth noting that the League of Nations, an organization whose central purpose was to avert another world war, and the forerunner to the modern-day United Nations, remained in place until April 1946—a year *after* the end of World War II. What Chamberlain could never recover from was the waving of that infamous piece of paper that became an emotional symbol of the lost hope for peace that he had promised.

But for future generations to vilify Chamberlain and paint him as a coward is both unfair and illogical. Who in his shoes would not have pursued every available course to avoid such a war? And who could have foreseen the depths of Hitler's depravity and insanity—as evidenced by his persecution of the Jews across Europe? As I referenced in an earlier chapter, the drawings by some the children held in Nazi death camps that are on display at the Jewish Cemetery in Prague are almost too difficult to look at because of the chilling picture they paint of unimaginable suffering as seen through a child's eyes. A similar portrait of lost innocence is brilliantly conveyed in Roberto Benigni's extraordinary film *Life Is Beautiful*, which received the Best Foreign Film Award at the 1998 Academy Awards[20]—and if you see only one subtitled movie in your life, make it this one. So monstrous and inconceivable were the reports that were filtering through about Nazi death camps early on in the war that even Churchill did not believe them.

Recognizing his popularity and patriotism, Churchill urged Chamberlain to remain in the cabinet and become the chancellor again after Chamberlain's resignation—and although he declined, on his first appearance in the House of Commons, members of Parliament from both parties loudly and enthusiastically cheered him. He remained a popular and respected voice, and he worked hard to bring the Conservative Party and Parliament as a whole in line behind Churchill until his death from bowel cancer later that year. Those who knew Chamberlain and who lived in those times applauded his tireless efforts for peace—and forgave him for having the same lack of foresight that most of them had been guilty of. Yet those who know him only as a figure in history seem unable to forgive him, *not* because of his failure to avert war—because likely no one could have—but for his naiveté in waving a piece of paper that unleashed the false hope for peace.

If you break a social contract and thereby halt the momentum of a movement, particularly one of that magnitude, it can be impossible to recover even generations later, as our continued vilification of Chamberlain illustrates. To that end, it might be extremely wise for Tony Hayward to avoid taking a vacation in New Orleans anytime soon.

RIGHTEOUSNESS IS NO DEFENSE

When Tony Blair marched triumphantly into 10 Downing Street in 1997 as the first Labour prime minister in fourteen years, he was considered a man of the people.[21] Blair had successfully repositioned his party to appeal to the naturally conservative-minded voters in the south of England—and his left-of-center political agenda and personal charisma had given Labour its largest parliamentary victory in a generation.[22] British voters had established a bond with Tony Blair and New Labour since his ascendency to the leadership in 1994, and his election victory of 1997 was based on a social contract that stated: *Britain needs new, progressive policies and a new face to present to the rest of the world. The country, its institutions, and its infrastructure need modernizing, and we must be seen as a global leader, rather than the fifty-first state of the United States.* Therefore, in order to live up to his social contract and perpetuate the political culture shift, Blair needed to be both "a new man and his own man."

Perhaps the height of Prime Minister Blair's popularity both in the United Kingdom and internationally came in June 1999 when then Serbian leader Slobodan Milosevic (now deceased, and a convicted war criminal) accepted NATO's peace terms, and the war in Kosovo ended.[23] Blair's leadership and the perception that he had pushed the United States under a weakened President Clinton to both increase air strikes against Serbia and threaten a ground invasion was taken as evidence that Blair was living up to his contract. These events were dramatized recently in the insightful 2010 HBO film *The Special Relationship* that starred Michael Sheen as Tony Blair and Dennis Quaid as Bill Clinton.[24] Sheen had previously portrayed Blair in the 2006 film *The Queen*[25] and seems to have a gift for morphing into distinctive public figures, having also played the noted broadcaster David Frost in *Frost/Nixon* (2008),[26] and the legendary English football manager Brian Clough in *The Damned United* (2009).[27]

In Tony Blair, the British public saw a leader with the moral fiber to take on those engaged in genocide, one who was willing and able to do so without having to follow America's lead. But for anyone prepared to look at what this signaled about his leadership moving forward, the evidence was there in plain sight. Prime Minister Blair believed in a doctrine that accepted it was morally justifiable to invade another sovereign nation when that country had failed to protect its own citizens—or worse, when the country had shown itself willing to commit genocide against its own people. He also believed that the United Kingdom should walk in lockstep with the United States in pursuing this new agenda around the world.

Whatever one's beliefs about the rights or wrongs of this doctrine, clearly this wasn't the typical philosophy of a progressive left-of-center politician. Where was the focus on domestic policy and the willingness to act independently from the United States? This was a prime minister who was driven by a deep sense of morality in keeping with his own religious beliefs and who valued his partnership with the United States above all others—in part because of the platform it afforded both him and the United Kingdom on the world stage. In assessing his subsequent leadership during the buildup to and ultimate invasion of Iraq, no one should therefore be surprised that he became President George W. Bush's staunchest ally.

Now a UN special envoy to the Middle East, Tony Blair stated in his recent memoir, *A Journey: My Political Life*,[28] that people expect their leaders to lead, even when the decisions are necessarily unpopular. Although that is certainly true, in a democracy, leaders serve at the will of the people who elect them, and it's essential that these leaders understand the nature of the social contract their support is based upon. In the eyes of many of the British people, Blair's support for the Iraq War made him seem like a hawkish puppet of the United States rather than "a new man and his own man," as his social contract demanded.

In the 2003 romantic comedy *Love Actually*, a prime minister played by Hugh Grant, who is modeled after Tony Blair,[29] publicly stands up to a lecherous American president—and that moment in the film generated a lot of discussion in the United Kingdom because it touched a nerve about how the British people had come to feel let down by Blair. Ironically, as probably the most astute politician of his generation, Blair likely *did* understand the nature of his social contract—and *was* acting as his own man, and out of a sense of righteousness, when he chose to break it. Ironically, he is quoted as saying in relation to the film that as prime minister there were times when he'd very much liked to have done a *Love Actually*!

Acting out of a sense of righteousness is often used as justification by those who choose to go against the wishes of their Disciples—acting counter to what drove their movement in the first place. Like Tony Blair, the NFL players in contractual dispute with their owners in 2011 fully understood the nature of the social contract they'd entered into with their fans, but unlike Blair they chose to act on that understanding. In March 2011, the football players union (NFLPA) opted to decertify,[30] causing the National Football League (NFL) to lock out the players—after the breakdown of talks around a new collective-bargaining agreement (CBA)—and it's said that the business world had too many acronyms!

Like politicians, athletes have the ability to inspire powerful emotions in us, although these emotions are more likely to be positive as we choose our favorite athletes and teams and define ourselves in part through our choices. Football stars can be arrested for taking drugs or for drunk driving, and generally it won't impact our support for them. They can publicly admit to embarrassing indiscretions and, if anything, it probably will only endear them to us more—that is, so long as they are prepared to go on *Leno, Letterman,* or *Ellen* and offer a sincere mea culpa. What we can't forgive a favorite athlete for, however, is choosing not to play.

Football has become unquestionably America's most popular sport. By many estimates the game's annual revenue is between $9 billion and $10 billion. The previous CBA determined how revenue should be shared between the club owners and the players. On one side of the argument you had billionaire owners claiming that the recession and the need to update or replace stadiums had impacted their profits—and that therefore they needed a greater percentage of revenue than the previous CBA had allowed them. On the other side, you had the NFLPA arguing that the game had never been more popular, and that the owners wouldn't open their books fully to pinpoint why they needed a greater percentage of revenue.

So in the midst of a recession, where the average fan was (and is) struggling to make ends meet and was having to make difficult choices just to pay for groceries or the mortgage, you had the obscene spectacle of billionaire owners like Jerry Jones of the Dallas Cowboys engaged in a legal spat with elite quarterbacks like Tom Brady of the New England Patriots, with each attempting to make a logical case for getting his slice of the biggest pie in the sport, while the fans couldn't even afford the crumbs. Sports radio hosts speculated about which side was doing better in the court of public opinion, while the situation drew closer to what seemed like an inevitable monumental legal battle—with the NFL hiring heavyweight attorney David Boies of Clinton-impeachment fame.

Generally, the fans were angry with all sides in the dispute, but if forced to take sides in the early part of 2011, they were leaning toward the players—because the NFL was, and is, a relatively intangible entity, and fans found it extremely hard to side with the bosses on principle. Also the fact that *Forbes* included all thirty-two NFL teams in its list of the top fifty most valuable sports franchises in the world in July 2011 probably didn't help the owners' cause! However, the nature of the fans' social contract with their favorite player, whether it be Drew Brees of the New Orleans Saints or Peyton Manning then of the Indianapolis Colts,[31] was such that as the dispute dragged on and threatened to interrupt the start of the season, the focus of the fans' anger began to switch.

The NFL fans' social contract with their favorite player states: *I am not a gifted athlete like you, so I will live vicariously through you and feel I am sharing in your successes. I'm happy for you to be paid millions because of the pleasure you bring on the football field, and I'm happy for you to get more than your fair share from the owners because they are greedy like most bosses. In return you will give 110 percent when you play—as I would if I had your talent.*

For a football player it's really a good deal, and it explains why a majority of fans initially sided with the players. The fan who is living vicariously through the players expects them to drive fast cars, live in impressive homes, and date beautiful women. Fans will also tolerate certain indiscretions by players because, in a sense, it shows that these stars are only human. But the essential part of fans living their lives vicariously through the players is sharing in their exploits on the football field—and if the players didn't play, they removed the centerpiece of the fans' projected experience, and *that* fans would not forgive or forget! Because the owners remained in the background, and fans didn't place them on a pedestal—paradoxically, the owners didn't run a similar risk of angering fans if the dispute had impacted the regular season.

Football became America's game in part because baseball gave up the mantle when players went through their own labor disputes. The 1994–1995 baseball strike was the fourth in-season lockout in twenty-two years, and the cancellation of the 1994 World Series was a tipping point for baseball fans. It became increasingly difficult for a fan to identify with a player who would set aside the chance to play in a World Series for any reason, let alone a labor dispute.[32] The ongoing steroids scandal that continues to undermine the accomplishments of a generation of stars has made it even harder for a baseball fan to identify with the athletes, or to imagine him- or herself making the same choices as his or her favorite player.

The nature of a social contract with star athletes demands first and foremost that they actually play—so that the fans can share in their exploits. Whatever the reason for not playing, however righteous the argument, if the players don't play, they have no personal value to the fan—and if players consciously choose not to play for any reason other than injury, the fan can't identify with their decision as, in their shoes, the fans would play at any cost.

Demonstrating an insightful understanding of the nature of their social contract with the fans, and having driven a hard bargain with the owners, the players wisely brought the dispute to a conclusion before it impacted the 2011 regular season,[33] although the Hall of Fame game sadly became a casualty. Whether the financial pressure on both sides drove a settlement, or whether the negotiators simply stepped up,[34] it was the players who benefited the most, as they would have incurred the lion's share of the fans' wrath if games had been cancelled.

The 2011 NBA dispute provided an instant and immediate point of comparison, as the players and owners in this instance failed to resolve their differences until the first portion of the 2011–2012 season had been lost. The basis of the dispute was, as ever, the amount of money that the players receive versus the owners and teams, although in this case you had a large number of NBA teams actually losing money. And while both sides eventually came to their senses and avoided the loss of an entire season, corralled by NBA commissioner David Stern, the apathy of fans at the delayed start of the season was palpable. Fans already struggled to find the same degree of affinity with this generation of aloof NBA stars like Kobe Bryant and LeBron James, relative to the populist eras of Magic Johnson and Michael Jordan, and the delayed 2011 season has only reinforced that sense of detachment. For a fan there is no greater sin than failing to play, and the NBA has a higher mountain to climb than ever as a result in trying to match the NFL's popularity.

So whether it's a politician like Tony Blair making a difficult decision, or whether it's an organization like the NFLPA, in the end they owe their position to the Disciples, and to consciously ignore their Disciples' wishes will inevitably lead to breaking their social contract and halting their culture shift—and once stalled, it's often impossible to regain the momentum.

SORRY SHOULDN'T BE THE HARDEST WORD

In 1990, *60 Minutes* aired a report suggesting that various people had been injured when their cars rapidly accelerated on their own.[35] At that time Audi, the German carmaker owned by Volkswagen, was relatively unknown in the United States.[36] People didn't know where Audis were made, and they had only a vague notion that they were different because of Audi's focus on quattro® (all-wheel drive), which generally was available only on trucks at that time. Audi's response to the negative report was to dispute the claims. Audi proceeded to explain, somewhat indelicately, that there was nothing wrong with the cars that accelerated rapidly—they went on to imply that the problem was due to driver error. If you drove an Audi at that time, you already struggled to justify your choice of car, and although the claims of unintended acceleration were subsequently disproved, the damage was done. Audi was almost driven out of the US market altogether.

The social contract for a committed Audi driver at that time stated: *Audi is different. But it functions brilliantly, so I'm happy to stand apart because I feel like my choice makes me smarter.* So when Audi blamed drivers for unintended acceleration, it not only insulted its customers but also broke the terms of its social contract by portraying those customers as incompetent. Today, Audi is prospering again in the United States with an eye-catching fleet of cars, but it took two decades of slowly rebuilding the image of the brand to fully recover from the unintended acceleration implosion. And even now if you Google "Audi unintended acceleration," you'll still receive more than one hundred thousand hits.

The enduring lesson of Audi's struggles in the 1990s wasn't lost on Toyota twenty years later when Toyota dealt with various recalls. Understanding that the essential nature of the social contract with its audience is to make them feel smart about their purchase, Toyota simply took responsibility and provided its drivers with fresh evidence to justify their purchases.[37] While Toyota is not out of the woods yet in terms of the damage done to its image as a maker of quality vehicles, it may have turned the corner with its unambiguous apology.

While Audi in the 1990s may be the poster child for brands that failed to say sorry—and paid the price by breaking their social contract, conversely, Jack in the Box restaurants in the 1990s were a testament to the redemptive power of an effective and inventive apology. Robert O. Peterson founded Jack in the Box in 1951 in San Diego, California. His first restaurant, on the Pacific Coast Highway in Long Beach, featured a giant clown's head on top of the building, and it revolutionized service by having a two-way intercom system that allowed customers to order, pull up to the drive-through window and instantly receive their order[38]—creating a template that the rest of the fast-food industry soon followed, and that we universally enjoy today.

In 1968, after Peterson sold the company to the pet-food manufacturer Ralston Purina, Jack in the Box experienced its most prolific period of growth in the early 1970s, and the restaurants began to be franchised. But in the process the former company-owned stores—which had taken pride in food preparation and quality control—began to resemble other, more generic fast-food restaurants like McDonald's, the market leader then, as now. As a result, the chain began to struggle and its ambitious East Coast expansion plan had to be put on hold.

In the early 1980s, as the company continued to lose market share, it decided to go for broke and initiated a marketing campaign where it literally blew up the Jack in the Box icon in order to signal a fundamental change of direction. Jack in the Box announced it would no longer compete with McDonald's for families with young children and instead would target older and more affluent (yuppie) customers. The restaurants were remodeled, and the menus and advertising were changed accordingly. Ralston Purina even attempted to change the name to Monterey Jack's but made a quick reversal when both the franchisees and the customers objected.

Although the change in direction enabled Jack in the Box to begin to rebound, in 1985 Ralston Purina decided to sell the company to the management team—and by 1987 sales had reached $655 million, while the chain boasted 897 restaurants. But then, with Jack in the Box suffering in the face of the national recession of 1990–1991, the sky fell in! In 1993, four children died and hundreds became sick in Seattle, California, Idaho, and Nevada after eating undercooked and contaminated meat from Jack in the Box restaurants. The *E. coli* epidemic resulted in millions in lost revenue and paid settlements in wrongful-death lawsuits, and bankruptcy was imminent. It's very often only in a time of crisis that a company will take a risk and roll the dice, and so Jack in the Box decided to throw a Hail Mary pass, and launched a bold new advertising campaign.

With a campaign conceived by its agency Secret Weapon Marketing—and harking back to the spectacle in the early 1980s where the company literally blew up the Jack in the Box icon—the company decided to bring a fictional Jack character back to fix the mess and refocus the company. In the launch commercial, Jack had a pingpong ball head and a business suit and was shown striding into the office building to reclaim his rightful role as CEO. In a revenge attack for having been blown up a decade earlier, Jack headed to the boardroom where the current board was meeting and detonated an explosive device—signaling the end of the old regime and the beginning of the new era.

While the apology was neither literal nor austere, the message to customers was explicit—the company had lost its way, and it was time to return to its original values and practices. It also wasn't without risk, however, to use humor at a time when a serious public spotlight was firmly fixed on the company. But it proved to be a highly effective strategy nonetheless, and the "Jack's Back" campaign went on to run for almost fifteen years, winning numerous industry awards and enabling the company to grow to the point where it now operates 2,200 restaurants nationally.

Just as we all make mistakes, people understand that companies sometime screw up or lose their way, although perhaps not as dramatically or as tragically as Jack in the Box had done. It wasn't the first company to offer a mea culpa to its customers, nor would it be the last. Other companies in the fast-food industry, like Hardee's and most recently Domino's Pizza, have used advertising to acknowledge their shortcomings and pledge to do better. In the travel and tourism sector, progressive companies also have come to understand the importance of a powerful and personalized apology, as evidenced by the fact that Southwest Airlines recently hired what amounts to a chief "forgiveness" officer, whose sole job is to fire off homespun apologies to disgruntled passengers.

But a poorly judged and delivered corporate apology can also be enormously destructive as Netflix CEO Reed Hastings discovered in late 2011 when he received a barrage of derision after he posted what seemed like a humble-sounding apology, stating, "I messed up . . . we lacked respect and humility in the way we announced the separation of DVD and streaming video, and the price changes."[39] This, after angry customers had experienced a 60 percent price increase and on complaining had previously been met with a wall of "corporate speak." Because Hastings was two months late in his apology, failed to justify the price hike, and compounded his mistake by introducing another unpopular move—separating DVD and streaming video into two separate entities, a decision he quickly had to reverse—unsurprisingly, his apology did nothing to curb the free fall of the share price or the flood of departing members. Netflix stock had already plummeted by 50 percent at that point, and still had a way to go before hitting rock bottom.

After its famously unapologetic CEO Leona Helmsley was convicted of tax evasion in 1989,[40] even the Helmsley Hotel chain ran ads under the campaign line, "Say what you will, she runs a helluva hotel."[41] In the heightened emotional cauldron that a commercial culture shift generates, customers have the capacity to forgive if the apology is genuine and heartfelt—or if even the company appears to at least acknowledge how it's perceived—as a little honestly goes a long way.

The July 2011 scandal involving the *News of the World* Sunday newspaper in the United Kingdom and its admittance at having hacked into the mobile voice mail of crime victims, including the murdered British schoolgirl Milly Dowler, is testament to the fact that there are some transgressions from which you simply can't rebound, however effective the apology might be. And with hindsight, the only course of action left to James Murdoch, chairman of the parent company News International, was to close down the paper. While this move undoubtedly generated the required dramatic effect and was intended to send a very public message about the ethics of News International, cynics had some justification in feeling that this wasn't as difficult a move as it might have first appeared. The company was rumored (now confirmed) to already have had plans to make its popular weekly tabloid the *Sun* available on Sundays, thereby making this little more than a rebranding effort.

The reason that public outrage in the United Kingdom finally exploded was because of the underlying "good versus evil" nature of the story, with Milly Dowler on one side, and the "dark lord" of global media, Rupert Murdoch, on the other. In truth, nobody had really cared if the now-defunct *News of the World* had been hacking into the phones of celebrities, politicians, and even members of the Royal family. But to hack into the voice mail of a missing thirteen-year-old, giving her parents false hope that she might still be alive simply to gain an edge for a news story, was about as low as any member of the free press could sink.

James Murdoch thought he was taking the nuclear option when he closed down the *News of the World* and attempted to salvage some semblance of public goodwill by offering advertising space free to charities. But the continuing revelations about the extent of the hacking practice at the paper, the acknowledgment that someone at News Corp. had previously lied to a parliamentary subcommittee—and the continued presence of Rebekah Brooks, the former paper's editor in chief, in her role as chief executive of News International—ensured the outrage wasn't going to abate, even long after Brooks eventually stepped down.

People have an unwritten social contract with their preferred news source that roughly states, *I know you will do almost anything for a story, and that our craving for immediate headlines and scandal fuels your behavior, but there is a line that you don't cross, and the* News of the World *didn't so much cross it as vault over it!*

When people suspected that News Corp. was happily serving up the *News of the World* to take the fall, only because it already had plans to launch its daily tabloid *The Sun* on Sundays—and when it continued to protect Ms. Brooks from the angry mob, it was apparent that this organization, which prided itself on understanding the pulse of the people, had no sense of the underlying morality of its readers and viewers.

So the classic tale of good triumphing over evil appeared to have played out again as Mr. Murdoch was forced to back out of his take-over of BSkyB, losing the desired crown jewel in his empire, which he has sought for over a decade. But it is important to remember that it's we who enabled the *News of the World* to flourish in the first place, and because of our insatiable and at times unhealthy curiosity, News Corp. is unlikely to be on the back foot for long! And indeed the company rebounded almost immediately with News Corp.'s stock gaining over 4 percent in a single day after news of its backing away from the BSkyB deal was announced!

The nature of the social contracts that people create with brands like Audi and Jack in the Box have the same emotional foundation as the relationships they establish with celebrities or politicians. It's equally important, therefore, that when a celebrity takes a serious misstep he or she be prepared to make an equally convincing and unqualified apology. Take the example of Hugh Grant, who famously salvaged his career by simply finding the right way to say he was sorry and having his apology universally accepted by his Disciples and the wider Congregation. Hugh Grant had first come into the public spotlight after his leading role in *Four Weddings and a Funeral,* the breakout British hit movie of 1994, in which he played the debonair yet bumbling Charles who eventually gets the girl—in the person of Carrie, played by Andie MacDowell.

Grant's good looks and boyish English wit and charm quickly established him as an A-list leading man in Hollywood—akin to a present-day combination of his namesake Cary Grant and the British actor David Niven. *Vogue* once memorably described him as a man with a "professionally misanthropic mystique."[42] As with all Hollywood celebrities, Hugh Grant's personal life came under tremendous scrutiny, fueled in part by the fact that he was dating the beautiful actress and model Elizabeth Hurley of *Austin Powers* fame. So on June 27, 1995, when Grant was arrested in an LA vice operation for misdemeanor lewd conduct in a public place with prostitute Divine Brown, it appeared that his career might have received a terminal blow.[43] How could people accept him in movies as a suave and charming English sophisticate when he was cruising the red-light district on Sunset Boulevard?

The answer lies in the power of a complete and heartfelt apology. At the time Grant was in the midst of promoting his forthcoming movie, *Nine Months,* and was scheduled to appear on *The Tonight Show with Jay Leno.* In a move that surprised many, he kept his appointment with Leno and together they changed their collective stripes. Grant was applauded in his interview for not making any excuses for his behavior, stating famously, "I think you know in life what's a good thing to do and what's a bad thing, and I did a bad thing. And there you have it." *The Tonight Show* moved ahead of *The Late Show with David Letterman* for the first time after Grant's appearance, and it never relinquished the top spot until Conan O'Brien briefly took over the show from Leno in 2010.

Through the *Tonight Show* interview, Grant faced up to his shortcomings, opened himself up to the watching public, and apologized unreservedly for his embarrassing mistake. Not only did the public forgive him, but also his career has continued to blossom with successful movies like *About a Boy* and *Love Actually.* He even continued to date Elizabeth Hurley for another five years, providing further justification for the public that he warranted forgiveness. In 2007, when Grant allegedly assaulted paparazzo Ian Whittaker, he made no similar public comment. Punching out a member of the paparazzi, it seems, requires no apology!

So whether it's a brand or a personality, people do have the capacity to forgive, even in the context of a social contract, so long as the apology is both heartfelt and unequivocal—a lesson, it seems that many companies and particularly politicians seeking to perpetuate political culture shifts still struggle to learn.

NO SOCIAL CONTRACT, NO BREACH!

The great recession of 2008 and 2009 continues to leave us battling unemployment, a weakened economy, and a massive fiscal deficit. The underlying causes of the recession have been debated at length, but what is undeniable is that it began in the housing sector—in part due to uncontrolled and reckless subprime lending. When borrowers by the thousands began to default, the degree of exposure that banks and major financial institutions faced came to light—as the US government first bailed out Bear Stearns, then the famously "too big to fail" AIG, while allowing Lehman Brothers to go under. The events surrounding that period in the fall of 2008 were dramatized in the 2011 HBO film *Too Big to Fail,* starring William Hurt as then treasury secretary Henry ("Hank") Paulson who struggled in the eye of the rising financial tsunami.[44]

To find the genesis of this great recession, however, it's necessary to go back to October 22, 1999. Under pressure from congressional Republicans, President Clinton then enacted one of the most sweeping deregulations of the banking, insurance, and stock-trading systems in US history—effectively repealing the last remnants of the Glass-Steagall Act, which had been a cornerstone of Roosevelt's New Deal in 1933. A few commentators at the time noted that the deregulation would increase the monopolization of finance by a few mega corporations and weaken the position of consumers in relation to their creditors. They also suggested, with ominous foresight, that the move would impact the stability of the United States and world capitalism, as the banking and insurance industry became inextricably linked to volatile global stock markets.

For the average homeowners and investors, their banks were supposed to be a pillar of stability, a place where they kept their savings and secured their mortgages. In reality, deregulation meant that a bank was able to attach a virtual casino with a revolving door and borrow from customers' precious savings in order to gamble on the stock market—without effective oversight. With the benefit of hindsight, the coming tempest was foreseeable, yet within the financial industry as a whole they continued to operate in a state of denial.

After almost one trillion dollars of public money was pumped into the economy and the financial system to prop up everyone from AIG to GM—with Congress continuing to bicker over effective new regulation,[45] and with the economy struggling to recover—the intriguing question remains: Where the is sense of public outrage? There had been no mass street protests directed at the banks and other financial institutions whose poor judgment and dubious practices brought the economy to its knees—requiring a massive injection of public investment[46] and effectively throwing people's tax dollars into the squall in order to preserve their own savings!

Ally Bank recently ran a series of commercials, the most notable of which featured a dog that had been taught by an owner to say, "I love my bank,"[47] and who doesn't love talking animals! The message being that it is possible to have an emotional relationship with a financial institution. In reality, the very fact that most people view banks as utilities—rather than something with which they chose to establish a social contract—helps to explain the absence of righteous indignation and anger directed toward the banks, which persisted until the emergence of the grassroots "Occupy" movement in October 2011.

Banks are a place to secure, draw, transfer, and borrow money. The arrangement is seen as almost entirely transactional rather than emotional. Typically that would be a vulnerable place for any brand or business to find themselves, with clients who have no emotional connection to them. But the idea of switching banks is so loathsome and hassle filled for most people that, although they feel no particular affinity to their bank, they still won't switch. After Wachovia effectively failed and was acquired by Wells Fargo, only a tiny percentage of its customers switched—and indeed Wachovia continues to be rated at or near the top in terms of customer service today! Even as Bank of America was voted the second-worst company operating in America in the 2011 Consumerist.com poll behind only BP[48]—as it has continued to wield a heavy foreclosure axe—Bank of America has seen no noticeable dropoff in its customer base.

So why hadn't people gone out and switched to the banks that didn't take TARP money or that remained stable because of solid stewardship? Because banking has been seen as a commodity like electricity. If there's a power cut, we grumble about the power company but we don't switch to solar. Similarly, banks are seen as a necessary evil that we tolerate. And because people mostly had no emotional relationship with their bank in the first place, they had nowhere to direct their anger, and therefore no emotional basis to switch.

In order to establish a social contract with a brand or an institution there needs to be a human (emotional) element—and banks are more faceless than most other types of businesses or institutions. Just because we can't put a face on a bank, however, doesn't mean that the financial sector as a whole is immune from emotion. Bernie Madoff's illegal and despicable Ponzi scheme,[49] and the executives of AIG who sought to pay themselves bonuses immediately after receiving public bailout money,[50] are testament to the fact that corrupt or arrogant financial organizations can incur the wrath of the public, but only when there is a human face for our anger. Banks and financial institutions continued the practice of paying sizable bonuses to executives as the US and world economy teetered on the brink of double-dip recession in October 2011—finally generating street protests, as initially Wall Street and the Financial District were occupied—and the unrest spread to other large and small cities in the United States and around the world. It was telling that after a week of social-media-directed protests in the manner of the Egyptian uprising, in order to maintain momentum organizers sought a human focal point and began protesting outside the homes of select corporate CEOs.

Establishing a social contract can both distinguish you and be massively profitable as the basis for a culture shift—although for the leader it puts a powerful spotlight on you as the core personality at the heart of the company. But if people will come to you anyway because you're an essential commodity, and if they won't switch no matter how badly you screw up, then you might consider whether it's smart to even try to establish a social contract!

However, this remains the clear exception, as most brands in most sectors don't have the luxury of being faceless, undefined, and unaccountable—and are therefore required to play by an entirely different set of rules than many banks appear to be able to.

HANDLE WITH CARE

William Congreve's quote "Heaven has no rage like love to hatred turned"[51] in this context can be interpreted as meaning that the same passion that was aroused in creating a social contract can be unleashed against you if you break the terms. The benefit of establishing a social contract as the basis for a potentially lucrative political, populist, or commercial movement is enough to spark the interest of any businessman or businesswoman. Reaching the broader Congregation via earned social media rather than traditional paid media is naturally appealing.

But there is no such thing as reward without risk, and the emotional nature of people's commitment to a movement means that any misstep, betrayal, or overt contradiction can result in that same passion being used against you. A social contract is not a static agreement but a living, breathing entity that must be monitored and nurtured every day, and as it evolves, so does the movement, and you need to continuously reappraise what's expected of you in order to avoid breaking its terms and stalling momentum.

Disciples and ultimately the Congregation decide if you've broken the social contract, and if you want your movement to prosper, you'd better understand their terms.

CHAPTER 9

CREATING A CULTURE SHIFT IN THE AGE OF ILLOGIC

"Logic is the beginning of wisdom, not the end."
—Leonard Nimoy,
Star Trek VI: The Undiscovered Country, 1991

A s emotional beings in a time of information overload, we create culture shifts based on illogical leaps.

Sherlock Holmes and Mr. Spock are two of popular fiction's most endearing and enduring characters, and they have a lot in common with each other. Both were highly intelligent, both were outsiders who always seemed to be one step ahead of everyone around them, both exhibited an incredible attention to detail, and most of all, both were slavish in their belief in the power of fact-based logic.

In *Star Trek,* Leonard Nimoy's Spock was engaged in a continuous joust with William Shatner's Captain Kirk, who was determined to have him set aside logic and follow an emotional path, exhorting him to use his "human side."[1] Gene Roddenberry's Spock—supposedly based on legendary police chief William H. Parker, whom he had revered while with the LAPD—was forced at the end of most episodes to accept the emotional nature of humans and simply work around our shortcomings. The recent success of the 2009 *Star Trek* movie, starring Chris Pine and Zachary Quinto as the young Kirk and Spock,[2] demonstrates the enduring fascination we have with the characters as well as the central narrative exploring the tension between emotion and logic. And the forthcoming sequel to this latest film will not doubt prove to be equally successful.

Holmes's character stayed ahead of the criminals and the police by never jumping to a conclusion before he had done his due diligence. He believed that if you formed a hypothesis before you had all the facts, then you would inevitably head in the wrong direction. He was speaking to the phenomenon of illogical leaps, although a century ago people had more time to slow down and process information. And a new generation appears equally fascinated with the interplay between Holmes and his long-suffering companion, Dr. Watson, portrayed by Robert Downey Jr. and Jude Law in the 2010 film *Sherlock Holmes*,[3] and their pursuit of "elementary" truths.

Great characters in contemporary fiction have always served to help us see the world from a different perspective, revealing just how illogical our day-to-day behaviors and beliefs really are. Characters like Winston Groom's *Forrest Gump,* superbly portrayed by Tom Hanks in the multiple-Oscar-winning 1994 film of the same name,[4] appear to be oddities or simpletons who miss the nuances of the world around them—and yet in seeing the world through their eyes we come to understand the illogic of the society that we've created. Mary Chase's original stage play *Harvey* was turned into a movie in 1950 and starred the peerless James Stewart as Elwood P. Dowd, an amiable and endearing middle-aged man whose best friend just happens to be a six-foot, three-and-a-half-inch tall invisible white rabbit named Harvey.[5] Drawn from Celtic mythology, Harvey is a *pooka* and inseparable from Dowd, his fellow social outcast, much to the chagrin of Dowd's excitable sister Veta, played by Josephine Hull. The play was recently revived in London's West End, demonstrating its enduring appeal, with Dowd being played by Stephen Fry.

Harvey takes you on a journey that forces you to question your own perspective of what's normal and sane. We can all aspire to have Dowd's effortless sociability and comfort with his place in the world, and if the essential contributor to his enviable peace of mind is an imaginary white rabbit, we should all be lucky enough to have such a friend. Dowd retains a childlike image of the world, where soul mates are invisible and everyone he encounters represents an equal opportunity to find a new friend. Veta represents the rest of us "normal folk"—high-strung, desperately concerned about how her brother's delusion is limiting her daughter's marriage prospects, and convinced that Harvey is the result of Dowd's generous alcohol consumption. Ultimately Veta tries to cure Dowd's delusion and takes him to a mental institution to receive drug treatments that will "fix him." But like the chief psychiatrist at the clinic, who comes to recognize the enviable nature of Dowd's outlook—and as a result also starts seeing Harvey—we don't want Dowd to change and become normal like the rest of us. Unlike his world, ours is full of competitiveness and petty neurosis and prejudice, which keep us apart from other people. Dowd's character forces us to see that the way we live our lives (without Harvey) is often illogical, and that, delusion-based or not, Dowd's worldview is actually the sane one.

Chauncey—Chance the Gardener—is another character in contemporary fiction who has the same ability to let us see the illogical nature of the world we've created. The 1979 film *Being There*, based on Jerzy Kosinski's novel, was the great Peter Sellers's last film.[6] Chance is a middle-aged man who has spent his entire life working as a gardener behind the walled garden of a Washington, DC, home, only experiencing the world outside through television that he "likes to watch." Another apparent simpleton, Chance is forced out into the world for the first time with nothing but his suitcase when the old man who owns the house dies, and he takes us on a journey that reveals how our world might seem to someone who had just landed from Mars.

As the drama unfolds, Chance finds himself becoming the friend and confidante of Benjamin Rand, America's wealthiest and most powerful man, and his wife, who are played to perfection by Melvyn Douglas and Shirley MacLaine. Rand is effectively the power behind the presidential throne, and because of Chance's association with the dying Rand, and because Chance has no recorded past, the media and even the current president become convinced that Chance is Rand's chosen successor for the presidency. The film's great wisdom and charm is in allowing us to see how we project whatever we want to believe onto others, convincing ourselves that people and events are the way we imagine them to be and ignoring all evidence to the contrary. Chance becomes a vessel for everyone's hopes and ambitions, including Rand's lonely and lovesick wife, Eve, the Washington media, and the grandees of the (suggested) Republican Party—who eventually concur at Rand's funeral, "Gentlemen, I do believe that if we wish to hold onto the presidency, our one and only hope is Chauncey Gardener." Jerzy Kosinski's message is clear with his final closing line, "Life is a state of mind."

Even though his role earned him an Academy Award nomination, some saw Sellers's contained and sedate performance in *Being There* as a disappointing final role for the man who had created hilarity for a generation with his performances as Inspector Clouseau in Blake Edwards's *Pink Panther* films. Yet in many ways it was an apt finale for the comedic genius who struggled to define his own personality off the screen, as was showcased in the 2004 biographical film *The Life and Death of Peter Sellers*, in which Sellers was portrayed by the chameleon-like Geoffrey Rush. As Sellers once famously commented, "There used to be a me but I had it surgically removed."[7]

The people who encountered Chance were too busy imagining what he could be to see who he actually was. The Republican grandees were so desperate to hold onto the presidency and create a culture shift that they took an illogical leap, followed their Chief Disciple, and determined that Chance was the solution. And while Holmes and Spock hold continued appeal to many of us because we wish society could strike a better balance between reason and emotion, as *Being There* dramatizes, we are all emotional beings who will continue to rush to judgment before considering the logical answer. As a result, we will always be prone to create culture shifts that are based on illogical leaps.

Today the endless number of advertising messages, smartphone interruptions, and the continuous lure of social networking increase the necessity to process at lightning speed. As a result, we miss key pieces of a story and have to fill in the gaps with our own invention in order to make sense of it—the result being that we pile ignorance on top of our innate illogic. So this has become the age of illogic and, as Spock would no doubt conclude, we are simply being human in our response.

As a business leader keen to promote a product or see a brand's popularity increase and create a culture shift, how do you begin to craft an approach in this environment? And as a political operative, how do you create cultural momentum for your party or candidate? It's clear we are all driven by emotion and prone to take illogical leaps to match our own preconceived notions. We know that consumers will pick up only fragments of the message through traditional and digital advertising, and as it goes viral, social media will distort and modify it until it's unrecognizable from what we originally seeded. So the question becomes, is it even worth attempting to shape the public image of your company, your brand, or your candidate?

Well, I do believe it is, and I've used the themes from each of the chapters in order to summarize the key tenets required to create a culture shift in the age of illogic—as well as providing some more examples where each of the key ingredients for a culture shift have been present—with amazing results.

THE TEN KEY TENETS FOR CREATING A CULTURE SHIFT

1. Establish a Social Contract

Social contracts represent the essential ingredient in the creation of culture shifts, whether those shifts are historical, political, populist, or commercial in nature—and it's essential to recognize the key elements and conditions that are required in order for them to form:

- Social contracts are often underpinned by an emotional desire for change or to challenge societal norms.
- Illogical leaps are often the central currency of social contracts, and therefore they are essential to creating culture shifts.

- Social contracts spawn passionate Zealots, although Disciples ultimately perpetuate culture shifts.
- Social contracts today are universally celebrated and perpetuated through social media.

It doesn't matter what was intended when your brand, celebrity persona, or political candidacy was launched—the only things that matter are how it was received and processed, and the nature of the social contract that was established in order to create a culture shift. Consumers, customers, and fans decide the terms of social contracts, no matter how illogical those terms may be.

2. Enlist Disciples and the Congregation

Disciples are your greatest assets in convincing the wider Congregation to be part of a culture shift, and the more your efforts and decisions are geared toward arming them to make the case for you, the more efficient you can be and the more success you'll achieve.

- Unless Zealots are able to evolve and adopt the persona of Disciples, it may be necessary to abandon them, as it's the Disciples who will ultimately persuade and engage the wider Congregation and perpetuate the culture shift.
- This may seem callous, but the nature of Zealots is such that they have a polarizing influence and in the end can serve to limit broader participation in a culture shift.
- The Disciples who take more time to finally support you do so because they were studying you before making a commitment.

When the Disciples do come on board, they make a positive choice, believing in your ability to fulfill your purpose, and as a result will be longer-term advocates in perpetuating the culture shift—assuming you don't break the terms of the social contract.

3. Leverage Your Chief Disciple

CEOs, politicians, and even celebrity leaders may not have created the social contract that their Disciples established with them, yet they must be seen to adhere rigidly to the terms of the contract and provide the vision in order to create a culture shift.

- A Chief Disciple is a living, breathing encapsulation of the organization, and the standard-bearer for the terms of the social contract. He or she must inspire passion and commitment and be proactive in causing participation.
- He or she must display appropriate behavior at all times and be an advocate for the organization's values, as well as nurture the culture.
- He or she must be seen to both lead and be happy to learn from the Disciples at the same time.
- Rational actions are important, but no less so than the emotional manner in which he or she conduct him- or herself at work and at play.

If you are serious about establishing a social contract, having a Chief Disciple with these qualities in place and leveraging him or her accordingly is crucial because nobody will want to be part of creating a culture shift that doesn't have an inspirational leader.

4. Embrace Illogical Leaps

Accept that the image people hold isn't fair or logical, and commit to revealing the true nature of their illogic as the basis for creating a culture shift—rather than building from a corporate strategy or political program developed from a logical (insider's) viewpoint.

- Use projective techniques to reveal the nature of people's illogical leaps. Projective techniques adopted from psychotherapy enable you to unlock the unconscious or hidden motivations that are shaping people's belief systems—and therefore the basis of their illogical leaps.

- With the influence of social media, it's unrealistic to think that if a large swathe of society believes something about you that it won't be shared and perpetuated.
- Embrace the conversation—leverage it when it makes sense—and have a sense of humor about it.
- It's entirely possible, using a basket of relatively quick and inexpensive progressive digital-research tools, to understand the nature of these illogical leaps that are essential ingredients in the creation of culture shifts if the will exists to do so.

Whether you are attempting to shape your own image or that of a candidate, a company, or a brand in creating a culture shift, accept that the image people have created isn't logical, and commit to decoding the true nature of the illogical leap they have taken.

5. Use Social Media to Generate Emotion

Emotion is the driver that causes people to create a social contract. The experience of mass participation in a culture shift via social media can serve to generate emotion, but its primary role is still to allow people to connect, organize, and engage, as well as increasingly to provide companies with rich insights.

- Social media is a powerful medium, but still just one medium. It is dramatically less expensive to see your message carried organically via social media sites than it is to invest in traditional media, but it's easy to both overstate and mischaracterize social media's true value and purpose.
- The way information is shared is such that any message disseminated via social media will naturally be modified and reframed in the manner of "the telephone game," and you must accept that it may run counter to your original intent or wishes.

- Social media can encourage the digital equivalent of attention deficit disorder, so it should be used judiciously.
- While social media can help people organize support for you or spark an idea, once that has happened, you must be prepared step back and see what transpires organically.

Social media is central to the creation of a social contract in part because it helps to fuel the invention of illogical leaps, and it serves as an emotion beacon. As technology continues to allow for more personalized real-time interaction from any location, social media's potential for generating the heightened emotion that is the lifeblood of any culture shift will continue to increase.

6. Deliver Emotional Certainty

No matter how illogical it may appear, we strive for certainty in all of our choices and affiliations. And the allure of certainty is central to the establishment of social contracts and the creation of culture shifts, because by helping people make decisions, individuals and organizations generate trust and credibility.

- Accept that it isn't a lack of imagination or intelligence that causes people to look for simplicity in making their choices, it's the feeling of self-affirmation that they are smart and knowledgeable enough to make informed selections.
- When people feel confident in their choices and affiliations, it fuels the illusion of certainty that they seek from the world around them—and inevitably they feel more connected to the organization that gave them peace of mind.
- When certainty is lost, people feel an enormous resentment toward whomever is perceived to have taken it away from them.

Emotional certainty is a central currency in the establishment of any social contract and therefore of any related culture shift, and once the illusion of certainty is lost, usually the momentum is also lost.

7. Protect Your Principal Symbols

Whatever tangible form a symbol takes, it can become an encapsulating beacon for a culture shift as well as an emotional conduit for a shift's goals and beliefs. Without symbolism, organizations and brands can see a gradual erosion of their social contract, which makes the creation or adoption of an appropriate icon absolutely pivotal to perpetuating culture shifts.

- A political, cultural, or brand symbol is the standard-bearer for the terms of a social contract. It can inspire passion and commitment, and drive affinity and participation. While many symbols are passive, when one rises to this level it becomes integral to a culture shift's lore and its continued progress.
- A principal symbol's use and application must be fiercely protected and monitored to ensure it doesn't become polluted or associated with anything that runs counter to the culture shift.
- When a principal symbol is forgotten or relegated to make way for something that is thought to be more topical, in most cases it becomes necessary to revive it in order to reconnect with the Disciples. In the process, the culture shift's momentum can begin to stall, and all for the sake of short-term gain.

Just as Zealots, Disciples, and the Congregation create the terms of a social contract and perpetuate a culture shift, they also determine its principal symbolism. And if you are seen to remove a symbol with which they've established a close connection, it can feel as though you've interfered with something deeply personal in their lives.

8. Avoid a Breach

The benefit of establishing a social contract as the basis for a potentially lucrative political, populist, or commercial movement is enough to spark the interest of any businessman or businesswoman. Having your Disciples spreading the word organically and reaching the broader Congregation without having to invest heavily is understandably appealing.

- There is no such thing as reward without risk, and the emotional nature of people's commitment to a commercial or political culture shift means that any misstep, betrayal, or overt contradiction can be fatal.
- A social contract is not a static agreement, but a living, breathing entity that must be monitored and nurtured every day—as it evolves, so does the culture shift, and you need to continuously reappraise what's expected of you in order to avoid breaking its terms.
- Disciples and ultimately the Congregation decide if you've broken the social contract, and if you want your culture shift to progress, you'd better understand their terms.

The same passion that was aroused in creating a movement will be unleashed against you if you break the terms.

9. Ride Your Luck

While each of the previous eight tenets required in creating culture shifts are things that can be largely effected, if not controlled, luck and timing are inevitably less certain. Nevertheless, when circumstances conspire to give a movement unexpected momentum, like any great brand or politician, it's essential to be able to adapt in midstream to an opportunity that has arisen and ride your luck, rather than remaining strictly wedded to a plan or a strategy that hadn't accounted for the new dynamic.

10. Timing Is Everything

In the *Perfect Ten* examples outlined below, I'll provide some final demonstrations of political, populist, and commercial culture shifts, where each of the ten key tenets were in evidence, including good luck and timing—and the extraordinary and enduring results speak for themselves.

PERFECT TENS

Ronald Reagan

In the age of twenty-four-hour digital and television news coverage, an American president becomes akin to a distant uncle that you invited into your home, and who then decided to stay for four or sometimes eight years. In essence, no matter how much affection you have for him, you're still happy to see him go, and that is particularly true if he's proved to be as unpopular as President Jimmy Carter had by 1980. To that end, it's no surprise that at least in terms of public perception, every American president seems to be the antithesis of the previous one, and in following Jimmy Carter as the fortieth President of the United States, Ronald Reagan was no exception to the rule.

Today, the late Ronald Reagan is probably revered as much as any American president of the last century. And an amusing compilation video from the 2008 Republican primary campaign, which dramatized how each of the many candidates mentioned his name in an attempt to be associated with his legacy, illustrates the continued importance of Reagan as an electoral asset. But it was not always the case, and it's easy to forget how unlikely his rise to the presidency and immortality truly was. There is a moment in the classic 1985 movie *Back to the Future* where the time-traveling Marty McFly played by Michael J. Fox informs the "mad scientist" Doc Brown, portrayed by Christopher Lloyd, that Reagan is the president and—stunned—he exclaims, "The *actor*!?"[8] Always attuned to pop culture, Reagan actually quoted from the film in his 1986 State of the Union address.

Primarily known as a B-movie actor and then president of the Screen Actors Guild, Reagan first came to national attention as a political figure after his rousing speech in support of Barry Goldwater's candidacy in 1964. Reagan went on to serve two terms as governor of California and leveraged his position and profile to run for the presidency in 1968 and in 1976. Having established a social contract among right-leaning Zealots by the early 1970s, Reagan's speech at the 1976 Republican National Convention after narrowly losing to then vice president Gerald Ford convinced many Disciples that they might have chosen the wrong candidate. In comfortably defeating President Jimmy Carter in 1980, taking more than 50 percent of the popular vote, Reagan cemented his social contract with both Disciples and the Congregation based on his core principle of lowering taxes to stimulate the economy, less government interference in people's lives, the reaffirmation of states' rights, and a strong national defense. Reaganomics passed the grasp-ability test, and the foundational elements of a political culture shift—in the form of an established social contract driven by committed Disciples—were firmly in place. And like any great political leader, Reagan was the embodiment of an inspiring Chief Disciple with his natural charisma, his peerless communication skills, and his ability to simplify complex issues and stay on message.

As with any powerful culture shift, timing and a degree of self-generated luck came into play. With many people in the United States feeling that the country was on the wrong path under the Carter administration, the underlying desire for societal change was clearly present in 1980. And due in large measure to the efforts of Reagan's team behind the scenes, while he was giving his first inaugural address on January 20, 1981, fifty-two American hostages, held by Iran for 445 days, were being set free. This was the first example of Reagan's powerful use of symbolism as an integral part of driving his culture shift, and other examples were to follow: Reagan waving from his hospital window after surviving an assassination attempt; Reagan in front of the Brandenburg Gate in Berlin and challenging the soviet leader Mikhail Gorbachev to "Tear down this wall"; and Reagan at home in his beloved Rancho del Cielo, astride a horse and wearing his slouched cowboy hat. Ronald Reagan mastered the art of oratory and symbolism as a means of perpetuating his culture shift, and his graspable and oft-repeated principles, as well as his assured and accessible delivery, created the necessary sense of certainty for his Disciples and the wider Congregation. This assured him a second term in office, as well as a place in the hearts of the American people.

Of course, in the age before the Web and social media, Reagan had to rely on traditional media like television as well as grass-roots efforts to both organize and generate emotion among the Congregation. But such was his progressive use of the tools at his dis-posal at that time that it isn't difficult to imagine his campaign swiftly mastering any and all new mediums. And in reflecting on Reagan's unprecedented political culture shift of the 1980s, the only poten-tial question as to whether he created the *Perfect Ten* (template) for others to follow relates to whether or not he broke the terms of his social contract through the Iran-Contra affair.

The 1986 scandal that centered around whether the proceeds from arms' sales to Iran had been funneled to the Contra rebels in Nicaragua certainly created a breach in Reagan's social contract with his Disciples and the Congregation—as his approval numbers dropped from 67 percent to 46 percent in a single week.[9] The sense of certainty that people had in Reagan's ethics and in the control he had over every aspect of the administration was weakened, and perhaps revealed the illogical leap at the heart of his political culture shift—that someone of his years could be micromanaging the execu-tive branch of government, rather than simply acting as its figure-head and Chief Disciple.

However, history has shown that while Iran-Contra damaged Reagan's popularity and weakened his social contract at the time, ultimately it didn't undermine the culture shift that he had created—evidenced by the fact that every Republican candidate for the presidency will seek to associate him- or herself with his legacy, and promise to revive his policies in the forthcoming 2012 election. If Reagan's political culture shift doesn't rise to the level of a *Perfect Ten*, then it certainly comes closer than any other political legacy has, at least in my lifetime.

Harry Potter

Today the Harry Potter brand and franchise is estimated to be worth around $15 billion, making author J. K. Rowling, by some estimates, almost as rich as Queen Elizabeth II.[10] A far cry from the 2,500-pound advance that Rowling received from Bloomsbury for *Harry Potter and the Philosopher's Stone* in 1995 after eight different publishers had previously rejected the book.[11] The Harry Potter series has been translated into sixty-seven languages, has sold four hundred million books worldwide, has been turned into a Warner Bros. movie franchise, with each of the seven films listed in the thirty top-grossing films of all time. The Harry Potter brand has spawned eight video games and more than four hundred different commercial products, and it has become a theme park at Universal Studios Orlando. In creating Harry Potter on a delayed Manchester-to-London train journey, J. K. Rowling created the basis for one of the most powerful pop-culture shifts the world has ever known.[12]

I cannot begin to paint of picture of Harry Potter's world of magic and wizardry, so you'll have to skip this section if you've been living under a rock for the past sixteen years and know nothing about Harry, Hermoine, Ron, Hagrid, Voldemort, and Dumbledore—suffice it to say that Harry Potter's appeal transcends all age, race, gender, socioeconomic, and nationalistic boundaries. The Harry Potter series broadly fits into the category of fantasy literature, but at the same time the books are mysteries, thrillers, coming-of-age novels, as well as belonging to the "English boarding school" genre that authors like Thomas Hughes, George MacDonald Fraser, and Rudyard Kipling mastered for previous generations.

Harry Potter and the Philosopher's Stone was such a mammoth success in the United Kingdom that J. K. Rowling received $105,000 for the US rights to the book, which was an unheard-of sum of money at that time for an unknown children's author. For the US market, the name was changed to *Harry Potter and the Sorcerer's Stone* when it was launched in September 1998, and it effortlessly made the transition from initial Zealots through the Disciples and into the wider Congregation. Children engaged other children as well as their parents, who in reading it to their children fell in love with the book and told other parents—ensuring the organic migration that we now see happening via social media with any significant pop-culture shift.

Harry Potter's social contract was based on J. K. Rowling's ability to allow us to escape into a magical world of wizards, with characters whom we quickly came to love (or hate), but *also* into the world of our childhood, where we could share a common passion with our own children. So powerful was the allure of this world Rowling created that, as normally over-protective parents, we took an illogical leap and ignored the often-dark and adult plots and themes such as tyranny, bigotry, and most of all, death. And while the majority of critics have noted the positive cultural impact of the Harry Potter series, as represented by the myriad of literary awards it's received, some have commented on its dark themes in the manner of the *Christian Science Monitor*'s Jenny Sawyer in 2007, who wrote that the books represented a "disturbing trend in commercial storytelling and Western society."[13]

Of course, Harry Potter's draw is also built on the powerful use of symbolism and iconography, from Hogwarts to Hogsmeade to Horcruxes, which have been steadily revealed through the launch of each of the books and films—and even the book covers were given alternative designs in order provide symbolism for children versus adults. While Harry's life-threatening experiences pushed the boundaries of children's fiction in terms of the emotional and physical trials he was forced to overcome, there remained an underlying certainty that good would ultimately overcome evil, and that through it all Harry would bend but never break. This also served to strengthen Harry's unquestioned position as the Chief Disciple of his own culture shift, even as other characters were introduced and developed. And not coincidently, Harry Potter's ascent through the previous decade coincided with the rise of digital and social media, as Disciples young and old were able to gather online through blogs, podcasts, and fan sites—and *MuggleCast* and *PotterCast* have each become top fifty favorite podcasts.[14] Even as the books and films have come to an end, Rowling has offered continued engagement in the franchise through the Pottermore website. In the real world, Disciples were able attend the Harry Potter symposia, or wait outside a bookstore or movie theater at midnight with fellow Potterites, for the latest release.

Clearly not everyone knew the world was waiting for an English boy wizard with round-rimmed glasses, a nasty scar, and lot of family baggage, or else the eight publishers that initially rejected J. K. Rowling wouldn't still be drowning their sorrows. As with all pop-culture shifts—and few have scaled the heights of Harry Potter—a liberal amount of self-generated luck as well as excellent timing were also required. In reviewing *Harry Potter and the Deathly Hallows* in the *New York Times* on August 12, 2007, the late Christopher Hitchens praised J. K. Rowling for creating "a world of youthful democracy and diversity" in contrast to the typical (Western) school story "bound up with dreams of wealth and class and snobbery."[15] And either by luck or intent (and probably a little of both), Rowling has seemingly managed with each new book in the series to capture the prevailing cultural and political mood, as the arrival of *Deathly Hallows* coincided with the resurgence of the Democrats and the rise of Barack Obama in the United States during the last months of George W. Bush's administration.

At the same time, America has needed a magical place to escape to post–September 11, 2001, in the face of global terrorism, and through the ongoing suffering caused by related wars in Iraq and Afghanistan—and Harry has been there through all of it, distracting us from our daily troubles, as he's battled Voldemort and his own demons. To that end it's not surprising that *Time* magazine placed J. K. Rowling as the runner-up in its 2007 Person of the Year award,[16] behind Vladimir Putin—providing conclusive evidence that the powerful culture shift that Harry Potter has created rises to the level of a *Perfect Ten.*

Google

Do you remember Excite or Galaxy®? How about WebCrawler®, Lycos®, or Infoseek®? Or how about AltaVista® and MetaCrawler®? Whether they've reinvented themselves from their beginnings as a search engine like Yahoo!, or whether they've disappeared altogether like InfoSeek, how did it happen that seemingly overnight the world stopped using these search engines and started using Google instead?

Founded by Larry Page and Sergey Brin (the Google Guys) while still at Stanford University, and incorporated in 1998, the company's original mission statement was "to organize the world's information and make it universally accessible and useful"—which eventually was encapsulated into "Don't be evil." Today, Google runs about one million servers worldwide and processes over one billion search requests. And beyond Google search, the brand encompasses Gmail™, Google Analytics™, Google Books™, Google Chrome™, Google Desktop™, Google Earth™, Google Energy™, Google Talk™, Google Voice™, and now Google+ to name a few—while also having developed the Android™ mobile operating system and owning a number of leading websites, including YouTube, Blogger™, and Orkut™.[17] Little wonder that BrandZ lists Google as number one on its list of most valuable global brands.[18] In just fourteen years, the search engine that Page and Brin originally nicknamed "BackRub"—because of its ability to check back-links to determine the relevance of a site to a particular inquiry—has spawned one of the most powerful companies on the planet and created a culture shift the likes of which the world has seldom seen.

There is no single reason why using the Google search engine became the world's default way to search in the late 1990s, but rather a series of competitive advantages—which became apparent the *first* time you searched using Google, most notably: faster loading, simpler interface, and more-relevant results. Recognizing the superior nature of their search, Yahoo!, which initially hosted Google, quickly began showing Google's search results versus its own, providing a further endorsement. So the Zealots discovered that Google was superior and told the Disciples, and it took just *one* try for them to discover the same thing and inform the Congregation—the social contract was established organically, and the momentum for a global culture shift moved at warp speed. It's hard to think of a comparable environment where trial, adoption, and loyalty happen in virtually the same instant, except perhaps falling in love after the first kiss—and perhaps the *first search* effect was Google's true magic bullet in providing certainty that theirs was a superior product.

In the early search world, which seemed both complex and intimidating to many, the Google logo and interface stood out as being clean and friendly: appropriate and effective symbolism for a company whose mantra was "Don't be evil." And yet when you control the flow of the world's information more than any other company (or country for that matter), and you've placed a moral stake in the ground, the risk of breaching the terms of your social contract is ever-present. Google has had to make constant judgment calls around the world in relation to potential misuses of its products and services. In January 2010, Google threatened to pull out of the Chinese market altogether when it was revealed that hackers had targeted the Gmail accounts of a number of human-rights activists[19]—and while Google stopped short of leveling accusations at the Chinese authorities, the implication of state involvement was apparent. This had been a sensitive area for Google ever since it first launched Google.cn (China) in 2006, when Google was forced to agree to a degree of censorship of search results. And even in the face of vocal resistance from various Google shareholder groups, it was no surprise when Google.cn was shut down in March 2010, with all Web traffic being directed to Google.hk (Hong Kong).[20]

In assessing whether Google's dramatic ascent rises to the level of a *Perfect Ten* in terms of the global culture shift it created, the only potential caveat has to be in considering the role that luck and good timing played. Google arrived in the world at the exact moment when Web search was exploding, and it came up against competitors with utterly inferior products. But I don't believe you should penalize a team for having to play inferior competition (as the Bowl Championship Series does), which is why I included Google as the quintessential example of a commercial culture shift on a global scale. The world will be watching after its 2011 acquisition of Motorola Mobility and the slow adoption of Google+, where they face significantly tougher competition, to see if Google can maintain its *Perfect Ten* score.

PRACTICING WHAT I PREACH

I wrote this book, *Second That Emotion*, with the purpose of decoding why people choose to make fundamental shifts in their actions and affiliations, and how they establish the beliefs that determine their choices—so that anyone in the commercial or political realm could follow the template that I've outlined.

To that end, it would be extremely bizarre if I hadn't followed my own advice in both launching and marketing *Second That Emotion*. So I wanted to conclude by outlining the broad approach that I developed, along with my publishing, advertising, design, and PR partners, in attempting to create a culture shift around the book itself. I finished writing the manuscript six months ahead of schedule and determined to use that time to begin seeding information and interest in the book, through means of blogging, PR, and by developing a viral advertising campaign. I wanted to create curiosity and awareness that *Second That Emotion* was coming, and that it represented something different in the genre of business books—for one thing that it wasn't primarily about business! We were especially keen to spark social-media dialogue and debate, and even create antagonism toward the premise and myself if need be, in order to bring the book into the Zealots' consciousness and through them to reach Disciples.

Having spent twenty-five years working with some of the largest and most progressive companies in Europe and the United States, I was fortunate enough to know various senior executives in a number of these organizations. I've also come into contact with many influential people in the academic, advertising, marketing, media, and publishing worlds, as well as with politicos. And yes, I've typically used social media to maintain and strengthen those contacts. So in order to gain traction within these various professional communities, I reached out and encouraged those individuals whom I had marked as most likely to be prospective Disciples for *Second That Emotion,* and either bought them a copy of the book or badgered them to do so—with the intent that they'd establish a social contract and start spreading the word organically—and with a passion that would register with the Congregation.

Unlike some authors who have a preexisting following, I was relatively unknown within the broader business community, let alone among consumers. So the focus of our PR and e-mail effort was to begin to build my profile as the Chief Disciple of *Second That Emotion,* through strategic public appearances, interviews, and media events—and by leveraging my own contacts and the early-enlisted Disciples to introduce me to their professional and personal networks. We also went back and forth to ensure that the book had powerful graphic symbolism in the form of an encapsulating logo, featured both on the front cover and on my website, JeremyDHolden.com, as well as on every available physical and digital forum where the book could potentially be discussed. Endorsements from fellow authors, business leaders, educators, political figures, and thinkers were sought and included, in order to give prospective Disciples a feeling of certainty that the book had the potential to create a culture shift.

The illogical leap that I wanted Disciples, and ultimately the Congregation, to take was that someone who hadn't previously been published, and who wasn't a recognized expert in relation to either history or politics, was the best person to write a book that wrapped these subjects together with pop culture, business, and brand marketing, where I *was* considered an expert. We needed to make Disciples feel that I was *Second That Emotion*'s greatest asset for the very reason that I was the "ultimate generalist," and that only a Chief Disciple with my background and breadth of experiences could pull this strange literary cocktail together. And of course the timing needed to be perfect, and we needed a healthy dose of self-generated luck in order for *Second That Emotion* to gain momentum. Launching in September 2012, just as most people were engaged in the presidential election, and having many of the political and commercial topics included in the book being talked about, worked strongly in our favor.

And although *Second That Emotion* is off to a good start, whether it ultimately rises to the level of a culture shift remains to be seen and largely depends on whether we manage to avoid creating a breach in the social contract, either in promoting the book, or with a potential sequel or related spinoff. But the fact that you are reading it and have enjoyed *Second That Emotion,* and hopefully plan to tell your network about it, is evidence perhaps that the essential premise does make logical sense—remembering of course that "logic is the beginning of wisdom, not the end."

ACKNOWLEDGMENTS

David Baldwin, Mark Barden, Adrian Ho, Patrick Howie, Chris Grams, Keith Grossman, Ted Manger, Tom Richards, Domenico Vitale, and Jim Whitehurst. For your insights and kind endorsements after reading an advance draft of the book.

Stephen Berkov, Rod Brown, Walt Barron, Erin Bredemann, Jonathan Cude, Dave Cook, Matt Fischvogt, Doug Holroyd, Jason Musante, Lee Newman, Christin Prince, Jim Russell, and Chris Walsh. For leading the charge on the "Heist" journey.

Hilary Boys, Mike Branson, Fiona Gilmore, and Michael Peters. For giving me my start in the design industry and teaching me an enormous amount about the business.

Patty Briguglio and Janice Snook. For all your help in generating publicity for the book.

Dave Bryant. For introducing me to NLP as well as numerous projective research and planning techniques.

Denis Budniewski. For being my automotive and financial expert and advisor, as well as my partner on the Audi and NASDAQ experiences.

Daanesh Chanduwadia and Cameron McNaughton. For being my automotive experts, advising on Hyundai and various other automotive examples.

Andrew Delbridge. For being my strategy partner for a decade and so often helping to make my ideas bigger and better.

Dr. Bob Deutsch. For generously allowing me to quote from your inspiring work, and for your insight after reading an advance draft of the book.

Nora Fritz. For your great assistance in pulling the notes section together.

Susan Gianinno, Rob Feakins, Brian Skahan, Robin Koval, Linda Kaplan, Tricia Kenney, our strategy community, and everyone at Publicis Kaplan Thaler. For your great assistance with the marketing and promotion of the book.

Kevin Grealey, Janet Mehl, and Lisa Shearin. For your great assistance with proofing and copy proofing, refining the notes section, and dealing with my "englishisms."

Bill Goodenough, Phillip Lauder, Richard Williams, and Keith Young. For teaching me everything I needed to know about the pan-European design business.

(The late) Dee Holden. For sharing a love of writing with me and for everything else, Mum. (The late) Pat Holden for the many life lessons and investing in my education. Also my sisters, Kay Knight, Gill Holden-Rea, and Penny Holden, along with my ex-wife, Manda Holden, for all the ideas you imparted both knowingly and unknowingly.

John Jacobs (and his team at NASDAQ). For allowing me to reference the NASDAQ experiences, and for your insights and kind endorsement after reading an advance draft of the book. Also in loving memory of the irreplaceable Kate Stonehouse, a deeply missed friend and colleague.

Jeff Jones. For kindly endorsing the book as well as my use of the McKinney experiences.

Everyone at McKinney (past and present). For all those conscious and unconscious thoughts that you put in my head that found their way into this book.

Mac Merrell and Gary Knutson. For giving me my start in advertising in the United States. Also in memory of Bruce Hall, a sadly missed friend and colleague.

Steven L. Mitchell and his team at Prometheus Books. For stewarding me through the final phases of editing toward the book launch.

Meryl Moss. For being my trusted publicist.

Johan de Nysschen. For allowing me to reference the Audi experiences, and for your insights and generous endorsement after reading an advance draft of the book.

Monty and Virginia Parker. For being the world's most enthusiastic readers and listeners.

Natalie Perkins. For letting me access Clean Design's many talents and simply being you, my love.

Dr. Chester Phillips. For being my medical advisor and racquetball torturer.

Linda Regan. For championing the book initially within Prometheus Books.

Tanya Russell. For working around me and tolerating my spontaneous outbursts of singing.

Scott Scaggs. For helping to source the images for the book and for the initial *Second That Emotion* "ribbon design."

Cynthia Zigmund. For being my trusted literary agent and making this book possible.

NOTES

CHAPTER 1: THE ROLE OF SOCIAL CONTRACTS

1. Pew Research Center, "31% - Republicans Believe Obama Is a Muslim," The Data Bank, July 21–August 5, 2010, http://pewresearch.org/databank/dailynumber/?NumberID=1078 (accessed June 15, 2011).

2. Ed Henry and Ed Hornick, "Rage Rising on the McCain Campaign Trail," CNN Politics, October 10, 2008, http://articles.cnn.com/2008-10-10/politics/mccain.crowd_1_mccain-palin-mccain-campaign-obama-presidency?_s=PM:POLITICS (accessed June 15, 2011).

3. "Carlson Attempted to Downplay Republican Attacks on Cleland," Media Matters for America, July 30, 2004, http://mediamatters.org/research/200407300007 (accessed June 15, 2011).

4. Peter Baker and John F. Harris, "Clinton Admits to Lewinsky Relationship, Challenges Starr to End Personal 'Prying,'" WashingtonPost.com, August 18, 1998, http://www.washingtonpost.com/wpsrv/politics/special/clinton/stories/clinton081898.htm (accessed June 15, 2011).

5. "The Clinton Presidency—In Quotes," BBC News, http://news.bbc.co.uk/2/hi/americas/1114491.stm (accessed July 6, 2012).

6. Rhonda Schwartz, Brian Ross, Chris Francescani, "Edwards Admits Sexual Affair; Lied as Presidential Candidate," *Nightline*, ABC News, August 8, 2008, http://abcnews.go.com/Blotter/story?id=5441195 (accessed June 16, 2011).

7. "1979: Election Victory for Margaret Thatcher," On This Day, BBC News, May 4, http://news.bbc.co.uk/onthisday/hi/dates/stories/may/4/newsid_2503000/2503195.stm (accessed June 16, 2011).

8. "Margaret Thatcher," BBC History, 2012, http://www.bbc.co.uk/history/historic_figures/thatcher_margaret.shtml (accessed June 16, 2011).

9. James Moher, "The Winter of Discontent: What Can We Learn from History?" *BBC History Magazine*, 2011, http://www.historyextra.com/feature/winter-discontent-what-can-we-learn-history (accessed June 16, 2011).

10. Jennifer Rosenberg, "History Quotes: A Collection of History Quotes of the Week," About.com, http://history1900s.about.com/od/people/a/History-Quotes.htm (accessed July 6, 2012).

11. Mark Davies, "Thatcher's Famous Speeches," BBC News, March 22, 2002, http://news.bbc.co.uk/2/hi/1888158.stm (accessed June 16, 2011).

12. "Heseltine: Political CV," BBC News, April 27, 2000, http://news.bbc .co.uk/2/hi/uk_news/politics/727824.stm (accessed June 16, 2011).

13. *Wikipedia*, s.v. "United Kingdom general election, 1992," http://en .wikipedia.org/wiki/United_Kingdom_general_election,_1992 (accessed June 16, 2011).

14. "1997: Labor Routs Tories in Historic Election," On This Day, BBC News, May 2, http://news.bbc.co.uk/onthisday/hi/dates/stories/may/2/newsid _2480000/2480505.stm (accessed June 16, 2011).

15. William Horsley, "Fifty Years of Fraternal Rivalry," BBC News, March 19, 2007, http://news.bbc.co.uk/2/hi/europe/6453889.stm (accessed June 16, 2011).

16. *Wikipedia*, s.v. "Margaret Thatcher," http://en.wikipedia.org/wiki/ Margaret_Thatcher (accessed June 16, 2011).

17. *Wikipedia*, s.v. "Julius Caesar," http://en.wikipedia.org/wiki/Julius_Caesar (accessed June 16, 2011).

18. *Wikipedia*, s.v. "Second Triumvirate," http://en.wikipedia.org/wiki/ Second_Triumvirate (accessed June 16, 2011).

19. Henry Abbott et al., "Summer Forecast: Where Will LeBron Be in 2010– 11?" NBA, ESPN, September 16, 2008, http://sports.espn.go.com/nba/news/ story?page=LeBronFuture-080916 (accessed June 16, 2011).

20. *Wikipedia*, s.v. "Robert Downey, Jr.," http://en.wikipedia.org/wiki/Robert _Downey,_Jr. (accessed June 16, 2011).

21. "Robert Downey Jr: Actor's Toughest Role," People in the News, CNN .com, http://www.cnn.com/CNN/Programs/people/shows/downey/profile.html (accessed July 6, 2012).

22. Ibid.

23. *Wikipedia*, s.v. "Dove Campaign for Real Beauty," http://en.wikipedia.org/ wiki/Dove_Campaign_for_Real_Beauty (accessed June 16, 2011).

24. Dove, http://www.dove.us/ (accessed June 16, 2011).

25. Unilever, "Our Brands," http://www.unilever.com/brands/ (accessed June 16, 2011).

26. Alisa Priddle, "2009 Hyundai Genesis Sedan," Auto Shows, *Car and Driver*, January 2008, http://www.caranddriver.com/news/car/08q1/2009_hyundai _genesis_sedan-auto_shows (accessed June 16, 2011).

27. Warren Brown, "Hyundai's Mission Possible: Beat the Luxury Brands," WashingtonPost.com, April 1, 2007, http://www.washingtonpost.com/wp-dyn/ content/article/2007/03/29/AR2007032901431.html (accessed June 16, 2011).

28. Phil LeBeau, "Hyundai's Latest Assurance Program Could Be Trouble for

Competitors," CNBC.com, April 25, 2011, http://www.cnbc.com/id/42748675/
Hyundai_s_Latest_Assurance_Program_Could_Be_Trouble_for_Competitors
(accessed June 16, 2011).

29. Michele Norris, "A Year after Program, under 100 Hyundais Returned," NPR,
January 8, 2010, http://www.npr.org/templates/story/story.php?storyId=122372379
(accessed June 16, 2011).

30. This quotation originally appeared in *E. W. Howe's Monthly*, which was in
publication from 1911 to 1937. "Edgar Watson Howe Quotes," ThinkExist.com,
http://en.thinkexist.com/quotes/edgar_watson_howe/ (accessed June 16, 2011).

CHAPTER 2: PLAYERS IN A MOVEMENT

1. Ernesto Londoño, "Egyptian Man's Death Became Symbol of Callous
State," *Washington Post*, February 8, 2011, http://www.washingtonpost.com/wp-dyn/
content/article/2011/02/08/AR2011020806421.html?nav=emailpage (accessed
June 8, 2012).

2. Mark Memmott, "ElBaradei: Mubarak 'Should Leave Today,'" NPR,
January 30, 2011, http://www.npr.org/blogs/thetwo-way/2011/01/30/133348846/
elbaradei-mubarak-should-leave-today (accessed June 19, 2011).

3. "Mubarak Defies Egypt Uprising; Protest Rages On," CBS News, February
2, 2011, http://www.cbsnews.com/stories/2011/02/02/world/main7308454.shtml
(accessed June 19, 2011).

4. The Blair Witch Project, http://www.blairwitch.com/home.html (accessed
June 19, 2011).

5. *Wikipedia*, s.v. "*The Blair Witch Project*," http://en.wikipedia.org/wiki/The
_Blair_Witch_Project (June 19, 2011).

6. *Wikipedia*, s.v. "*The Last Broadcast* (film)," http://en.wikipedia.org/wiki/
The_Last_Broadcast_(film) (accessed June 19, 2011).

7. *Wikipedia*, s.v. "*Cannibal Holocaust*," http://en.wikipedia.org/wiki/
Cannibal_Holocaust (accessed June 19, 2011).

8. *Wikipedia*, s.v. "The Art of the Heist," http://en.wikipedia.org/wiki/The
_Art_of_the_Heist (accessed June 19, 2011).

9. *Wikipedia*, s.v. "Ron Paul," http://en.wikipedia.org/wiki/Ron_Paul (accessed
June 19, 2011). See also Congressman Ron Paul, http://paul.house.gov/index
.php?option=com_content&task=view&id=1806&Itemid=28 (accessed June 10, 2012).

10. "Official Results from Iowa Straw Poll," CNN Politics, August 12, 2007,
http://politicalticker.blogs.cnn.com/2007/08/12/official-results-from-iowa-straw
-poll/ (accessed June 21, 2011).

11. "Ron Paul's Election Results," RonPaul.com, November 5, 2008, http://en.wikipedia.org/wiki/Ron_Paul_presidential_campaign,_2008 (accessed June 21, 2011).

12. "Curtains for Ron Paul's Web Crusade?" *The Paulite Food Blog*, January 11, 2008, http://paulitefood.blogspot.com/ (accessed June 21, 2011). See following footnote.

13. Andy Greenberg, "Curtains for Ron Paul's Web Crusade," *Forbes*, January 11, 2008, http://www.forbes.com/2008/01/11/ron-paul-vote-tech-ebiz-cx_ag_0111 ronpaul.html (accessed June 10, 2012).

14. Jack Cafferty, "Ron Paul's 'Money Bomb'?" *The Cafferty File*, CNN, December 17, 2007, http://caffertyfile.blogs.cnn.com/2007/12/17/ron-paul's-"money-bomb"/ (accessed June 21, 2011).

15. Kevin Patterson, "Talk to Me Like My Father: Frontline Medicine in Afghanistan," *Mother Jones*, July/August 2007, http://www.motherjones.com/politics/2007/06/talk-me-my-father-frontline-medicine-afghanistan (accessed July 6, 2012).

16. *Wikipedia*, s.v. "Julian Assange," http://en.wikipedia.org/wiki/Julian_Assange (accessed June 21, 2011).

17. Paul Armstrong, "Are WikiLeaks Revelations Really Damaging for U.S.?" CNN, December 1, 2010, http://articles.cnn.com/2010-12-01/world/wikileaks.reaction_1_nuclear-program-wikileaks-military-personnel?_s=PM:WORLD (accessed June 21, 2011).

18. Susan Schmidt and James V. Grimaldi, "Abramoff Pleads Guilty to 3 Counts," WashingtonPost.com, January 4, 2006, http://www.washingtonpost.com/wp-dyn/content/article/2006/01/03/AR2006010300474.html (accessed June 21, 2011).

19. *Wikipedia*, s.v. "Casino Jack," http://en.wikipedia.org/wiki/Casino_Jack (accessed June 21, 2011).

20. Empowerment Partnership, "What Is NLP?" http://www.nlp.com/whatisnlp.php (accessed June 21, 2011).

21. David Walton, "Books in Brief: Nonfiction: Franklin and Winston," *New York Times*, January 4, 2004, http://www.nytimes.com/2004/01/04/books/books-in-brief-nonfiction-715530.html (accessed June 21, 2011).

22. *Wikipedia*, s.v. "*The Gathering Storm* (2002 film)," http://en.wikipedia.org/wiki/The_Gathering_Storm_(2002_film) (accessed June 21, 2011).

23. *Wikipedia*, s.v. "Into the Storm (film)," http://en.wikipedia.org/wiki/Into_the_Storm_(film) (accessed June 21, 2011).

24. Ollie Stone-Lee, "The Wartime Battle for Welfare?" BBC News, July 25, 2005, http://news.bbc.co.uk/2/hi/uk_news/politics/4713041.stm (accessed June 21, 2011).

25. Paul Reynolds, "Yalta Casts Its Shadow 60 Years On," BBC News, February 7, 2005, http://news.bbc.co.uk/2/hi/europe/4241863.stm (accessed June 21, 2011).

26. *Wikipedia*, s.v. "*My Life* (Bill Clinton autobiography)," http://en.wikipedia.org/wiki/My_Life_(Bill_Clinton_autobiography) (accessed June 21, 2011).

CHAPTER 3: I FOLLOW THE LEADER. HE FOLLOWS ME.

1. *Wikipedia*, s.v. "Caligula," http://en.wikipedia.org/wiki/Caligula (accessed June 23, 2011).

2. *Wikipedia*, s.v. "Battle of Actium," http://en.wikipedia.org/wiki/Battle_of_Actium (accessed June 23, 2011).

3. *Wikipedia*, s.v. "*I, Claudius*," http://en.wikipedia.org/wiki/I,_Claudius (accessed June 23, 2011).

4. Nick Bryant, "Elizabethan Holiday," BBC News, June 8, 2008, http://www.bbc.co.uk/blogs/thereporters/nickbryant/2008/06/elizabethan_holiday.html (accessed June 23, 2011).

5. "Prince William and Kate Middleton Reveal Wedding Plans," BBC News, January 11, 2011, http://www.bbc.co.uk/news/uk-12120099 (accessed June 23, 2011).

6. "22 November 1990: 'I'm Enjoying This!'" BBC News, updated August 26, 2009, http://news.bbc.co.uk/democracylive/hi/historic_moments/newsid_8190000/8190652.stm (accessed June 23, 2011).

7. *Wikipedia*, s.v. "Social Democratic Party (UK)," http://en.wikipedia.org/wiki/Social_Democratic_Party_(UK) (accessed June 23, 2011).

8. "SDP: Breaking the Mould," BBC News, January 25, 2011, http://news.bbc.co.uk/2/hi/uk_news/politics/1136223.stm (accessed June 23, 2011).

9. *Wikipedia*, s.v. "Nelson Mandela, Imprisonment," http://en.wikipedia.org/wiki/Nelson_Mandela#Imprisonment (accessed June 23, 2011).

10. *Wikipedia*, s.v. "*Cry Freedom*," http://en.wikipedia.org/wiki/Cry_Freedom (accessed June 23, 2011).

11. "Nobel Peace Prize 1993: Nelson Mandela Biography," NobelPrize.org, http://nobelprize.org/nobel_prizes/peace/laureates/1993/mandela-bio.html (accessed June 23, 2011).

12. Brian Montopoli and Robert Hendin, "What Is the Tea Party Movement?" CBS News, September 15, 2010, http://www.cbsnews.com/8301-503544_162-20016540-503544.html (accessed June 23, 2011).

13. Kate Milner, "Flashback 1984: Portrait of a Famine," BBC News, April 6, 2000, http://news.bbc.co.uk/2/hi/africa/703958.stm (accessed June 23, 2011).

14. "Number of Hungry People Worldwide Nears 1 Billion Mark, UN Agency Reports," UN News Centre, December 9, 2008, http://www.un.org/apps/news/story.asp?NewsID=29231 (accessed June 23, 2011).

15. *Wikipedia*, s.v. "Bob Geldof," http://en.wikipedia.org/wiki/Bob_Geldof (accessed June 23, 2011).

16. James Robinson, "BBC Marks 25th Anniversary of Live Aid with Bob Geldolf Drama," BBC News, July 14, 2010, http://www.guardian.co.uk/world/2010/jul/14/bob-geldof-live-aid-bbc2 (accessed June 23, 2011).

17. Richard Esposito et al., "IMF Chief Dominique Strauss-Kahn Charged with Rape, Sexual Abuse, Unlawful Imprisonment," ABC News, May 16, 2011, http://abcnews.go.com/International/imf-chief-dominique-strauss-kahn-charged-rape-sexual/story?id=13609991 (accessed June 23, 2011).

18. Liz Alderman and Katrin Bennhold, "A Favorite Emerges for Helm of IMF," *New York Times*, May 18, 2011, http://www.nytimes.com/2011/05/19/world/europe/19iht-profile.html (accessed June 23, 2011).

19. Aaron Smith, "Steve Jobs' Departure Pushes Apple Stock Down 2.25%," CNNMoney.com, January 18, 2011, http://money.cnn.com/2011/01/18/technology/apple_jobs/index.htm (accessed June 23, 2011).

20. Beth Bacheldor and Martin J. Garvey, "HP Reinvented," InformationWeek .com, May 13, 2002, http://www.informationweek.com/news/6502433 (accessed June 23, 2011).

21. "Jerry & Bill's Shoe Business," *Los Angeles Times*, September 8, 2008, http://articles.latimes.com/2008/sep/08/entertainment/et-webscout8 (accessed June 23, 2011).

22. *Wikipedia*, s.v. "Napster," http://en.wikipedia.org/wiki/Napster (accessed June 23, 2011).

23. *Wikipedia*, s.v. "*The Social Network*," http://en.wikipedia.org/wiki/The _Social_Network (accessed June 23, 2011).

24. *Wikipedia*, s.v. "*A&M Records, Inc. v. Napster, Inc.*," http://en.wikipedia.org/wiki/A%26M_Records,_Inc._v._Napster,_Inc. (accessed June 23, 2011).

25. Michael Simon, "The Complete iTunes History- SoundJam MP to iTunes 9," Mac Life, September 11, 2009, http://www.maclife.com/article/feature/the _complete_itunes_history?page=0%2C2 (accessed June 23, 2011).

26. "NASDAQ Selects Ad Agency McKinney & Silver," NASDAQ.com, August 7, 2001, http://www.nasdaq.com/Newsroom/news/pr2001/ne_section01_231.html (accessed June 23, 2011).

27. Nina Mehta, "Justice Department Saw Multiple Monopolies in NYSE–NASDAQ Deal," *Bloomberg Businessweek*, May 18, 2011, http://www.businessweek.com/news/2011-05-18/justice-department-saw-multiple-monopolies -in-nyse-nasdaq-deal.html (accessed June 23, 2011).

28. Sue Stock, "Researchers: CEO Voices Can Predict Company Performance,"

NewsObserver.com, March 2, 2011, http://www.newsobserver.com/2011/03/02/v-print/1023052/stock-tips-in-ceo-voices.html (accessed June 23, 2011).

29. John Mackey, "Winning the Battle for Freedom and Prosperity," WholeFoodsMarket.com, February 27, 2006, http://www2.wholefoodsmarket.com/blogs/jmackey/2006/02/27/winning-the-battle-for-freedom-and-prosperity/ (accessed June 23, 2011).

30. *Wikipedia*, s.v. "Patagonia (clothing)," http://en.wikipedia.org/wiki/Patagonia_(clothing) (accessed June 23, 2011).

31. *Wikipedia*, s.v. "Red Hat," http://en.wikipedia.org/wiki/Red_Hat (accessed June 23, 2011).

32. "RedHat Reports Second Quarter Results," RedHat.com, September 22, 2010, http://www.redhat.com/about/news/press-archive/2010/9/q2-2011 (accessed June 11, 2012).

33. "Jim Whitehurst: President and Chief Executive Officer," RedHat.com, 2011, http://www.redhat.com/about/companyprofile/management/whitehurst.html (accessed June 23, 2011).

CHAPTER 4: THE PSYCHOLOGY OF ILLOGICAL LEAPS

1. "Meet Dr. Bob," http://www.brain-sells.com/?p=1 (accessed July 7, 2011).

2. "Interview with Father and Stepmother of Serial Killer Jeffrey Dahmer," Transcripts, CNN, June 17, 2004, http://transcripts.cnn.com/TRANSCRIPTS/0406/17/lkl.00.html (accessed July 7, 2011).

3. Rita Healy, "The Columbine Papers: What Their Parents Knew," *Time*, July 6, 2006, http://www.time.com/time/nation/article/0,8599,1211059,00.html (accessed July 7, 2011).

4. "Is Norway Gunman the Missing Link of the Mysterious Knights Templar?" July 25, 2011, http://www.ibtimes.com/articles/186077/20110725/is-norway-gunman-the-missing-link-of-mysterious-order-temple-knights-templars-oslo-utoya-youth-camp.htm (accessed November 1, 2011).

5. *Wikipedia*, s.v. "Brad Pitt," http://en.wikipedia.org/wiki/Brad_Pitt (accessed July 7, 2011).

6. *Wikipedia*, s.v. "Jennifer Aniston," http://en.wikipedia.org/wiki/Jennifer_Aniston (accessed July 7, 2011).

7. *Wikipedia*, s.v. "Angelina Jolie," http://en.wikipedia.org/wiki/Angelina_Jolie (accessed July 7, 2011).

8. *Wikipedia*, s.v. "Tom Cruise," http://en.wikipedia.org/wiki/Tom_Cruise (accessed July 7, 2011).

9. "In Tense Moment, Cruise Calls Lauer 'Glib,'" *Today*, MSNBC.com, June 28, 2005, http://today.msnbc.msn.com/id/8344309/ns/today-entertainment/t/tense -moment-cruise-calls-lauer-glib/ (accessed July 7, 2011).

10. "Paul McCartney," Rock and Roll Hall of Fame, 1999, http://rockhall .com/inductees/paul-mccartney/ (accessed July 7, 2011).

11. *Wikipedia*, s.v. "Dudley Moore," http://en.wikipedia.org/wiki/Dudley _Moore (accessed July 7, 2011).

12. *Wikipedia*, s.v. "Hugh Laurie," http://en.wikipedia.org/wiki/Hugh_Laurie (accessed July 7, 2011).

13. *Wikipedia*, s.v. "*Wilde* (film)," http://en.wikipedia.org/wiki/Wilde_%28 film%29 (accessed July 7, 2011).

14. *Wikipedia*, s.v. "*Paperweight* (book)," http://en.wikipedia.org/wiki/ Paperweight_%28book%29 (accessed July 6, 2012).

15. *Wikipedia*, s.v. "Annie Lennox," http://en.wikipedia.org/wiki/Annie _Lennox (accessed July 7, 2011).

16. *Wikipedia*, s.v. "*Unlawful Killing* (film)," http://en.wikipedia.org/wiki/ Unlawful_Killing_%28film%29 (accessed July 7, 2011).

17. *Wikipedia*, s.v. "Yoko Ono," http://en.wikipedia.org/wiki/Yoko_Ono (accessed July 7, 2011).

18. "The War in Afghanistan: A Timeline," CBS News, December 1, 2009, http://www.cbsnews.com/stories/2009/12/01/ap/government/main5850224 .shtml (accessed July 7, 2011).

19. Sarah Kessler, "Starting a New Year's Resolution? Gympact Makes You Keep It or Pay," Tech, *Mashable*, http://mashable.com/2012/01/01/gympact-keep-it-or -pay/ (accessed July 6, 2012).

CHAPTER 5: SOCIAL MEDIA'S EMOTION BEACON

1. "Bing Search Overload Syndrome—Supermarket," YouTube video, 0:31, from a commercial for Bing, posted by "loganful100," February 2, 2011, http:// www.youtube.com/watch?v=1MDAY0ZLKfs (accessed July 12, 2011).

2. Louise Story, "Anywhere the Eye Can See, It's Likely to See an Ad," *New York Times*, January 15, 2007, http://www.nytimes.com/2007/01/15/business/ media/15everywhere.html?pagewanted=1 (accessed July 12, 2011).

3. Erin McCarthy, "The Science of *Limitless*: Fact vs. Fiction," PopularMechanics. com, March 18, 2011, http://www.popularmechanics.com/technology/digital/fact -vs-fiction/the-science-of-limitless-fact-vs-fiction (accessed July 12, 2011).

4. Sarah Dingle, "The Revolution Is Just a Tweet Away," *The 7:30 Report*,

ABC [Australian Broadcasting Company], September 2, 2011, http://www.abc.net .au/7.30/content/2011/s3134593.htm (accessed July 12, 2011).

5. Arden Farhi, "Osama bin Laden Dead, Ground Zero Celebrates," CBS News, May 2, 2011, http://www.cbsnews.com/stories/2011/05/01/national/main 20058786.shtml (accessed July 12, 2011).

6. Pablo Andreu, "'I'm on a Motherf**king Space Shuttle,' Tweets Captain Kelly," *Huffington Post*, May 16, 2011, http://www.huffingtonpost.com/pablo -andreu/im-on-a-motherfking-space_b_862550.html (accessed July 12, 2011).

7. "Howard Dean Profile," CNBC TV Profiles, CNBC.com, 2011, http://www .cnbc.com/id/30264284 (accessed July 12, 2011).

8. "Candidates/Howard Dean," CNN, 2004, http://www.cnn.com/ ELECTION/2004/special/president/candidates/dean.html (accessed July 12, 2011).

9. Joel Roberts, "Howard Dean's Internet Love-In," CBS News, February 11, 2009, http://www.cbsnews.com/stories/2003/06/04/politics/main557004.shtml (accessed July 12, 2011).

10. "They Did What, Said What?" *USA Today*, May 7, 2007, http://www.usa today.com/news/top25-meltdowns.htm (accessed July 12, 2011).

11. Blake Morrison, *USA Today*, Campaign 2004, "Dean Scream Gaining Cult-like Status on Web," January 21, 2004, http://www.usatoday.com/news/politics elections/nation/2004-01-22-dean-usat_x.htm (accessed July 12, 2011).

12. Claire Cain Miller, "How Obama's Internet Campaign Changed Politics," *New York Times*, November 7, 2008, http://bits.blogs.nytimes.com/2008/11/07/ how-obamas-internet-campaign-changed-politics/ (accessed July 12, 2011).

13. "Tina Sinatra: Mob Ties Aided JFK," *60 Minutes*, CBS News, February 11, 2009, http://www.cbsnews.com/stories/2000/10/05/60minutes/main238980.shtml (accessed July 12, 2011).

14. "Interview Transcript: Rep. Gary Condit," ABC News, August 23, 2001, http://abcnews.go.com/Primetime/story?id=131905&page=1 (accessed July 12, 2011).

15. "Complaint against Congressman Gary A. Condit (D) of California," JudicialWatch.org, July 10, 2001, http://www.judicialwatch.org/cases/64/Condit HouseComplaint.htm (accessed July 12, 2011).

16. *Wikipedia*, s.v. "Chandra Levy," http://en.wikipedia.org/wiki/Chandra _Levy (accessed July 12, 2011).

17. Dana Blanton, "FOX News/Opinion Dynamics Poll: Condit Constituents Split Their Judgment," FOX News, July 23, 2001, http://www.foxnews.com/ story/0,2933,30258,00.html (accessed July 12, 2011).

18. "Condit Loses in California Primary," Inside Politics, CNN.com, March

6, 2002, http://edition.cnn.com/2002/ALLPOLITICS/03/06/condit.election/index.html (accessed July 12, 2011).

19. Kevin Hayes, "Chandra Levy Murder: Ingmar Guandique Sentenced to 60 Years in Prison," CBS News, February 11, 2011, http://www.cbsnews.com/8301 -504083_162-20031530-504083.html (accessed July 12, 2011).

20. "Marc Dutroux: Belgium to Free Ex-wife Michelle Martin," BBC News, May 10, 2011, http://www.bbc.co.uk/news/world-europe-13344408 (accessed July 12, 2011).

21. *Wikipedia*, s.v. "Zicam," http://en.wikipedia.org/wiki/Zicam (accessed July 12, 2011).

22. Gardiner Harris, "F.D.A. Warns against Use of Popular Cold Remedy," *New York Times*, June 16, 2009, http://www.nytimes.com/2009/06/17/health/policy/17nasal.html (accessed July 12, 2011).

23. Christina Warren, "'Toy Story 3' Builds Online Buzz with 1980s-Inspired Commercials," Mashable.com, April 27, 2010, http://mashable.com/2010/04/27/toy-story-3-viral-video/ (accessed July 12, 2011).

24. Willis Wee, "Apple iAd to Revolutionize Mobile Advertising," *Tech in Asia*, April 9, 2010, http://www.penn-olson.com/2010/04/09/apple-iad-to-revolutionize -mobile-advertising/ (accessed July 12, 2011).

25. "Toy Story 3 Becomes Highest-Grossing Animated Film of All Time," *New York Post*, August 13, 2010, http://www.nypost.com/p/entertainment/movies/toy_ story_becomes_highest_grossing_L2rznj6TjhDph2aOycDTYN (accessed July 12, 2011).

26. Pepsi, http://www.pepsi.com/ (accessed July 10, 2012).

27. "Diet Coke Passes Pepsi to Become No. 2 Soda in US," CBS News, March 17, 2011, http://www.cbsnews.com/stories/2011/03/17/business/main20044412. shtml (accessed July 12, 2011).

28. Dale Buss, "Is Pepsi Refresh Distracting PepsiCo from the Cola Wars?" March 17, 2011, http://www.brandchannel.com/home/post/2011/03/17/Cola -Wars.aspx (accessed July 12, 2011).

29. "Social Media's Massive Failure," *Ad Contrarian*, March 21, 2011, http://adcontrarian.blogspot.com/2011/03/social-medias-massive-failure.html (accessed July 12, 2011).

30. Matthew Ingram, "Facebook Ranks below Airline Industry in Customer Satisfaction," Gigaom.com, July 20, 2010, http://gigaom.com/2010/07/20/facebook-ranks-below-airline-industry-in-customer-satisfaction/ (accessed July 12, 2011).

31. "Zeitgeist 2010: How the World Searched," Google Zeitgeist, http://www .google.com/intl/en/press/zeitgeist2010/ (accessed July 12, 2011).

32. BrainJuicer, http://www.brainjuicer.com/ (accessed July 12, 2011).

33. Evernote, http://www.evernote.com/ (accessed July 12, 2011).

34. foursquare, https://foursquare.com/ (accessed July 12, 2011).

35. WeePlaces, http://www.weeplaces.com/ (accessed July 12, 2011).

36. Ning, http://get.ning.com/social-website?&keyword=.ning&creative =6657528298&matchtype=b&source=1&network=g&placement=&keywordID ={keywordID}&m_campaign=brand&m_source=google&m_medium=search&m _content=brand&m_matchtype=b&m_term=.ning&gclid=CKmogc3G_KkCFct95Q od3RPhaQ (accessed July 12, 2011); Facebook, http://www.facebook.com (accessed July 12, 2011).

37. Delicious, http://www.delicious.com/ (accessed July 12, 2011); Instapaper, http://www.instapaper.com/ (accessed July 12, 2011).

CHAPTER 6: THE SANCTUARY OF CERTAINTY

1. Ollie Williams, "Where the Premier League's Players Come From," BBC Sport, August 13, 2009, http://news.bbc.co.uk/sport2/hi/football/eng_prem/ 8182090.stm (accessed July 14, 2011).

2. "Manchester United Fixtures," BBC Sport, 2011, http://news.bbc.co.uk/ sport2/hi/football/teams/m/man_utd/fixtures/default.stm (accessed July 14, 2011).

3. *Wikipedia*, s.v. "Leeds United A.F.C. and Manchester United F.C. rivalry," http://en.wikipedia.org/wiki/Leeds_United_A.F.C._and_Manchester_United _F.C._rivalry (accessed July 14, 2011).

4. "Barcelona Wins 2011 Champions League Final 3–1," CBS News Sports, May 28, 2011, http://www.cbsnews.com/stories/2011/05/28/sportsline/main200 67086.shtml (accessed July 14, 2011).

5. Mike Ozanian, "Manchester United Again the World's Most Valuable Soccer Team," *Forbes*, April 18, 2012, http://www.forbes.com/sites/mikeozanian/ 2012/04/18/manchester-united-again-the-worlds-most-valuable-soccer-team/ (accessed June 14, 2012).

6. "Kenyan Man Commits Suicide over Arsenal Loss," ClickAfrique.com, May 6, 2009, http://www.clickafrique.com/Magazine/ST010/CP0000003462.aspx (accessed July 14, 2011).

7. "Moment of Silence to be Observed at Duke Game," TarHeelBlue.com, March 7, 2008, http://tarheelblue.cstv.com/sports/m-baskbl/spec-rel/030708aad .html (accessed July 14, 2011).

8. *Wikipedia*, s.v. "Carolina–Duke rivalry," http://en.wikipedia.org/wiki/ Carolina%E2%80%93Duke_rivalry (accessed July 14, 2011).

9. *Wikipedia*, s.v. "New England Patriots," http://en.wikipedia.org/wiki/New _England_Patriots (accessed July 14, 2011).

10. Larry Dorman and Liz Robbins, "Woods Is Silent as Spin Takes on Life of Its Own," *New York Times*, November 28, 2009, http://www.nytimes.com/2009/11/28/ sports/golf/29woods.html (accessed June 14, 2011).

11. Sean Martin, "Q&A: 2010 PGA Champ Martin Kaymer," *Golfweek*, July 7, 2011, http://www.golfweek.com/news/2011/jul/07/q-2010-pga-champ-martin -kaymer/ (accessed July 14, 2011).

12. Johnette Howard, "Borg–McEnroe vs. Federer–Nadal," ESPN.com, June 10, 2011, http://sports.espn.go.com/espn/commentary/news/story?id=6645028 (accessed July 14, 2011).

13. "Congress to Probe BCS Antitrust Issues," ESPN.com, March 25, 2009, http://sports.espn.go.com/ncf/news/story?id=4015667 (accessed July 14, 2011).

14. Thayne Hallyburton, "Introducing the 2008 NCAA Tournament Cinderellas: The Davidson Wildcats," *Bleacher Report*, March 19, 2008, http:// bleacherreport.com/articles/13821-introducing-the-2008-ncaa-tournament -cinderellas-the-davidson-wildcats (accessed July 14, 2011).

15. Chris Leyden, "NCAA Tournament 2011: Kansas vs. VCU Preview," *Bleacher Report*, March 26, 2011, http://bleacherreport.com/articles/645962-ncaa -tournament-2011-kansas-vs-vcu (accessed July 14, 2011).

16. "The Flat-Tax Revolution," *Economist*, April 14, 2005, http://www .economist.com/node/3861190 (accessed July 14, 2011).

17. Michael Kinsley, "Steve Forbes's Flat Tire," *Washington Post*, August 7, 2005, http://www.washingtonpost.com/wp-dyn/content/article/2005/08/05/ AR2005080501490.html (accessed July 14, 2011).

18. Julie Borowski, "Congressional Leaders Call for Flat Tax," *FreedomWorks*, December 1, 2010, http://www.freedomworks.org/blog/jborowski/congressional -leaders-call-for-flat-tax (accessed July 14, 2011).

19. iPhone, http://www.apple.com/iphone/apps-for-iphone/ (accessed July 14, 2011).

20. Daniel Eran Dilger, "New 'iPad Is Iconic' Ad Touts 60,000 Apps," AppleInsider.com, January 25, 2011, http://www.appleinsider.com/articles/11/ 01/25/new_ipad_is_iconic_ad_touts_60000_apps.html (accessed July 14, 2011).

21. "Albert Einstein Quotes," BrainyQuote, http://www.brainyquote.com/ quotes/quotes/a/alberteins133991.html (accessed July 14, 2011).

22. "Angry Birds," iTunes Preview, http://itunes.apple.com/us/app/angry -birds/id343200656?mt=8 (accessed July 14, 2011).

23. Ben Rooney, "Is Angry Birds Bigger Than Mickey Mouse?" *Wall Street*

Journal, January 24, 2011, http://blogs.wsj.com/digits/2011/01/24/inflating-the
-social-games-bubble-in-europe/?mod=rss_WSJBlog&mod= (accessed July 14, 2011).

24. Ibid.

25. Tom Cheshire, "In Depth: How Rovio Made Angry Birds a Winner (and What's
Next)," Wired.co.uk, March 7, 2011, http://www.wired.co.uk/magazine/archive/2011/
04/features/how-rovio-made-angry-birds-a-winner (accessed June 14, 2012).

26. "Angelina Jolie Addicted to Angry Birds," WNC News, April 11, 2011,
http://www.worldnewsco.com/5843/angelina-jolie-addicted-to-angry-birds/
(accessed July 14, 2011).

27. *Wikipedia,* s.v. *"The Hangover Part II,"* http://en.wikipedia.org/wiki/The
_Hangover_Part_II (accessed July 14, 2011).

28. *Wikipedia,* s.v. *"Arthur* (2011 film)," http://en.wikipedia.org/wiki/
Arthur_%282011_film%29 (accessed July 14, 2011).

29. *Wikipedia,* s.v. "Classic Malts of Scotland," http://en.wikipedia.org/wiki/
Classic_Malts_of_Scotland (accessed July 14, 2011).

30. "The Six Classic Malts of Scotland," http://www.awa.dk/whisky/clasmalt
.htm (accessed July 14, 2011).

31. *Wikipedia,* s.v. *"Sideways,"* http://en.wikipedia.org/wiki/Sideways (accessed
July 14, 2011).

32. *Wikipedia,* s.v. "'The Soup Nazi,'" http://en.wikipedia.org/wiki/The
_Soup_Nazi (accessed July 14, 2011).

33. *Wikipedia,* s.v. *"Predictably Irrational,"* http://en.wikipedia.org/wiki/
Predictably_Irrational (accessed July 14, 2011).

34. Scott Mayerowitz, "Steven Slater, JetBlue Flight Attendant out on Bail,"
ABC News, August 10, 2010, http://abcnews.go.com/US/steven-slater-jetblue
-flight-attendant-bail-emergency-slide/story?id=11367793 (accessed July 15, 2011).

35. *Wikipedia,* s.v. *"The Accidental Tourist,"* http://en.wikipedia.org/wiki/The
_Accidental_Tourist (accessed July 15, 2011).

36. "Fact Sheet," Soutwest.com, http://www.southwest.com/html/about
-southwest/history/fact-sheet.html (accessed July 15, 2011).

37. "Sign of the Times: Astrology Story Soars Like a Comet," *Star Tribune,*
January 14, 2011, http://www.startribune.com/lifestyle/style/113100139.html
(accessed July 15, 2011).

38. Rob Brezsny, "Here We Go Again with the 'Zodiac Is Wrong' Scam," Free
Will Astrology, 2010, http://www.freewillastrology.com/guest_astros.html (accessed
July 15, 2011).

39. Eric Francis, "Attention All Astronomers—The World Is Flat," *Planet Waves,*
January 13, 2011, http://planetwaves.net/pagetwo/daily-astrology/your-zodiac-
sign-is-not-wrong/ (accessed July 15, 2011).

CHAPTER 7: SIGNS, SYMBOLS, AND ICONS

1. *Wikipedia*, s.v. "Legio IX Hispana," http://en.wikipedia.org/wiki/Legio _IX_Hispana (accessed July 20, 2011).

2. *Wikipedia*, s.v. "*The Eagle of the Ninth*," http://en.wikipedia.org/wiki/The_ Eagle_of_the_Ninth (accessed July 20, 2011).

3. Malcolm Jack, "What Really Happened to the Roman Ninth Legion?" *Heritage Key*, September 9, 2009, http://heritage-key.com/rome/what-really -happened-roman-ninth-legion (accessed July 20, 2011).

4. *Wikipedia*, s.v. "Massacre of the Ninth Legion," http://en.wikipedia.org/ wiki/Massacre_of_the_Ninth_Legion (accessed July 20, 2011).

5. IMDb, s.v. "*The Eagle* (2011)," http://www.imdb.com/title/tt1034389/ (accessed July 20, 2011).

6. *Wikipedia*, s.v. "Aquila (Roman)," http://en.wikipedia.org/wiki/ Aquila_%28Roman%29 (accessed July 20, 2011).

7. Peter Bowen, "What Is the Meaning of the Eagle?" Focus Features, January 11, 2011, http://www.focusfeatures.com/article/what_is_the_meaning_of_the _eagle_?film=the_eagle (accessed July 20, 2011).

8. *Wikipedia*, s.v. "Battle of the Teutoburg Forest," http://en.wikipedia.org/ wiki/Battle_of_the_Teutoburg_Forest (accessed July 20, 2011).

9. "The Bald Eagle—An American Emblem," American Bald Eagle Information, http://baldeagleinfo.com/eagle/eagle9.html (accessed July 20, 2011).

10. *Wikipedia*, s.v. "*The Name of the Rose*," http://en.wikipedia.org/wiki/The_ Name_of_the_Rose (accessed July 20, 2011).

11. *Wikipedia*, s.v. "*The Da Vinci Code* (film)," http://en.wikipedia.org/wiki/ The_Da_Vinci_Code_%28film%29 (accessed July 20, 2011).

12. IMDb, "The Name of the Rose (1986)," http://www.imdb.com/title/ tt0091605/ (accessed July 20, 2011).

13. "Deception/Lying: Umberto Eco," Quoteland.com, http://www.quote land.com/rate/Umberto-Eco-Quotes/2746/ (accessed July 20, 2011).

14. *Wikipedia*, s.v. "Swastika," http://en.wikipedia.org/wiki/Swastika (accessed July 20, 2011).

15. "Thule Society," *Crystal Links*, 2011, http://www.crystalinks.com/thule .html (accessed July 20, 2011).

16. *Wikipedia*, s.v. "*Mein Kampf*," http://en.wikipedia.org/wiki/Mein_Kampf (accessed July 20, 2011).

17. "Origins of the Swastika," BBC News, January 18, 2005, http://news.bbc .co.uk/2/hi/uk_news/magazine/4183467.stm (accessed July 20, 2011).

18. "Treaty of Versailles, 1919," United States Holocaust Memorial Museum, January 6, 2011, http://www.ushmm.org/wlc/en/article.php?ModuleId=10005425 (accessed July 20, 2011).

19. "Adolf Hitler Quotes, ThinkExist.com, http://thinkexist.com/quotation/how_fortunate_for_leaders_that_men_do_not_think/221282.html (accessed July 10, 2012).

20. Ibid.

21. *Wikipedia*, s.v. "Nazi symbolism," http://en.wikipedia.org/wiki/Nazi_symbolism (accessed July 20, 2011).

22. *Wikipedia*, s.v. "File: Three sevens.svg," http://en.wikipedia.org/wiki/File:Three_sevens.svg (accessed July 20, 2011).

23. "Harry Says Sorry for Nazi Costume," BBC News, January 13, 2005, http://news.bbc.co.uk/2/hi/4170083.stm (accessed July 20, 2011).

24. "Donkey, Democratic," BBC News, March 28, 2000, http://news.bbc.co.uk/2/hi/in_depth/americas/2000/us_elections/glossary/c-d/689655.stm (accessed July 20, 2011). "Elephant, Republican," BBC News, March 28, 2000, http://news.bbc.co.uk/2/hi/in_depth/americas/2000/us_elections/glossary/e-f/689757.stm (accessed July 20, 2011).

25. *Wikipedia*, s.v. "Thomas Nast," http://en.wikipedia.org/wiki/Thomas_Nast (accessed July 20, 2011).

26. Steven Heller, "The 'O' in Obama," *New York Times*, November 20, 2008, http://campaignstops.blogs.nytimes.com/2008/11/20/the-o-in-obama/ (accessed July 20, 2011).

27. *Wikipedia*, s.v. "Solidaryca," http://en.wikipedia.org/wiki/Solidaryca (accessed July 20, 2011).

28. *Wikipedia*, s.v. "Barack Obama 'Hope' poster," http://en.wikipedia.org/wiki/Barack_Obama_%22Hope%22_poster (accessed July 20, 2011).

29. "Jim Fitzpatrick—Update," JimFitzpatrick.com, http://www.jimfitzpatrick.ie/update/che.html (accessed July 20, 2011).

30. "South Africa Holiday: National Flag," SouthAfricaHoliday.org, 2011, http://www.southafricaholiday.org.uk/history/national_flag.htm (accessed July 25, 2011).

31. IMDb, s.v. "*Invictus* (2009)," http://www.imdb.com/title/tt1057500/ (accessed July 25, 2011).

32. Bass, http://www.bass.com/history/ (accessed July 25, 2011).

33. "Happy Birthday, Coca-Cola!" The Coca-Cola Company, May 7, 2010, http://www.thecoca-colacompany.com/presscenter/happy_birthday_coca-cola.html (accessed July 25, 2011).

34. Sofia Zoey, "FedEx Logo—History," Logo Design Maestro, February 7,

2011, http://www.logodesignmaestro.com/blog/famous-logo-designs/fedex-logo-history-at-logodesignmaestro/ (accessed July 25, 2011).

35. *Wikipedia*, s.v. "*Cast Away*," http://en.wikipedia.org/wiki/Cast_Away (accessed July 25, 2011).

36. *Wikipedia*, s.v. "Swoosh," http://en.wikipedia.org/wiki/Swoosh (accessed July 25, 2011).

37. IMDb, "*Without Limits* (1998)," http://www.imdb.com/title/tt0119934/ (accessed July 25, 2011).

38. *Wikipedia*, s.v. "*Playboy*," http://en.wikipedia.org/wiki/Playboy (accessed July 25, 2011).

39. William F. Buckley Jr., "Norman Mailer, RIP," *National Review Online*, November 14, 2007, http://www.nationalreview.com/articles/222822/norman-mailer-r-i-p/william-f-buckley-jr (accessed July 25, 2011).

40. James Rosen, "W-Hef-B: Bill Buckley, Playboy, and the Struggle for the Soul of America," Real Clear Politics, July 30, 2008, http://www.realclearpolitics.com/articles/2008/07/whefb_bill_buckley_playboy_and.html (accessed July 25, 2011).

41. Ibid.

42. Rolling Thunder, Inc., http://www.rollingthunder1.com/ (accessed July 25, 2011).

43. "Maya Lin," Art21, PBS, 2011, http://www.pbs.org/art21/artists/lin/card1.html (accessed July 25, 2011).

44. Denise Kersten Wills, "The Vietnam Memorial's History," *Washingtonian*, November 1, 2007, http://www.washingtonian.com/articles/people/the-vietnam-memorials-history/ (accessed July 25, 2011).

45. "Maya Angelou Upset over MLK Memorial Inscription," August 31, 2011, ABC News, http://abcnews.go.com/blogs/headlines/2011/08/maya-angelou-upset-over-mlk-memorial-inscription/ (accessed July 10, 2012).

46. America's Favorite Architecture, http://www.favoritearchitecture.org/afa150.php (accessed July 25, 2011).

47. *Wikipedia*, s.v. "Thomas E. Franklin," http://en.wikipedia.org/wiki/Thomas_E._Franklin (accessed July 25, 2011).

48. "Alfred North Whitehead Quotes," ThinkExist.com, http://thinkexist.com/quotation/symbolism_is_no_mere_idle_fancy_or_corrupt/163381.html (accessed July 25, 2011).

CHAPTER 8: BREAKING A SOCIAL CONTRACT CAN BE TERMINAL

1. "Beyond Petroleum," BP.com, 2011, http://www.bp.com/sectiongeneric article.do?categoryId=9028308&contentId=7019491 (accessed August 11, 2011).

2. "About the Station," BP.com, 2011, http://www.bp.com/sectiongeneric article.do?categoryId=2222&contentId=7028375 (accessed August 11, 2011).

3. "Gulf of Mexico Oil Spill," *New York Times*, April 25, 2010 (updated April 24 2012), http://topics.nytimes.com/top/reference/timestopics/subjects/o/oil _spills/gulf_of_mexico_2010/index.html (accessed August 11, 2011).

4. "Boycott BP," Facebook, http://www.facebook.com/pages/Boycott-BP/ 119101198107726 (accessed August 11, 2011).

5. "BP Spills Coffee," YouTube video, 2:49, posted by "UCBComedy," June 9, 2010, http://www.youtube.com/watch?v=2AAa0gd7ClM (accessed August 11, 2011).

6. "BP CEO Tony Hayward Apologizes for His Idiotic Statement: 'I'd Like My Life Back,'" *Business Insider*, June 2, 2010, http://www.businessinsider.com/bp -ceo-tony-hayward-apologizes-for-saying-id-like-my-life-back-2010-6 (accessed August 11, 2011).

7. Brian Vastag, "BP Makes $1 Billion Down Payment on Gulf Restoration," *Washington Post*, April 21, 2011, http://www.washingtonpost.com/national/ environment/bp-makes-1-billion-down-payment-on-gulf-restoration/2011/04/21/ AF5374KE_story.html (accessed August 11, 2011).

8. Stephanie Condon, "How Much Does BP Owe for Gulf Oil Spill?" CBS News, May 3, 2010, http://www.cbsnews.com/8301-503544_162-20004034-503544 .html (accessed August 11, 2011).

9. Jennifer A. Dlouhy, "BP Ad Talley: Nearly 100 Million," *Chron Business*, September 2, 2010, http://www.chron.com/disp/story.mpl/business/7182730 .html (accessed August 11, 2011).

10. Jeff Brady, "BP to Resume Paying Dividends to Shareholders," NPR, February 1, 2011, http://www.npr.org/2011/02/01/133415617/bp-to-resume -paying-dividends-to-shareholders (accessed August 11, 2011).

11. "Congratulations BP: You're the Worst Company in America!" Consumerist. com, April 18, 2011, http://consumerist.com/2011/04/congratulations-bp-youre -the-worst-company-in-america.html (accessed August 11, 2011).

12. *Wikipedia*, s.v. "*The Audacity of Hope*," http://en.wikipedia.org/wiki/The _Audacity_of_Hope (accessed August 11, 2011).

13. *Wikipedia*, s.v. "Neville Chamberlain," http://en.wikipedia.org/wiki/ Neville_Chamberlain (accessed August 11, 2011).

14. *Wikipedia,* s.v. "Anschluss," http://en.wikipedia.org/wiki/Anschluss (accessed August 11, 2011).

15. *Wikipedia,* s.v. "Timeline of World War II," http://en.wikipedia.org/wiki/Timeline_of_World_War_II (accessed August 11, 2011).

16. *Wikipedia,* s.v. "Sudetenland," http://en.wikipedia.org/wiki/Sudetenland (accessed August 11, 2011).

17. *Wikipedia,* s.v. "Munich Agreement," http://en.wikipedia.org/wiki/Munich_Agreement (accessed August 11, 2011).

18. IMDb, s.v. "*The King's Speech* (2010)," http://www.imdb.com/title/tt1504320/ (accessed August 11, 2011).

19. "Peter Ustinov Quotes," BainyQuote.com, http://www.brainyquote.com/quotes/quotes/p/peterustin386382.html (accessed August 11, 2011).

20. *Wikipedia,* s.v. "*Life Is Beautiful,*" http://en.wikipedia.org/wiki/Life_Is_Beautiful (accessed August 11, 2011).

21. "1994: Labour Chooses Blair," On This Day, BBC News, July 21, http://news.bbc.co.uk/onthisday/hi/dates/stories/july/21/newsid_2515000/2515825.stm (accessed August 11, 2011).

22. "1997: Labour Routs Tories in Historic Election," On This Day, BBC News, May 2, http://news.bbc.co.uk/onthisday/hi/dates/stories/may/2/newsid_2480000/2480505.stm (accessed August 11, 2011).

23. *Wikipedia,* s.v. "NATO," http://en.wikipedia.org/wiki/NATO (accessed August 11, 2011).

24. IMDb, s.v. "*The Special Relationship* (2010)," http://www.imdb.com/title/tt1117646/ (accessed August 11, 2011).

25. IMDb, s.v. "*The Queen* (2006)," http://www.imdb.com/title/tt0436697/ (accessed August 11, 2011).

26. IMDb, s.v. "*Frost/Nixon* (2008)," http://www.imdb.com/title/tt0870111/ (accessed August 11, 2011).

27. IMDb, s.v. "*The Damned United* (2009)," http://www.imdb.com/title/tt1226271/ (accessed August 11, 2011).

28. Tony Blair, *A Journey: My Political Life* (New York: Vintage Books/Random House, 2011).

29. IMDb, s.v. "*Love Actually* (2003)," http://www.imdb.com/title/tt0314331/ (accessed August 11, 2011).

30. Chris Mortensen and Adam Schefter, "Sources: NFLPA to Decertify by March 3," ESPN, February 28, 2011, http://sports.espn.go.com/nfl/news/story?id=6161468 (accessed August 15, 2011).

31. Sal Paolantonio, "Star QBs Call for Sides to Reach Deal," ESPN, July 13, 2011, http://espn.go.com/nfl/story/_/id/6765018/nfl-lockout-tom-brady-peyton-manning-drew-brees-call-deal (accessed August 15, 2011).

32. "1994 Strike Was a Low Point for Baseball," ESPN, August 10, 2004, http://sports.espn.go.com/mlb/news/story?id=1856626 (accessed August 15, 2011).

33. "NFL Lockout: NFLPA Executive Committee Approves Settlement; Hello, Football," ESPN, July 25, 2011, http://seattle.sbnation.com/seattle-seahawks/2011/2/9/1985448/nfl-lockout-cba-talks-negotiations-nflpa-union-meetings#nfl-lockout-nflpa-executive-committee-approves-settlement (accessed August 15, 2011).

34. Peter King, "Making Sense of the New CBA and How It Will Affect the Game," *Sports Illustrated*, July 25, 2011, http://sportsillustrated.cnn.com/2011/writers/peter_king/07/24/labor/index.html (accessed August 15, 2011).

35. *Wikipedia*, s.v. "*60 Minutes*," http://en.wikipedia.org/wiki/60_Minutes (accessed August 15, 2011).

36. *Wikipedia*, s.v. "Audi," http://en.wikipedia.org/wiki/Audi (accessed August 15, 2011).

37. "Recall Information," Toyota, http://www.toyota.com/recall/ (accessed August 15, 2011).

38. *Wikipedia*, s.v. "Jack in the Box," http://en.wikipedia.org/wiki/Jack_in_the_Box (accessed August 15, 2011).

39. "Netflix CEO Apologizes, Renames DVD Division Qwikster," September 19, 2011, Fox News, http://www.foxnews.com/tech/2011/09/19/netflix-splits-in-two-renames-dvd-division-qwikster/ (accessed July 10, 2012).

40. *Wikipedia*, s.v. "Leona Helmsley," http://en.wikipedia.org/wiki/Leona_Helmsley (accessed August 15, 2011).

41. *Wikipedia*, s.v. "Joyce Beber," http://en.wikipedia.org/wiki/Joyce_Beber (accessed August 15, 2011).

42. *Wikipedia*, s.v. "Hugh Grant," http://en.wikipedia.org/wiki/Hugh_Grant (accessed August 15, 2011).

43. Ibid.

44. "HBO Movies: *Too Big to Fail*," http://www.hbo.com/movies/too-big-to-fail/index.html (accessed August 15, 2011).

45. "Advocated Assail Bank Deal," CNNMoney.com, October 22, 1999, http://money.cnn.com/1999/10/22/news/bankfolo/ (accessed August 15, 2011).

46. Jen Duck et al., "U.S. Will Invest $250B to Bail Out Banks," ABC News, October 14, 2008, http://abcnews.go.com/Politics/Economy/story?id=6028477&page=1 (accessed August 15, 2011).

47. "Ally Bank 'Rufus' Commercial," YouTube video, 0:31, from a commercial for Ally Bank, posted by "amrevolutions," April 3, 2011, http://www.youtube.com/watch?v=Qe7socrbG5o (accessed August 15, 2011).

48. "Worst Company in America Elite 8: Bank of America vs. Walmart,"

Consumerist.com, April 6, 2011, http://consumerist.com/2011/04/worst -company-in-america-elite-8-bank-of-america-vs-walmart.html (accessed August 15, 2011).

49. Robert Lenzner, "Bernie Madoff's $50 Billion Ponzi Scheme," *Forbes*, December 12, 2008, http://www.forbes.com/2008/12/12/madoff-ponzi-hedge-pf -ii-in_rl_1212croesus_inl.html (accessed August 15, 2011).

50. *Wikipedia*, s.v. "AIG bonus payments controversy," http://en.wikipedia.org/ wiki/AIG_bonus_payments_controversy (accessed August 15, 2011).

51. "William Congreve Quotes," BrainyQuote.com, http://www.brainyquote .com/quotes/quotes/w/williamcon100903.html (accessed August 15, 2011).

CHAPTER 9: CREATING A CULTURE SHIFT IN THE AGE OF ILLOGIC

1. *Wikipedia*, s.v. "*Star Trek*," http://en.wikipedia.org/wiki/Star_Trek (accessed August 17, 2011).

2. *Wikipedia*, s.v. "*Star Trek* (film)," http://en.wikipedia.org/wiki/Star_ Trek_%28film%29 (accessed August 17, 2011).

3. IMDb, s.v. "*Sherlock Holmes* (2009)," http://www.imdb.com/title/tt0988045/ (accessed August 17, 2011).

4. IMDb, s.v. "*Forrest Gump* (1994)," http://www.imdb.com/title/tt0109830/ (accessed August 17, 2011).

5. *Wikipedia*, s.v. "*Harvey* (film)," http://en.wikipedia.org/wiki/ Harvey_%28film%29 (accessed August 17, 2011).

6. IMDb, "*Being There* (1979)," http://www.imdb.com/title/tt0078841/ (accessed August 17, 2011).

7. *Wikipedia*, s.v. "*The Life and Death of Peter Sellers*," http://en.wikipedia.org/ wiki/The_Life_and_Death_of_Peter_Sellers (accessed August 17, 2011).

8. IMDb, "Memorable Quotes for *Back to the Future* (1985)," http://www .imdb.com/title/tt0088763/quotes (accessed August 17, 2011).

9. *Wikipedia*, s.v. "Ronald Reagan," http://en.wikipedia.org/wiki/Ronald _Reagan (accessed August 17, 2011).

10. Susan Thompson, "Business Big Shot: Harry Potter Author J. K. Rowling," *The Times*, April 2, 2008, http://business.timesonline.co.uk/tol/business/movers _and_shakers/article3663197.ece (accessed August 17, 2011).

11. John Lawless, "Nigel Newton," *Bloomberg Businessweek*, May 30, 2005, http://www.businessweek.com/magazine/content/05_22/b3935414.htm (accessed August 17, 2011).

12. *Wikipedia*, s.v. "Harry Potter," http://en.wikipedia.org/wiki/Harry_Potter (accessed August 17, 2011).

13. Jenny Sawyer, "Missing from Harry Potter—A Real Moral Struggle," *Christian Science Monitor*, July 25, 2007, http://www.csmonitor.com/2007/0725/p09s02-coop .html (accessed August 17, 2011).

14. *MuggleCast*, http://www.mugglenet.com/mugglecast/ (accessed August 17, 2011); *PotterCast*, http://www.the-leaky-cauldron.org/pottercast/?p=1856 (accessed August 17, 2011).

15. Christopher Hitchens, "The Boy Who Lived," *New York Times*, August 12, 2007, http://www.nytimes.com/2007/08/12/books/review/Hitchens-t.html (accessed August 17, 2011).

16. Nancy Gibbs, "Person of the Year 2007 Runners-Up: J. K. Rowling," *Time*, December 19, 2007, http://www.time.com/time/specials/2007/personoftheyear/ article/0,28804,1690753_1695388_1695436,00.html (accessed August 17, 2011).

17. *Wikipedia*, s.v. "Google," http://en.wikipedia.org/wiki/Google (accessed August 17, 2011).

18. "BrandZ Top 100: Google Beats Coca-Cola, GE, Microsoft for Top Brand Honors," *Marketing Charts*, April 22, 2008, http://www.marketingcharts.com/direct/ brandz-top-100-google-beats-coca-cola-ge-microsoft-for-top-brand-honors-4303/ (accessed August 17, 2011).

19. Andrew Jacobs and Miguel Helft, "Google, Citing Attack, Threatens to Exit China," *New York Times*, January 12, 2010, http://www.nytimes.com/2010/01/13/ world/asia/13beijing.html?pagewanted=all (accessed August 17, 2011).

20. Chris Lefkow, "Google Stops Censoring Search Results in China," *Discovery News*, March 22, 2010, http://news.discovery.com/tech/google-china-censorship .html (accessed August 17, 2011).

INDEX

AAAA. *See* American Association of Advertising Agencies (AAAA)

ABC (network), 121

About a Boy (movie), 204

Abramoff, Jack, 55

Academy Awards, 25, 28, 126, 149, 189, 190, 212

accidental Disciples. *See* Disciples

Accidental Tourist, The (Tyler), 152

Actium, Battle of, 62, 158

Acura® (car), 34

Adams, John, 161

adaptability, 219

Adbusters (magazine), 41–42

ADD. *See* Attention Deficit Disorder (ADD)

ADHD. *See* Attention Hyperactivity Disorder (ADHD)

adoption curve, 37

AFC. *See* African National Congress (ANC)

Afghanistan, war in, 52, 104–105, 226

"African Child" (music video), 71

African National Congress (ANC), 65–66, 173

Afrikaner Weerstandsbeweging [Afrikaner Resistance Movement] (AWB), 166

AIG (American International Group, Inc.), 205, 207

Air America (movie), 28

Air Southwest, 152

air travel, difficulties in, 151–53

Al-Fayed, Dodi, 97

Al-Fayed, Mohamed, 97

Allen, Keith, 97

Ally Bank, 206

Ally McBeal (TV series), 29

al-Qaida, 90, 104, 105

AltaVista®, 226

"alter egos," 107–108

Amazon.com, Inc., 77

American Association of Advertising Agencies (AAAA), 78

American Institute of Architects, 179

American International Group. *See* AIG (American International Group, Inc.)

American Nazi Party, 177

"America's Favorite Architecture" (American Institute of Architects), 179

ANC. *See* African National Congress (ANC)

Android™, 226

Angelou, Maya, 180

Angels & Demons (Brown), 162

Angivarian Wall, Battle of, 160

Angry Birds®, 145–46, 147, 154

Aniston, Jennifer, 91–92

anosmia, 122–23

"Anschluss," 188

Anthony, Casey, 93–94

Antony, Marc. *See* Marc Antony

apologies, importance of, 151, 197–204

Apotheker, Leo, 74

Apple, Inc., 10, 73, 74, 75, 76–77, 97–98, 124, 131–32, 144–45, 183
    having one of top eight logos, 174
    See also iPad®; iPhone®; iPod®; iTunes®

aquila, 158

Aquila, Marcus Falvius (fictional character), 159

Arcade Fire (band), 133

architectural symbols, 178–83

Archlight (fictional character), 47

Ariely, Dan, 110, 149–50

Arizona Diamondbacks (NFL team), 140

Arminius (also known as Hermann), 160

Arsenal (British Premier League), 136, 138

Arthur (1981 movie), 95, 147

Arthur (2011 movie), 147

Artisan Entertainment, 44, 45

"Art of the Heist, The" (ad campaign), 46–48

Assange, Julian, 52–54, 55

Associated Press, 173

astrology, 154–56

A3 (car), 46–48

Attenborough, Richard, 28

Attention Deficit Disorder (ADD), 113, 133, 217

Attention Hyperactivity Disorder (ADHD), 113

Audacity of Hope (Obama), 187–88

Audi® (car), 34, 46–48, 106, 197–98, 203

auditory communication, 56

Augustus Caesar (emperor), 26, 62, 157, 158

Austin Powers (movie), 203

AWB. *See* Afrikaner Weerstandsbeweging [Afrikaner Resistance Movement] (AWB)

Axe®, 31, 87

Babar (Brunhoff), 168

Bachmann, Michele, 66

"BackRub." *See* Google®

Back to the Future (movie), 220–21

Ballmer, Steve, 74, 77, 78

Bandler, Richard, 56

Bank of America Corporation, 206

Barcelona (Spanish football team), 138

Bartlett, Josiah "Jed" (fictional character), 117

baseball, 138, 140, 196

basketball, 27–28, 30, 138–39, 141–42, 154, 196–97

Bass Ale Brewery, 174

BBC, 57–58, 67, 89

Bear Stearns Companies, Inc., The, 205

Beatles (band), 95, 100

Beck, Glen, 66

Beijing Olympics, 101

Being There (movie), 211–12

Belichick, Bill, 139

Benigni, Roberto, 190
Berlin Wall, fall of, 24, 182
"Beyond Petroleum" (BP advertising campaign), 185
Bezos, Jeff, 77
"Big Shift, The," 42
Biko, Steve, 65
Bill & Melinda Gates Foundation, 74
billboards, interactive, 131
Bing® (search engine), advertisement for, 113
bin Laden, Osama, 115
Black, Jack, 146
Blair, Tony, 16, 23, 63, 64, 191–93, 197
Blair Witch Project, The (movie), 43–46, 118
Blogger™, 226
Bloomsbury (publisher), 223
Blue Devils. *See* Duke University, basketball team
Blue Ribbon Sports, 176
blue torch as symbol for Conservative Party, 166
BMW® (car), 34, 106
boar as a symbol, 159
Boies, David, 195
Bono (musician), 67, 68, 70
Boomtown Rats (band), 67
Borg, Björn, 141
Boston Red Sox (MLB team), 138
Boudica (queen), 158
Bowerman, Bill, 176
Bowl Championship Series (NCAA BCS), 141, 228
"Boycott BP" campaign, 186

Boy George (musician), 68
BP p.l.c., 185–87, 206
Brady, Tom, 139, 194
BrainJuicer®, 129
Brand, Russell, 71, 147
Brandenburg Gate (Berlin), 222
brands
    adoption curve, 37
    banks as faceless brands, 207
    brand loyalty, 185
    brand-opinion research, 56, 85, 106–107, 109, 111, 129–30
    CEOs as Chief Disciples, 71–77
    CEOs as chief emotion officer, 77–83
    and the Congregation, 39, 55
    creating a culture shift, 10, 16, 178, 182, 186, 209–30
        Google® as an example of a perfect culture shift, 226–28
    and cue framing, 56
    as cults, 97–98, 112–13
    and Disciples, 38, 52, 54, 55, 74–75, 78, 80–81, 84, 127, 148, 151, 154, 175, 176, 177–78, 183–84, 227, 229
        appeal of icons/logos, 171
        Apple® Disciples, 74, 76, 97, 144–45, 147, 183
        response to Zealot-favored CEOs, 75–76
        Southwest Airlines Company, 152–53
    examples of branding, 174, 213
        FedEx Corporation, 174–75
        Google®, 226–28

Harry Potter series, 223–26
Nazism, 165–66
Nike, Inc., 176
Obama 2008 campaign, 169–70
Playboy magazine, 177–78
and illogical leaps, 15, 19, 85, 86, 87, 105–106, 111–12
creating affinity to, 86
undoing illogical leaps about, 106–109
minimizing choice to ease selection process, 147–51
negative branding, 15, 187, 198
rebranding, 147–49, 199–200, 201
and social contracts, 30–35, 36, 73, 83, 105, 127, 135, 153, 183, 198, 203–204, 207, 214, 216
and social media, 72, 116, 123–28, 130
and symbolism, 157–84, 218
top eight logos representing brands, 174–78
using viral movements, 46–48
and Zealots, 55, 87
See also corporations and CEOs
BrandZ, 226
Brazil, 72
Brees, Drew, 195
Breivik, Anders Behring, 89, 90
Brezny, Rob, 155
Brin, Sergey, 226
Britain
football (soccer) in, 136–38
monarchy in, 63

politics and political parties, 16, 20–25, 58, 63–64, 166, 188–93, 197
riots in 2011, 42, 132
British Open (golf), 140–41
British Trademark Act of 1875, 174
Brooks, Rebekah, 202
Brown, Dan, 161
Brown, Divine, 203
Brown, Doc (fictional character), 220–21
Brunhoff, Laurent de, 168
Brutus, 25, 26
Bryant, Kobe, 197
BSkyB, 202–203
Buckley, William F., 177
Budweiser® (beer), 107
Buerk, Michael, 67
buildings as symbols, 178–83
burro [donkey], 168
Burton, Richard, 93
Busby, Matt, 137
Bush, George W., 16, 105, 117, 193, 225
businesses. *See* corporations and CEOs
buyer's remorse, 86

Cadillac® (car), 106, 140
Caesar, Julius, 25–27, 62, 109, 157–59
Cafferty, Jack, 51
Cain, Hermann, 67, 143
Caligula (emperor), 61–62, 160
Cameron, David, 23
Campaign for Liberty, 48, 49
Campaign for Real Beauty® (Dove®), 30–32

"Candle in the Wind" (song), 97

Cannae, Battle of, 103

Cannes Film Festival, 97

Cannibal Holocaust (movie), 44

Cardoza, Dennis, 121

Carson, Eve, 138

Carter, Jimmy, 220, 221

Casino Jack (movie), 55

Cassius, 25, 26

Cast Away (movie), 175

Castro, Fidel, 65

Catcher in the Rye, The (Salinger), 89

CBA. *See* collective-bargaining agreement (CBA)

celebrities
and cue framing, 56
as Disciples in humanitarian causes, 67–69
endorsing Angry Birds®, 146, 147
illogical leaps in ways we view, 90–98
other races and cultures, 99–103
social contracts with, 27–30, 203–204, 224
See also leadership

cell structure for managing businesses, 79–80

Center for Constitutional Rights, 53

Central Park (Zoo) Menagerie Scare, 168–69

certainty, 135–56
emotional certainty and culture shifts, 217–18
lack of certainty in air travel, 151–53

and loss of momentum, 153–56
using repetition to ensure, 146–47

Chamberlain, Neville, 188–91

Chambers, John, 77

Chan, Jackie, 102

Chance the Gardner (fictional character), 211–12

Chaplin (movie), 28

Chapman, Graham, 90

Chapman, Mark, 89

Charles (prince), 63

Chase, Mary, 210

Chelsea (British Premier League), 136

Chicago Sun-Times (newspaper), 45

Chief Disciples. *See* Disciples

China, 65, 72, 101–102, 182, 227–28

choice, minimizing to ease selection process, 147–51, 153

Chouinard, Yvon, 80–81

Christian Science Monitor (newspaper), 224

Christopher, Tommy, 50

Chrome™, 226

Chrysler Corporation, 33

Chung, Connie, 121

Church, Thomas Haden, 149

Churchill, Clementine, 58

Churchill, Winston, 57–59, 188, 190–91

CIA (US), 56

Cicero, 61

Cisco Systems, Inc., 77

Clarke, Darren, 140–41

Classic Malts of Scotland® collection, 147–49, 150

Claudius (emperor), 62, 160

Clegg, Nick, 23

Cleland, Max, 15

Cleopatra, 62, 158

Cleveland Cavaliers (NBA team), 27–28

Clinton, Bill, 16–17, 59, 192, 205

Clinton, Hillary, 17, 49, 53

Clooney, George, 106

closed-source software, 81

Clough, Brian, 69, 192

Clouseau, Inspector (fictional character), 212

CNN (network), 49, 51, 114

Coca-Cola Company, The, 126, 127
    having one of top eight logos, 174

cognitive dissonance, 85, 86–87
    parents not seeing aggression in killers, 87–90
    See also illogical leaps

Coke®, 126, 127

Coldplay (band), 71

collective-bargaining agreement (CBA), 194

Collins, Phil, 68

Columbine High School killers, 88–89

Combs, Sean, 71

common cold and Zicam®, 122–23

communications modalities, 56

concentration camps, 166

Condit, Gary, 121

Congregation, 37–60, 82, 184, 218
    and access to music, 76
    and brands, 39, 55
    of business software users, 82
    categorizing public figures as, 55–59

and celebrities, 71, 76

and culture shifts, 60, 71, 77, 84, 127, 133, 214, 218

and Disciples, 43, 44, 45–46, 48, 54, 59, 60, 65, 66, 208, 214, 219, 224

discovery of Google® by, 227

efforts to reach for *Second That Emotion* (Holden), 229

need for confidence and certainty, 142

and politics
    the "Dean Scream," 118
    in Egypt, 41
    in Nazi Germany, 165
    and Occupy Wall Street protests, 42
    and Ronald Reagan, 221, 222
    Ron Paul's campaigns, 48, 52

and social contracts, 184, 208, 218
    broken social contracts, 203, 208, 219

and social media, 43, 44, 128–32

and test of leadership, 83–84

and viral movements, 43–48

and wine, 149

and Zealots, 59, 60, 65, 83, 214, 224

Congreve, William, 185, 208

Connery, Sean, 161

Conservative Party (British), 20–24, 64, 166, 191

Consumerist.com, 187, 206

Contra rebels, 222
Cook, Peter, 95
Cook, Tim, 75–76
Corona® (beer), 107
corporations and CEOs
    as Chief Disciples, 71–77
    as chief emotion officer, 77–83
    commercial symbolism, 174–78
    examples of perfect cultural
      shifts
        Google®, 226–28
    and the great recession of 2008
      and 2009, 204–207
    impact of CEO on company's
      stock performance, 78–79
    protests against CEOs, 207
    use of social media, 123–28,
      130
    See also brands; leadership
Council of the People's Commissars
    of Russia, 62
Court of Appeals for Ninth Circuit
    (US), 76
Cox, John H., 49
Cradup, Billy, 176
Cragganmore (Scotch malt), 148
credit-card debt, 107–108, 110–11
crime prevention, 132
Crispin Porter + Bogusky (adver-
    tising agency), 74
Cruise, Tom, 70, 94–95, 98, 130
Cry Freedom (Woods), 65
cue framing, 56–57
cultures and illogical leaps, 99–103
culture shifts
    brands creating, 10, 16, 178,
      182, 186, 209–30

and certainty, 135–56
and the Congregation, 60, 71,
    77, 84, 127, 133, 214, 218
and Disciples, 60, 71, 77, 84,
    127, 133, 142, 154, 214, 215,
    218, 219
and emotions, 114–15, 133, 209
examples of
    Angry Birds®, 146
    Apple, Inc., 76–77
    Audi® A3® campaign, 46–48
    Blair Witch Project (movie),
      43–46, 118
    BP p.l.c., 186
    Dove® Campaign for Real
      Beauty®, 30–32
    efforts to create for *Second
      That Emotion* (Holden),
      228–30
    FedEx Corporation, 175
    Google® as an example of
      a perfect culture shift,
      226–28
    Harley-Davidson, Inc., 178
    Harry Potter series as an
      example of a perfect
      culture shift, 223–26
    humanitarian cultural shifts,
      67–71, 125–27
    NCAA March Madness, 154
    Nike, Inc., 176
    Patagonia, Inc., 80
    Playboy magazine, 178
    in politics, 20–22, 42–43,
      48–52, 62–67, 118–20,
      144, 164–66, 170–71, 173–
      74, 192, 197, 204, 212

Red Hat, Inc., 81–83
Ronald Reagan as an
   example of a perfect
   culture shift, 220–23
single-malt whiskey, 147–49,
   150–51
Southwest Airlines
   Company, 152–53
Toy Story 3 (movie), 124
Vietnam Veterans Memo-
   rial, 179
Whole Foods Market, Inc., 79
and the grasp-ability of ideas,
   142–47
halting a cultural shirt, 197, 201
and illogical leaps, 106–107,
   123, 130, 209–30
and mass participation, 216
pop-culture shifts, 90, 96, 145,
   146, 147, 175, 221, 223, 224,
   225, 230
and social contracts, 15–16, 30,
   81, 84, 123, 127, 128–32, 135,
   138, 162, 164, 174, 207
and social media, 116, 119, 120,
   126, 127, 128–32, 133
and social psychology, 87
and symbolism, 162, 222
and viral movements, 43–48
and Zealots, 60, 71, 77, 84, 127,
   133, 218
Curious Case of Benjamin Button, The
   (movie), 91
Current TV® (network), 42
Curry, Stephen, 142
Curse of the Blair Witch (TV show),
   45

Dahmer, Jeffrey, 87–89
Dahmer, Lionel, 87–89
Dallas Cowboys (NFL team), 136,
   140, 194
Dallas Mavericks (NBA team), 30
Dalwhinnie (Scotch malt), 148
Damned United, The (movie), 69, 192
Damon, Matt, 173
Davidson, Carolyn, 176
Davidson College basketball team,
   142
Da Vinci Code, The (Brown), 161
Da Vinci Code, The (movie), 90
Dean, Howard, 49, 116–18, 123
decimation, definition of, 159
decision-making process
   and the Congregation, 39, 214
   and cue framing, 56
   and Disciples, 38, 59, 60, 214
   emotional basis for, 9, 10, 28,
      106–108, 217
   social contracts' role in, 16
Deepwater Horizon oil spill, 185–87
de Klerk, F. W., 65
Delicious®, 130
Dell, Michael, 77, 78
Dell Inc., 77
Delta Air Lines, Inc., 82
DeMint, Jim, 66
Democracy for America, 117
Democratic Party (DNC), 116–17,
   120, 166–69
Demolition Man (movie), 132
Depp, Johnny, 148
Derby County (British Football
   League Championship), 69
Deutsch, Bob, 85–86, 99

Diageo PLC, 147

Diana (princess), 96–97, 98

DiCaprio, Leonardo, 18

Diet Coke, 126

Diet Pepsi®, 126

Disciples, 37–60

accidental Disciples, 67–71

and businesses and brands, 38, 52, 54, 55, 74–75, 78, 80–81, 84, 127, 145, 151, 154, 175, 176, 177–78, 183–84, 227, 229

appeal of icons/logos, 171

Apple® Disciples, 74, 76, 97, 144–45, 147, 183

response to Zealot-favored CEOs, 75–76

Southwest Airlines Company, 152–53

and celebrities, 67–69, 70–71, 146, 147, 148, 203, 215

characteristics of, 15, 38, 39, 41, 46, 54, 60, 69, 70, 80, 81, 83, 151, 164, 214, 230

identifying leaders and groups as Disciples, 55–59

test of leadership, 83–84

Chief Disciples, 183, 212

celebrities as humanitarian Chief Disciples, 67–71

CEOs as Chief Disciples, 71–77

CEOs as chief emotion officer, 77–83

Harry Potter (fictional character) as, 224

Jeremy Holden as for *Second That Emotion*, 229–30

as leaders for mass participation, 64–67

role of, 69–71

Ronald Reagan as, 221

and social contracts, 215

and test of leadership, 83–84

and the Congregation, 39, 43, 44, 45–46, 48, 54, 59, 60, 66, 208, 214, 219, 224

and culture shifts, 60, 71, 77, 84, 127, 133, 142, 154, 214, 215, 218, 219

pop-culture shifts, 145, 146, 147, 175

efforts to reach for *Second That Emotion* (Holden), 229

in humanitarian causes, 67–69, 70–71, 127

and mass participation, 64–67

and motivation, 38, 67

and peer-to-peer music sharing, 75–77

in politics, 48–55, 118, 193, 221–22

Nazi Germany, 164, 165

Obama 2008 campaign, 52, 119–20, 171

role of political consulting, 54–55

Ronald Reagan, 221

Ron Paul's campaigns, 48, 52, 67

Tea Party movement, 66

and pop-culture shifts, 146

and protest movements, 40–41, 42, 43, 59, 60, 65–66

response to music-sharing, 76
and social contracts, 45, 84,
    119, 127, 128, 152–53, 184,
    197, 214, 215, 218
    breaking social contracts, 208
    spreading word because of
        social contract, 208
and social media, 47, 119, 123,
    127, 128–32
as source of leadership
    in humanitarian cultural
        shifts, 67–71
    perpetuating movements, 83
    in political cultural shifts,
        64–67
    test of leadership, 83–84
and sports, 193, 197
and viral movements, 43–48
and Zealots, 38, 39, 42, 48, 54,
    59, 74–75, 83
    Zealots acting as Disciples,
        60, 65, 66
Disney. *See* Walt Disney Company,
    The
Diva (album), 96
Djokovic, Novak, 141
Dr. Dre (musician), 75
Domino's Pizza, Inc., 200
Donald, Luke, 140
donkey as symbol for the Demo-
    cratic party, 166–69
"Don't be evil" (Google mantra),
    226, 227
"Dot-Bomb" era (2002), 77, 78
"Do They Know It's Christmas"
    (song), 68
Douglas, Alfred (Bosie), 96

Douglas, Melvyn, 211
Douglass, Frederick, 180
Dove®, 30–32, 72, 87
Dowd, Elwood P. (fictional char-
    acter), 210–11
Dowd, Veta (fictional character),
    210–11
Dowler, Milly, 201, 202
Downey, Robert, Jr., 28–30, 210
Dr. Dre (musician), 75
Duke University
    basketball team, 138–39, 141
    Fuqua School of Business,
        78–79
Dumbo (movie), 168
Dutroux, Marc, 122

Eagle, The (movie), 158
eagle as a symbol, 158–61, 162, 166
Eagle of the Ninth, The (Sutcliff), 158,
    159
Eastwood, Clint, 18, 173
eBay, Inc., 74
Ebert, Roger, 45
Eboracum fortress, 158
Eco, Umberto, 161–62
E. coli epidemic, 199
Economist (journal), 142–43
eco-Zealots, 186
Eden, Anthony, 188
Edward IV (king), 136
Edwards, Blake, 212
Edwards, Elizabeth, 17–18
Edwards, John, 17–18, 118
Egypt
    protests in, 40–41, 59, 65, 115,
        126, 128, 207

use of commercial branding, 174

Einstein, Albert, 145

Elantra® (car), 35

ElBaradei, Mohammed, 40–41

electronic gaming, 47, 50, 113, 131, 223

Angry Birds®, 145–46, 147, 154

rise of, 113

elephant as symbol for the Republican party, 166–69

"Elephant's Child, The" (Kipling), 168

Elizabeth II (queen), 22, 63, 96, 223

Ellen (TV series), 194

Ellison, Larry, 77, 78

emotions

companies' efforts to use social media to generate, 123–28

and culture shifts, 114–15, 133, 209

and the decision-making process, 9, 10, 28, 106–108, 217

emotional certainty, 217–18

and illogical leaps, 10, 107, 109, 133

impact of social media, 115–20, 121–23, 126, 216–17

importance of leadership, 77–83, 180

and information overload, 113–15

and movements, 10–11, 15–16, 115, 122, 183, 219

and social contracts, 207, 216–17

of sports fans, 135–42, 154

Endeavour space shuttle, 116

Endurance (Japanese TV show), 100

Espionage Act (US), 53

ESPN (network), 114

Ethiopia, famine in, 67–69, 71

eulogy for a favorite brand, 107

Eurythmics (band), 96

Evernote®, 129

Everton (British Premier League), 136

E.W. Howe's Monthly, 1911–1937 (Howe), 13

Excel® (car), 33

Excite, 226

Eyes Wide Shut (movie), 94

Facebook®, 31, 76, 128, 130

January 2008 Facebook election, 49

use of

"Boycott BP" campaign, 186

Michelle Martin campaign, 122

Pepsi Refresh Project®, 125

to promote *Toy Story 3*, 124

protests in Egypt, 40, 115

for research, 130

Fair & Lovely®, 32

Fairey, Shepard, 171, 173

Falklands War, 21, 24

Fanning, Shawn, 75–76

fans' relationships to sports teams, 135–42

during labor disputes, 193–97

sports arena as symbols for, 182

faux documentaries, 43–46

FBI (US), 18, 56

FDA (US) attempt to ban Zicam®, 122–23

FDR. *See* Roosevelt, Franklin Delano

Federal Bureau of Prisons (US), 121

Federer, Roger, 141

FedEx Corporation, 174–75
    having one of top eight logos, 174

Fedora Project, 81

Ferguson, Alex, 137

Fifth Element, The (movie), 132

Filmcritic.com, 45

Finney, Albert, 58

Fiorina, Carly, 74

Firdos Square, Bagdad, photo of pulling down Hussein's statue, 182

Firing Line (TV series), 177

Firth, Colin, 189

Fitzpatrick, Jim, 171–73

flags as powerful political symbols, 173–74
    "flag-raising photograph" at Ground Zero, 180–81
    raising flag at Iwo Jima, 181

"flat tax," 142–44

"Flat-Tax Revolution, The" *(Economist)*, 142–43

Flickr®, 129

Fonteyn, Margot, 85

football
    American football, 139–40, 193–95
    British football, 136–38

Football Association Community Shield (formerly Charity Shield), 136

Football League (British), 136

Forbes, Steve, 142–43, 144

Forbes (magazine), 137, 144, 195

Ford, Gerald, 221

Ford Motor Company, 33

"forgiveness" officer, 200

Forrest Gump (movie), 210

Fortune 500 companies, 79

Foster, Jodie, 89

foursquare®, 130

Four Weddings and a Funeral (movie), 203

Fox, Michael J., 220

FOX News (network), 121

Franklin, Benjamin, 135, 153, 161

Franklin, Thomas E., 180

Franklin and Winston (Meacham), 57

Freeman, Morgan, 173

French Revolution, 62–63

Friedman, Thomas L., 42

Friends (TV series), 91

Frost, David, 192

Frost/Nixon (movie), 192

Fry, Stephen, 95–96, 210

Fulham (British Premier League), 136

Fun-Vii® (car), 131–32

Fuqua School of Business (Duke University), 78–79

Gadhafi, Muammar, 102, 103

gaidouri [donkey], 168

Galaxy®, 226

Gambino, Carlo, 119

gaming, electronic. *See* electronic gaming

Gandhi (movie), 28

Garcia, Mannie, 173

Gardener, Chauncey (fictional character), 211–12

Gates, Bill, 61, 74, 84, 127

Gathering Storm, The (movie), 57–58

Geldorf, Bob, 67–69, 70, 71

General Motors Corporation. *See* GM (General Motors Corporation)

Genesis (band), 68

Genesis® (car), 34, 35

"Genius Bar," 183

George VI (king), 189

Germanicus, 160

Get Him to the Greek (movie), 71

Ghonim, Wael, 40

Giamatti, Paul, 149

Gibson, Mel, 29

Gilding, Paul, 42

Gingrich, Newt, 143

Girl, Interrupted (movie), 91

Givens, Robin, 91

Glass-Steagall Act, 205

Gleeson, Brendan, 58

Glenkinichie (Scotch malt), 148

GM (General Motors Corporation), 33, 205

Gmail™, 226, 227

Godfather Pizza, 67

Godzilla, 100

Gold Effie Award, 78

Golden Globe Awards, 96

Goldsmith, Harvey, 68

Goldwater, Barry, 221

golf, 140–41

Gonzalez, Tony, 151

Google®, 118, 123
  brands encompassed within the Google family, 226
  as an example of a perfect culture shift, 226–28

Google+®, 128

Google Maps™, 133

Google Street View ™, 133

Google Zeitgeist™, 129
  See also Android™

Gorbachev, Mikhail, 25, 222

Gore, Al, 16, 59, 117

Gotti, John, 55

Grammy Award, 96, 133

Grant, Hugh, 146, 193, 203–204

Grape Restaurant (chain), 150

grasp-ability of ideas, 142–47

Graves, Robert, 62

Great Disruption, The (Gilding), 42

great recession of 2008 and 2009, 204–207

Great Seal of the United States, 160–61

Green movement, 186

Grindler, John, 56

Groom, Winston, 210

Ground Zero, 115, 180–81

group dynamics, 9

Guandique, Ingmar, 121–22

Gulf of Mexico oil spill, 185–87

GymPact® app for New Year's resolutions, 109–10, 111

Hadrian (emperor), 158

Hagel, John, III, 42

Hall of Fame game, 196

Hangover Part II, The (movie), 146

Hanks, Tom, 161, 175, 210
Hannibal Barca, 102–103
Hardee's Food Systems Inc., 200
Harley-Davidson, Inc., 178
Harold & Kumar Go to White Castle
    (movie), 112
Harper's Weekly (newspaper), 168
Harris, Eric, 88–89
Harris, Wayne, 88–89
Harry (prince), 166
Harry Potter series (Rowling)
    as an example of a perfect
        culture shift, 223–26
    *Harry Potter and the Deathly
        Hallows* (Rowling), 225
    *Harry Potter and the Philosopher's
        Stone* (Rowling) [also known
        as *Harry Potter and the Sorcerer's
        Stone*], 223, 224
Harvey (Chase), 210–11
Hastings, Reed, 200–201
Havel, Václav, 65
Hawaii Five-0 (TV series), 56
Haxan Films, 44, 45
Hayward, Tony, 186
HBO, 57–58, 192, 205
Head & Shoulders®, 71
Heath, Ted, 20
Hefner, Hugh, 177
Helios House in Los Angeles, 185
Helmsley, Leona, 201
Helmsley Hotels, 201
Henry VI (king), 136
Hermann (also known as
    Arminius), 160
Heseltine, Michael, 22–23, 26
Hewlett-Packard Company, 74

himar [donkey], 168
Hinckley, John, Jr., 89
historical figures, social contracts
    with, 20–27
Hitchens, Christopher, 225
Hitler, Adolf, 58, 163, 164–65,
    188–91
Holden, Jeremy (efforts to launch
    and market *Second That Emotion*),
    228–30
Holder, Eric, 53
Holmes, Sherlock (fictional char-
    acter), 209, 210, 212
Holocaust, 166
Hoover, J. Edgar, 18–19
"Hope" poster (Fairey), 171–72, 173
horoscopes, 154
horse as a symbol, 159
House (TV series), 96
House of Lancaster, 136–37
House of York, 136–37
Houston Texans (NFL team), 136
Howe, Edgar Watson, 13, 36
Howe, Geoffrey, 22, 26
Huffington Post (online news), 43
Hull, Josephine, 210
Hunter, Rielle, 17
Hurley, Elizabeth, 203, 204
Hurt, William, 205
Hussein, Saddam, 103, 104, 105
    photo of residents pulling
        down statue of, 182
Hyundai Assurance program, 34–35
Hyundai Motor Company, 33–35

I, Claudius (Graves), 62
iAd®, 124

IBM, 132
    having one of top eight logos, 174
iconography. *See* symbolism
illogical leaps, 10
    attempts to create meaning, 114
    and brands, 15, 19, 85, 86, 87,
        105–106, 111–12
        creating affinity to, 86
        undoing illogical leaps
            about, 106–109
    cognitive dissonance, 85, 86–87
        parents not seeing aggres-
            sion in killers, 87–90
    and culture shifts, 106–107,
        123, 130, 209–30
    and emotions, 10, 107, 109, 133
    and personal relationships,
        87–90
    projective techniques to undo
        illogical leaps, 106
    psychology of, 85–112
    for *Second That Emotion*
        (Holden), 230
    and social contracts, 14, 15–16,
        17, 18, 21–22, 26, 28, 36,
        105–12, 213
    and social media, 120–23, 130
    and sports fans' devotion, 138
    used as basis of reactions
        in *Being There* (movie), 212
        to Bill Clinton, 16–17
        to Casey Anthony, 31
        to Chandra Levy, 121
        to China and the Olympics,
            101–102
        to Dove® Campaign for Real
            Beauty®, 31

and Harry Potter series, 224
to Hyundai Assurance
    program, 35
to John Edwards, 17–18
leading to war, 103–105
to LeBron James, 28
to Margaret Thatcher,
    21–22
New Year's resolutions,
    109–10
Obama as an Arab, 14
to other races and cultures,
    99–103
to Princess Diana's death,
    96–97
to Robert Downey Jr., 29
and Ronald Reagan, 222
to shape personal relation-
    ships, 87–90
to strangers and celebrities,
    90–98
to White Castle® burgers,
    111–12
to Yoko Ono, 99–101
to Zicam®, 122–23
IMF. *See* International Monetary
    Fund (IMF)
Immersive Labs, 131
India, 72
Indiana Jones and the Last Crusade
    (movie), 90
Indianapolis Colts (NFL team), 195
Indica Gallery, 99
Infiniti® (car), 34
information overload, 113–15,
    120–23
Infoseek®, 226

Instapaper®, 130
Intel Corporation, 77
interactive media, 131–32
International Monetary Fund
    (IMF), 72–73
Into the Storm (movie), 58
Invictus (movie), 173
iPad®, 144–45, 183
iPhone®, 10, 73–74, 76, 97, 124,
    131–32, 144–45, 183
iPod®, 76
Iran-Contra affair, 222
Iraq War
    and illogical leaps, 103–105
    impact of on Tony Blair, 193
Ironclad (movie), 90
"Iron Lady." *See* Thatcher, Margaret
Iron Lady, The (movie), 24
Iron Man (movie), 29
iTunes®, 76
Ivanhoe (movie), 90
Iwo Jima flag-raising photograph,
    181

jackass, 168
Jack in the Box restaurants, 198–
    200, 203
Jackson, Michael, 68
Jacksonville Jaguars (NFL team),
    140
James, LeBron, 27–28, 30, 197
Janiszewski, Jerzy, 171
Japan, illogical leaps concerning,
    99–101, 102
Jay-Z (musician), 71
J. Edgar (movie), 18
Jefferson, Thomas, 161

Jenkins, Roy, 64
JeremyDHolden.com, 229
Jerry Maguire (movie), 70
JetBlue Airways Corporation, 151
Jews and Nazi Germany, 163,
    165–66, 188, 190
Jobs, Steve, 73, 74, 75, 76–77, 97–98
John, Elton, 97
Johnson, Magic, 197
Jolie, Angelina, 91–92, 146
Jones, Jerry, 194
Jordan, Michael, 176, 197
Journey, A: My Political Life (Blair),
    193
"Just Do It" (Nike, Inc.'s mantra),
    176
Justice Department (US), 53, 78
Just So Stories (Kipling), 168
JWT Specialized Communications,
    Inc., 113

Kaymer, Martin, 140
Kedward, Elly, 44
Kelleher, Herb, 152
Kelly, Mark E., 116
Kennedy, John F., 119
Kerry, John, 118
Kidman, Nicole, 94
"KillerKelly's" Tweets, 116
killers and illogical leaps, 87–90
kinesthetic communication, 56
King, Martin Luther, Jr., 180
King, Rollin, 152
King's Speech, The (movie), 63, 189
Kipling, Rudyard, 168
Kirk, James (fictional character),
    209

Klebold, Dylan, 88–89
Knight, Phil, 176
Knights Templar Order, 89, 90
Kosinski, Jerzy, 211–12
Kosovo, war in, 192
Krasner, Lee, 70
Krohn, Friedrich, 163
K Street, 55
Kubrick, Stanley, 94
Kung Fu Panda 2 (movie), 146
Kunkle, Parke, 154, 155–56

labor disputes in sports, 193–97
Labour Party (British), 23, 58, 64,
    166, 191
Lady Gaga (musician), 71
Lagarde, Christine, 73
Laguvulin (Scotch malt), 148
Lancaster, House of, 136–37
Langdon, Robert (fictional char-
    acter), 161
Last Broadcast, The (movie), 44
Late Show with David Letterman, The
    (TV series), 204
Lauer, Matt, 95
Laurie, Hugh, 95–96
Law, Jude, 96, 210
Leader, Lindon, 175
leadership, 61–84
    celebrities as, 55–59, 84, 215
        humanitarian aid leader-
            ship, 67–69, 70–71, 125
    Chief Disciples, 183, 212
        celebrities as humanitarian
            Chief Disciples, 67–71
        CEOs as Chief Disciples,
            71–77

CEOs as chief emotion
    officer, 77–83
Harry Potter (fictional char-
    acter) as, 224
Jeremy Holden as for *Second
    That Emotion*, 229–30
as leaders for mass partici-
    pation, 64–67
role of, 69–71
Ronald Reagan as, 221
and social contracts, 215
and test of leadership,
    83–84
corporate leaders, 55, 72–73,
    74–83, 84, 186, 213, 215
    CEOs as chief emotion
        officer, 77–83
Disciples as source of, 64–71, 83
emotional importance of,
    77–83, 180
Hitler on leadership, 165
inspirational/spiritual leaders,
    66, 74, 84, 177, 215
leaders for mass participation,
    64–67
moving toward or away from
    leaders, 56, 57, 59
need to have only one leader,
    61–64
opinion leaders, 42
personifying leaders and
    groups, 55–59
political leaders, 17, 20–24, 27,
    41, 52, 55, 61–67, 102–103,
    187, 188–90, 191–93, 215,
    221–22
and social contracts, 73, 207

sports leaders, 69, 182
test of leadership, 83–84
and Zealots, 32, 54, 60, 65, 66, 74–75, 83
League of Nations, 190
Leary, Macon (fictional character), 152
Le Bon, Simon, 68
Leeds United (British Football League Championship), 69, 136–37, 138
Legio IX Hispana [Ninth Legion] of Rome, 157–60
Lehmann Brothers Holdings, Inc., 205
Lenin, Vladimir, 62, 65
Lennon, John, 89, 95, 99–101
Lennox, Annie, 96
Leno (TV series), 194
Leno, Jay, 204
Lessig, Lawrence, 43
Less Than Zero (movie), 28
Letterman (TV series), 194
Letterman, David, 33, 118
Letters from the Earth (Twain), 113
Levy, Chandra, 121–22
Lewinsky, Monica, 16
Lewis, Juliette, 91
Lewis Moberly (design agency), 148
Lexus® (car), 34
Liberal Democrats (British), 23, 64
Libertarian Party, 51
Libya, illogical leaps concerning, 102–103, 115
lies, repetition of, 165
Lie to Me (TV series), 56
Life (magazine), 180–81

Life and Death of Peter Sellers, The (movie), 212
Life Is Beautiful (movie), 190
Limbaugh, Rush, 66
Limitless (movie), 114
Lin, Maya, 178
Live Aid movement, 67–69, 70
Liverpool (British Premier League), 136
Lloyd, Phyllida, 24
logic
    importance of fact-based logic, 209, 230
    lack of when making choices, 112
    See also illogical leaps
logos. *See* symbolism
London riots (2011), 42–43, 132
Love Actually (movie), 193, 204
Lowery, Louis, 181
loyalty, 185, 227
luck and culture shifts, 219
Lycos®, 226
Lynx®, 31

MacDowell, Andie, 203
Mackey, John, 79–80
MacLaine, Shirley, 211
Madoff, Bernie, 207
Madonna (musician), 75
Mailer, Norman, 177
Major, John, 23
Manchester City (British Premier League), 136
Manchester United (British Premier League), 136–38
Mandela, Nelson, 59, 65–66, 173

manipulative propaganda, 15

Manning, Peyton, 195

Mara Slavatrucha (Latin American gang), 121

Marc Antony, 26, 62, 158

March Madness, 141–42, 154

Margot Fonteyn: Autobiography (Fonteyn), 85

Marius, Gaius, 159

Martin, Chris, 71

Martin, Michele, 122

Martin Luther King National Memorial, 180

MartketSite Tower, 182

Massachusetts Institute of Technology Communications Forum, 50

mass participation, 116, 216

Masters Tournament (golf), 140

Mayew, William, 78–79

McCain, John, 13–15, 66, 129

McCartney, Paul, 95

McCartney, Stella, 95

McDonald's Corporation, 199
    having one of top eight logos, 174

McEnroe, John, 141

McFly, Marty (fictional character), 220

McIlroy, Rory, 140, 141

McKinney (advertising agency), 46, 77

McTeer, Janet, 58

Meacham, Jon, 57

Meetup.com®, 50, 117

Mein Kampf (Hitler), 163

Memphis Police Department, 132

Mentalist, The (TV series), 56

Mercedes-Benz® (car), 34, 106

Mercury, Freddie, 68

MetaCrawler®, 226

Metallica (band), 75

Meyer, Roelf, 173

Miami Heat (NBA team), 27, 30

Michael, George, 68

Microsoft Corporation, 74, 77, 81, 113

Middleton, Kate, 63

Miller Lite® (beer), 107

Milosevic, Slobodan, 192

Ming, Yao, 102

Minnesota Planetarium Society, 154

Minority Report (movie), 130–31

Minotaur as a symbol, 159

Mr. and Mrs. Smith (movie), 91

momentum
    gaining, 34, 60, 66, 74, 117, 207, 219, 227, 230
    loss of, 153–56, 183, 184, 191, 197, 208, 218

Monroe, Marilyn, 97

Monterey Jack's (alternative name for Jack in the Box), 199

Monty Python and the Holy Grail (movie), 90

Moore, Dudley, 95, 147

Mother Jones (magazine), 37

motivations, 56, 86, 109
    and Disciples, 38, 67
    hidden motivations, 106, 107, 108, 215–16
    negative motivation, 110–11
    understanding unconscious motivations, 107–108
    of a White Castle® burger lover, 111–12
    and Zealots, 38, 40

Motorola Mobility, 228

Mourning Bride, The (Congreve), 185

movements, 9, 13, 112
    and emotions, 10–11, 15–16,
        115, 122, 183, 219
    failure of, 19, 65, 183, 191, 208
    group dynamics that shape, 41
    need for a leader, 41, 65, 66, 67,
        84. *See also* leadership
    perpetuating a movement, 71,
        80, 83, 184, 219
    players in a movement. *See* Con-
        gregation; Disciples; Zealots
    signs, symbolism, and iconog-
        raphy, 157–84
    social contracts and creation of,
        13–36, 83–84, 208, 219
    and test of leadership, 83–84
    viral movements, 43–52, 118,
        124
    See also culture shifts; illogical
        leaps

moving away or toward something,
    56–57

MTV (network), 45

Mubarak, Hosni, 40–41, 59, 65, 115

Mugabe, Robert, 59

MuggleCast (podcast), 225

Munich Agreement, 189

murders and illogical leaps, 87–90,
    93–94, 122

Murdoch, James, 201, 202

Murdoch, Rupert, 201–203

music-sharing, 75–76

My Life (Clinton), 59

Myrick, Daniel, 44

Myspace®, 49, 121

Nadal, Rafael, 141

Name of the Rose, The (Eco), 161

Napster, Inc., 75–76

NASA (US), 116

NASDAQ, 77–78, 182

Nast, Thomas, 168–69

National Enquirer (newspaper), 146

National Football League (US),
    136, 139–40, 193–95

National Governors Association,
    116

National Portrait Gallery, 173

National Review (magazine), 177

National September 11 Memorial &
    Museum at Ground Zero, 180–81

NATO, 51, 52, 53, 192

Natural Born Killers (movie), 28

Navy Seals (US), 115

Nazi Germany, 164–65
    and Neville Chamberlain,
        188–91
    and the symbolism of the swas-
        tika, 162–66

NCAA
    Bowl Championship Series,
        141, 228
    March Madness, 141–42, 154

negative branding, 15, 187, 198

negative motivation, 110, 111

Nelson, Willie, 68

NetBase®, 129

Netflix, Inc., 200–201

Neuro-Linguistic Programming™
    (NLP), 56

Newcastle Brown Ale®, 107

New England Patriots (NFL team),
    139, 194

New Jewish Cemetery (Prague), 181–82, 190
New Orleans Saints (NFL team), 195
New Republic (magazine), 51
News International, 201–203
News of the World (newspaper), 201–203
New Year's resolutions, 109–110, 111
New York Herald (newspaper), 168–69
New York Times (newspaper), 42, 95, 113, 225
New York Yankees (MLB team), 138, 140
Ney, Bob, 55
NFLPA, 194
Nicholas II (tsar), 62
Nike, Inc., 176
   having one of top eight logos, 174
Nimoy, Leonard, 209
9/11, 104, 105
   National September 11 Memorial & Museum at Ground Zero, 180–81
Nine Months (movie), 204
Ning®, 130
Ninth Legion [Legio IX Hispana] of Rome, 157–60
Niven, David, 203
NLP. *See* Neuro-Linguistic Programming™ (NLP)
Noland, Chuck (fictional character), 175
NYSE (New York Stock Exchange), 78

Obama, Barack, 50, 141, 225
   campain in 2008, 13–14, 52, 119–20, 169–70, 171–73
   judging whether he has brought change, 187–88
   Republican Party "Obama as an Arab" theory, 13–15
Obama, Michelle, 119
Oban (Scotch malt), 148
O'Brien, Conan, 204
Occupy Wall Street (OWS) protests, 41–43, 206, 207
Octavian, 26, 62, 157, 158
Ogilvy & Mather (advertising agency), 30–32
Olbermann, Keith, 42
Omondi, Suleiman, 138
"100 Photographs That Changed the World" (*Life* magazine), 180–81
Ono, Yoko, 99–101, 102
open social ethnography, 129
"open-source" software, 81–83
Ophiuchus (as thirteenth sign of the zodiac), 155
Oracle Corporation, 77, 78, 81
Orkut™, 226
Owen, David, 64
OWS. *See* Occupy Wall Street (OWS) protests

Page, Larry, 226
Palin, Sarah, 66
Paloma Picasso perfume, 86
Paltrow, Gwyneth, 91
Paperweight (Fry), 96
Parker, Sean, 75–76

Parker, William H., 209

Patagonia, Inc., 80–81

Patterson, Kevin, 37, 52, 60

Paul, Rand, 48, 66

Paul, Ron, 48–52, 55, 66–67, 118, 143

Paulson, Henry "Hank," 205

Pearl Harbor, 101

PepsiCo, Inc., 125–27
    Pepsi Refresh Project®, 125–27

perception
    decoding social-media perceptions, 128–32
    illogic nature of, 85, 105–106, 112
    as reality, 35

Perot, H. Ross, 178

Perry, Katy, 71

Perry, Rick, 66, 143

personal relationships and illogical leaps, 87–90

personification as way to understand illogical leaps, 106

persuasion, 9

Peterson, Robert O., 198

Pew Research Center, 14

PGA Championship (golf), 140

photographs as iconographic symbols, 180–82

physical iconography, 178–83

Pienaar, Francois, 173

Pine, Chris, 209

Pink Panther (movies), 212

Pinterest®, 128

Pitt, Brad, 90–92, 98

Pixar Animation Studios, Inc., 98, 124–25, 127

Plastic Ono album, 99

Platt, Lew, 74

Playboy Enterprises, Inc. (having one of top eight logos), 174
    Playboy (magazine), 177–78

Poland, 171

Police (band), 68

politics and political figures, 128–32
    British politics
        Margaret Thatcher, 20–23, 24–25, 64
        Neville Chamberlain, 188–91
        political parties, 20–25, 58, 63–64, 166, 191–93
        Tony Blair, 16, 23, 63, 64, 191–93, 197
    campaigning for "flat tax," 142–44
    and cue framing, 56
    and the great recession of 2008 and 2009, 204–207
    political cultural shifts, 64–67
    political symbolism, 166–74
    Ronald Reagan as an example of a perfect culture shift, 220–23
    social contracts with political figures, 16–19
        Barack Obama, 119–20
        Bill Clinton, 17
        Howard Dean, 117
        impact of breaking a social contract, 188–93, 222
        J. Edgar Hoover, 19
        John Edwards, 18
        Ronald Reagan, 221

Ron Paul, 51
   Steve Forbes, 144
use of social media
   Howard Dean, 116–18
   Obama 2008 campaign,
      13–14, 52, 119–20, 169–70
   Ron Paul primary campaign
      in 2008, 118–19
use of Zealots, Disciples, and
   Congregation, 48–55
See also leadership
Pollock, Jackson, 70
Pompey the Great, 25, 157
Ponzi scheme, 207
pooka, 210
pop-culture shifts. *See* culture shifts
Portland State University, 176
Potter, Harry (fictional character).
   See Harry Potter series (Rowling)
PotterCast (podcast), 225
Pottermore website, 225
Pound (movie), 28
Power of Pull, The (Hagel), 42
Praetorian Guard, 62
precession, 154–56
Predictably Irrational (Ariely), 110,
   149–50
predictive technology, 132
Prefontaine, Steve "Pre," 176
Premier League (British), 136
Procter & Gamble, 31, 72
progressive lifestyle, 79–81
projective techniques to undo illog-
   ical leaps, 106
propaganda, use of, 14–15, 40, 62,
   164–65, 186

Quaid, Dennis, 192
qualitative research. *See* research
Queen, The (movie), 96, 192
Queen (band), 68
Queens Park Rangers (British
   Premier League), 136
Quinto, Zachary, 209

races and illogical leaps, 99–103
racism, 51
Radian6®, 129
Ralston Purina, 198–99
Ramaphosa, Cyril, 173
Rand, Benjamin (fictional char-
   acter), 211–12
Rand, Eve (fictional character), 212
Rankin. *See* Waddell, John Rankin
Reagan, Ronald, 21, 25, 89
   as an example of a perfect
      culture shift, 220–23
reality and perception, 35
Real Madrid (Spanish football
   team), 138
rebranding, 147–49, 199–200, 201
recession of 2008 and 2009, 204–207
"Red Army" of Manchester United,
   137
Redgrave, Vanessa, 58
Red Hat, Inc., 81–83
red rose as symbol for Labour Party,
   166
"red triangle" logo of Bass Ale, 174
Republic, Lost (Lessig), 43
Republican Party (GOP), 142
   and the "Obama as an Arab"
      theory, 13–15
   "Rockefeller Republicans," 117

and Ronald Reagan, 220, 221
and Ron Paul, 49, 51
symbol for, 166–69
and the Tea Party movement,
48, 51, 66–67
research
brand-opinion research, 56, 85,
106–107, 109, 111, 129–30
closed digital qualitative
research, 129–30
Neuro-Linguistic Program-
ming™ (NLP), 56
open social ethnography to
monitor social media, 129
qualitative research and illogical leaps, 106–109
use of Facebook® for research, 130
resignation and air travel, 151
respect and illogical leaps, 95–96
Revie, Don, 137
River Runs through It, A (movie), 91
Roberts, Nisha (fictional character), 46–47
Rock and Roll Hall of Fame, 95
Rockwell, George Lincoln, 177
Roddenberry, Gene, 209
Rolling Stone (magazine), 174, 178
"Rolling Thunder," 178
Rome, 61–62, 157–60, 162
and Hannibal Barca, 102–103
and Julius Caesar, 25–27, 62,
109, 157–59
Romney, Mitt, 143
"Ron Paul Girl" (viral video), 50
Roosevelt, Franklin Delano, 57, 58, 59
Rovio Entertainment, 145–46, 154
Rowling, J. K., 223–26

Rugby World Cup, 173
Runyan, Richard, 174
Rush, Geoffrey, 212
Russian National Unity Party, 166
Russian Revolution, 62

Said, Khaled, 40, 115
St. Paul's Cathedral, photo of
during the Blitz, 182
Salinger, J. D., 89
Samarra bowl, 163
Sánchez, Eduardo, 44
Sanfilippo Syndrome, 125
Sanskrit meaning of the swastika, 163
Saul, Ben, 53
Sawyer, Jenny, 224
scholastic method of reasoning, 161
Schutzstaffel [protection
squadron], 165
Scientology, 95
Sci-Fi Channel (network), 45
Scott, Adam, 69
"Scream, the," 117–18, 123
Screen Actors Guild, 221
SDP. *See* Social Democratic Party
(British)
Second That Emotion (Holden), strate-
gies to launch and market, 228–30
Secret Weapon Marketing (adver-
tising agency), 199–200
Seinfeld, Jerry, 74
Seinfeld (TV series), 149
selection process
minimizing choice to ease,
147–51, 153
need to feel smart, 153–54, 217
Sellers, Peter, 211, 212

semiotics. *See* signs

Sender, Sol, 169–71

serekh, 174

"Service Crew" of Leeds United Football Club, 137

Seven (movie), 91

Sextus, 157

ShareThis® widget, 129

Shatner, William, 209

Sheen, Martin, 117

Sheen, Michael, 192

Sherlock Holmes (movie), 29, 210

Shields, Brooke, 95

Shultz, Howard, 73, 77–78

sidereal zodiac, 155

Sideways (movie), 149

signs. *See* symbolism

simplicity, desire for, 153

Sinatra, Frank, 119

single-malt whiskey, 147–49, 150–51

Sisulu, Walter, 65

60 Minutes (TV series), 197

Slater, Steven, 151

smell, loss of, 122–23

Smith, Will, 45

Smithsonian Institution, 173

Snelling, Richard, 116

soccer. *See* football, British football

social contracts, 13–36

    benefit of establishing, 208

    breaking social contracts, 32, 185–208, 214, 219

        Google® relationship with China, 227–28

        Iran-Contra affair, 222

        Neville Chamberlain, 188–91

        role of apologies, 197–204

        Tony Blair, 191–93

    with celebrities, 27–30, 224

        Hugh Grant breaking of the social contract, 203–204

    and certainty, 135–56, 217–18

    with companies or brands, 30–35, 36, 83, 105, 127, 135, 183, 198, 203–204, 214, 216

        Apple and Starbucks, 73–74

        Audi® (car), 47, 198

        Dove® Campaign for Real Beauty®, 31

        Facebook®, 128

        Hyundai Assurance program, 35

        needing a human or emotional element, 207

        News of the World, 202

        Patagonia, Inc., 80–81

        Pepsi Refresh Project®, 126–27

        Red Hat, Inc., 82

        role of Zealots and Disciples, 75

        Southwest Airlines Company, 152–53

        Whole Foods Market, Inc., 79–80

    and the Congregation, 184, 208, 218

        broken social contracts, 203, 208, 219

    and the creation of movements, 13–36, 83–84, 208, 219

    and culture shifts, 15–16, 30, 81, 84, 123, 127, 128–32,

135, 138, 162, 164, 174, 207, 213–14
and Disciples, 45, 84, 119, 127, 128, 152–53, 184, 197, 214, 215, 218
    breaking social contracts, 208
    Chief Disciples, 215
and emotions, 207, 216–17
in history, 20–27
    Julius Caesar, 26
    Margaret Thatcher, 21
and illogical leaps, 14, 15–16, 17, 18, 21–22, 26, 28, 36, 105–12, 213
and leadership, 73, 207
need to monitor and nurture, 219
non-negotiability of, 36
with political figures, 16–19
    Barack Obama's with Disciples, 119–20
    Bill Clinton, 17
    Howard Dean, 117
    J. Edgar Hoover, 19
    John Edwards, 18
    Neville Chamberlain, 189–90
    Ronald Reagan, 221
    Ron Paul, 51
    Steve Forbes, 144
    Tony Blair, 191–92
and signs, symbols, and iconography, 157–84, 218
in sports, 196
    Manchester United (British Premier League), 138

National Football League, 195
and test of leadership, 83–84
and Zealots, 36, 184, 214, 218, 221
Social Democratic Party (British), 64
social media, 72, 113–33
and creating a culture shift, 127
decoding perceptions about, 128–32
and Disciples, 47, 123, 127, 128–30
efforts to reach for *Second That Emotion* (Holden), 229
and emotions, 115–20, 121–23, 126, 216–17
and illogical leaps, 15, 120–23, 130
power of, 118–19
requiring fast information processing, 212
and social contracts, 15, 214, 217
true value of, 132–33
use of
    Dove® Campaign for Real Beauty®, 31
    to fight FDA ban of Zicam®, 122–23
    to generate sales, 123–28
    by NASA, 116
    in Pepsi Refresh Project®, 125–27
    for Pepsi Refresh Project®, 125–27
    to promote *Toy Story 3*, 124–25, 127, 128

for protest movements, 40,
42–43
viral movements, 43–48
Audi® A3 campaign, 46–48
Blair Witch Project, The,
43–46, 118
Ron Paul's campaigns,
48–52, 118
Toy Story 3, 124
and Zealots, 38
See also Facebook®; Myspace®;
Twitter®; YouTube™
Social Network, The (movie), 76
Sofitel Hotel, 72
Solidarity movement, 65
"Solidarnosc" logo, 171
Somalia, famine in, 70, 71
Sonata® (car), 35
sorry shouldn't be hardest word to
say, 197–204
Sosigenes of Alexandria, 109
SoundJam MP, 76
"Soup Nazi," 149
South Africa, 59, 65–66, 166, 173
Southwest Airlines Company,
152–53, 154, 200
Space Invaders®, 145
Special Relationship, The (movie), 192
Spielberg, Steven, 130–31
spin doctors. *See* manipulative
propaganda
Spock, Mr. (fictional character),
209, 212, 213
sports
and culture shifts, 154
fans' relationships to sports
teams, 135–42

impact of labor disputes on,
193–97
and social contracts, 27–28, 30
sports arena as symbols for
fans, 182
See also leadership
Springsteen, Bruce, 68, 70
SS-Totenkopfverbände [concentra-
tion camp unit], 166
Stalin, Joseph, 58
Stallone, Sylvester, 132
Stanford University, 226
Starbucks Corporation, 73, 77
having one of top eight logos, 174
Star Trek (TV series and movies), 80
*Star Trek VI: The Undiscovered
Country* (movie), 209
StarTribune (newspaper), 154
Steel, David, 64
stereotyping. *See* illogical leaps, way
we view other races and cultures
Stern, David, 197
Stewart, Dave, 96
Stewart, James, 210
Sting (musician), 67, 68, 70
strangers and illogical leaps, 90–98
Strauss-Kahn, Dominique, 72
Streep, Meryl, 24, 25
Sturmabteilung [storm troopers],
165
Suburbs, The (album), 133
Sudetenland, 188–89
Summer Olympics in Munich, 176
Sun (British tabloid), 201, 202
Sundance Film Festival, 45
Super Bowl (NFL), 139
Sutcliff, Rosemary, 158

Sutherland, Donald, 158
swastika as a symbol, 162–66
Sweden, 53
"Swoosh" logo for Nike, Inc., 176
symbolism, 157–84
    and culture shifts, 162, 222
        protecting symbols repre-
            senting, 218
    in Harry Potter series, 224
    iconography in Harry Potter
        series, 224
    logos
        as commercial symbolism,
            174–78
        efforts to reintroduce Jack
            in the Box restaurants'
            logo, 199–200
        Hyundai logo, 33
        Obama '08 logo, 169–70,
            171, 173
        as simple stories, 170
        "Solidarnosc" logo, 170
        Ronald Reagan's use of, 221–22

Taliban, 104
Talisker (Scotch malt), 148
Tar Heels. *See* University of North
    Carolina, basketball team
TARP money (for banks), 33, 42,
    206
Tatum, Channing, 158
Tatum, Virgil (fictional character),
    46–47
taxation, 142–44
Taylor, Elizabeth, 93
Taylor, Peter, 69
teams. *See* names of specific teams,

    e.g., Dallas Cowboys, Leeds
        United Football Club, etc.; sports
Tea Party movement, 48, 51, 66–67
"telephone game," 133, 216
10 (movie), 95
tennis, 141
Tetris®, 145
Teutobrug Forest, Battle of the,
    159–60
Thapsus, Battle of, 157
Thatcher, Margaret, 20–23, 24–25,
    64
Thelma & Louise (movie), 90
Theory of Semiotics, A (Eco), 161
"thinkering" groups, 86
Thompson, Tommy, 49
Thorburn, David, 50
Thornton, Billy Bob, 91, 92
Thule Society, 163
Tiananmen Square protests, 65, 182
Tide®, 71
Timberlake, Justin, 76
Time (magazine), 226
timing and culture shifts, 220, 230
TODAY Show (TV series), 95
Tokyo Motor Show, 131–32
Tolson, Clyde, 18, 19
Tonight Show with Jay Leno, The (TV
    series), 204
Too Big to Fail (movie), 205
Total Wine & More (stores), 150
Tottenham Hotspurs (British
    Premier League), 136
Towton, Battle of, 136–37
Toyota Motor Corporation, 131–32,
    198
Toy Story 2 (movie), 124

Toy Story 3 (movie),promoting of, 124–25, 127–28, 132–33

Transportation Security Administration (TSA), 151

Trebia, Battle of the, 103

trust and illogical leaps, 99–100

TSA. *See* Transportation Security Administration (TSA)

Tunisia, protests in, 115, 128

Twain, Mark, 113, 133

Twitter®, 31, 42, 43, 97, 115, 125, 129, 151

Tyler, Anne, 152

UEFA Champions League, 137, 138

Ultravox (band), 68, 69

unconscious motivations, understanding, 107–108

Unilever, 30–32

United Distillers UK PLC, 147–49

United Federation of Planets, 80

United Kingdom. *See* Britain

United Nations, 51, 67
    UN Refuge Agency (UNHCR), 71, 92
    weapons inspectors, 104, 105

United States
    eagle as a symbol, 160–61
    See also names of specific agencies, e.g., CIA, FBI, Justice Department

Universal Studios Orlando, 223

University of Bologna, 161

University of Connecticut basketball team, 141

University of Florida basketball team, 141

University of Kansas basketball team, 141

University of Kentucky basketball team, 141

University of North Carolina basketball team, 138–39, 141

Unlawful Killing (movie), 97

Ure, Midge, 68, 69

US Open (golf), 140

Ustinov, Peter, 189

US Track and Field Olympic Trials, 176

U2 (band), 68

Van Gogh, Theo, 70

Van Gogh, Vincent, 70

Varus, Publius Quinctilius, 159–60

Velvet Revolution, 65

Venkatachalam, Mohan, 78–79

Versailles, Treaty of, 164

Vietnam Veterans Memorial, 178–79

"Vinca script," 162–63

viral movements
    Audi® A3 campaign, 46–48
    Blair Witch Project, The, 43–46, 118
    Ron Paul's campaigns, 48–52, 118
    Toy Story 3, 124

Viren, Lasse "the Flying Finn," 176

Virginia Commonwealth University basketball team, 142

Visible Measures®, 129

visual communication, 56

Vogue (magazine), 203

Voldemort (fictional character), 223, 226

Volkswagen AG, 46

Wachovia Corporation, 206
Waddell, John Rankin, 30
Walesa, Lech, 59, 65, 171
Wall Street Journal (newspaper), 126
Walt Disney Company, The, 124–25, 127, 168
war, illogical leaps leading to, 103–105
"War Guilt Clause," 164
War of the Roses, 136–37
Warwick, Dionne, 68
Watson, Dr. (fictional character), 210
"We Are All Khaled Said," 40
"We Are the World" (song), 68
Webb, Jim, 178
WebCrawler®, 226
WeePlaces, 130
Weller, Paul, 68
Wells Fargo and Company, 206
West Ham United (British Premier League), 136
West Wing, The (TV series), 117
White Castle® burgers, 111–12
Whitehead, Alfred North, 157, 183
Whitehurst, Jim, 82
Whitman, Meg, 74
Whittaker, Ian, 204
Whole Foods Market, Inc., 79–80
Wiji software, 131
WikiLeaks, 52–54
Wilde, Oscar, 96
"Wilderness Downtown, The," online project, 133
Wild Wild West (movie), 45
William (prince), 63
William of Baskerville (fictional character), 161

Williams, Steve, 69
Willis, Bruce, 132
wine and difficulty of selection, 149–51
Without Limits (movie), 176
wolf as a symbol, 159
Woods, Donald, 65
Woods, Tiger, 69, 140, 176
World of Warcraft (online game), 50
World Trade Center, 180
World Trout Initiative, 81
Wright, Jeremiah, 14

Yahoo! Inc., 80, 227
Yalta Conference, 58
Yankelovich Partners (research group), 114
Yarborough, Ian (fictional character), 46–47
York, House of, 136–37
Young, Paul, 68
YouTube™, 31, 129, 226
    "Boycott BP" campaign, 186
    and Pepsi Refresh Project®, 125
    Ron Paul on, 49–50

Zealots, 37–60
    appeal of icons/logos, 171
    and categorizing public figures, 55–59
    and the Congregation, 59, 60, 65, 83, 214, 224
    and corporations and brands, 55, 75–76, 87
    and culture shifts, 60, 71, 77, 84, 127, 133, 218
    desiring choices, 148

and Disciples, 38, 39, 42, 48, 54, 59, 75, 83
    Zealots acting as Disciples, 60, 65, 66
discovery of Google, 227
and Dove® Campaign for Real Beauty®, 31, 32, 87
eco-Zealots, 186
efforts to reach for *Second That Emotion* (Holden), 229
and leadership, 32, 54, 60, 65, 66, 74–75, 83
    leaders beginning as Zealots, 65
and motivation, 38, 40
in Nazi Germany, 164, 165
and Occupy Wall Street protests, 43
and "open-source" software movement, 81–83

and politics, 48–55
    Barack Obama, 120
    Howard Dean, 116–18
    role of political consulting, 54–55
and protests in Egypt, 40, 42
as purists, 83
and social contracts, 36, 184, 214, 218, 221
and social media, 123, 128–32
and the Tea Party movement, 66
and viral movements, 43–48
Zemeckis, Robert, 175
Zhang, Yifan, 110
Zicam®, 122–23
zodiacal constellations, 154–56